THE SPRINGS OF NAMJE

THE SPRINGS OF NAMJE

*A Ten-Year Journey from the Villages of Nepal
to the Halls of Congress*

ஒ

Rajeev Goyal

BEACON PRESS
BOSTON

Beacon Press
25 Beacon Street
Boston, Massachusetts 02108-2892
www.beacon.org

Beacon Press books are published under the auspices of the Unitarian
Universalist Association of Congregations.

15 14 13 12   8 7 6 5 4 3 2 1

This book is printed on acid-free paper that meets the uncoated paper
ANSI/NISO specifications for permanence as revised in 1992.

Text design by Kim Arney
Map designed by Priyanka Bista

Some names and identifying characteristics of people mentioned in
this work have been changed to protect their identities.

Library of Congress Cataloging-in-Publication Data

Goyal, Rajeev.
The springs of Namje : a ten-year journey from the villages
of Nepal to the halls of Congress / Rajeev Goyal.
p. cm.
ISBN 978-0-8070-0175-2 (alk. paper)
1. Peace Corps (U.S.)—Nepal.   2. Rural development—Nepal.   I. Title.
HC60.5.G69 2012
361.6—dc23   2012009321

To Priyanka and my parents

Contents

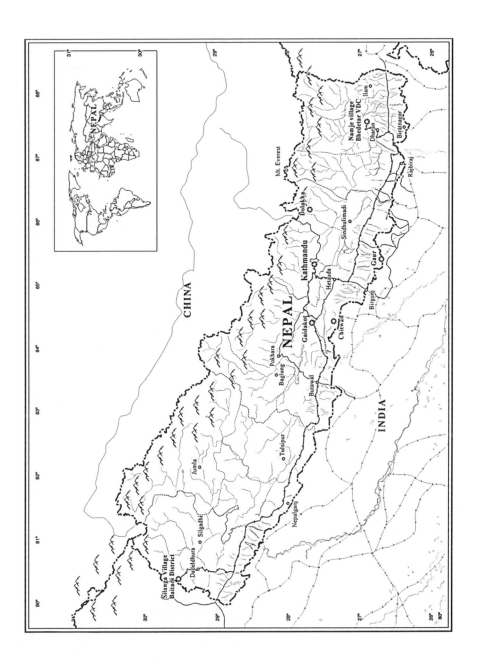

Foreword

I've never felt comfortable in Washington, DC. Maybe it's the way the city dies every night, the five o'clock crowds fleeing to the suburbs, until parts of downtown seem as lifeless as Arlington Cemetery. Or maybe it's all those monuments, the big blocks of marble scattered around town like the reminders of some earlier, more inspired civilization. Even the bustle of a weekday morning can leave me feeling depressed. There are so many young people, and they move with such purpose; the city is full of highly educated aides and interns who run the place on a day-to-day basis. And yet the stories that come out of Washington seem eternal: gridlock in the Senate, logjams in the House; presidential backpedaling and partisan politics. Whatever happens to all that youthful energy?

But the place felt different when I saw it with Rajeev Goyal. In the summer of 2010, I researched a *New Yorker* magazine profile of Rajeev, and I spent part of a week with him on Capitol Hill, where he was lobbying to increase support for the Peace Corps. He had no formal training for this job, although he told me that he had learned useful lessons during his time as a volunteer teacher in a Nepalese village called Namje. His mentor, a schoolteacher named Tanka Bhujel, had taught him that politics is personal, and not really about rules and systems. "Politics is the *dur-tee* game," Tanka Sir used to say happily, although he didn't mean this statement in a cynical way. He believed that politics requires creativity and guile, and that it should be seen as a human game—there should be lightness and joy to the process.

This was how Rajeev approached Washington. To him, it was simply another village, and the fact that he was an outsider—the son of Indian immigrants, short and dark skinned—only made it easier for him to capture people's attention. (Tanka Sir was also a misfit, a member of an obscure caste in Namje.) After Rajeev began his work on Capitol Hill, he memorized the photographs of every member of the House and Senate. He learned the DC equivalent of village-well routes: the obscure places where even the great and mighty have to tread. He recognized Senator

Bob Corker at Reagan National Airport. He struck up a conversation with Representative Russ Carnahan at a Starbucks on Pennsylvania Avenue. He ran into Representative Peter Welch late one night at Cosi, and he encountered Representative Dennis Kucinich at Le Pain Quotidien. He spent hours hanging around the small rotunda that connects the Cannon and Longworth House Office Buildings, where he met dozens of officials. In 2009 the Peace Corps received the largest single-year increase in its history, and many people told me that Rajeev's campaign deserved much of the credit for the new funding.

In 2010 I spent two and a half days with Rajeev, and I watched him track down fifteen different senators without a single appointment. One afternoon, he approached Senator Dianne Feinstein at the end of a meeting on military intelligence. After introducing himself, Rajeev asked for more support for the Peace Corps, but the senator said it would be hard in the current economic climate.

"Look at the foreign military finance," Rajeev said, and he pulled a copy of the proposed budget out of his pocket. "It's almost $5.5 billion, and that includes a $1.2 billion increase. All we're asking for is dust compared to that. It's $46 million."

The senator raised her eyebrows. "Just dust?" she said.

"That's it."

"Well, we'll take a look at it."

She turned to go, but Rajeev persisted. "Look at this money!" he said. "A $1.2 billion increase for foreign militaries, and nine hundred million for Pakistan counterinsurgency."

The numbers caught the senator's attention, and she asked Rajeev to repeat them. Less than a year later, the figure for Pakistan would seem even more jarring, when it was discovered that Osama bin Laden had spent years living in a mansion fewer than a thousand yards from a military academy in Pakistan. But even in 2010, a $900 million increase for the Pakistani military seemed like a lot. It was more than twice the entire Peace Corps budget.

The senator took Rajeev's paper, thanked him, and called to an aide: "Give this to Rich." And then she was gone, and Rajeev was off to find another Washington village-well route.

—〰—

There was a time when the Peace Corps didn't have to scramble for support. After John F. Kennedy founded the program in 1961, it was administered by his brother-in-law, Sargent Shriver, who made sure that it grew fast. By 1966 more than fifteen thousand volunteers were serving around the world, and Kennedy had once remarked that the program would make a difference when that figure reached one hundred thousand. But the number of volunteers decreased in the late 1960s, when the Vietnam War turned many young people against any kind of government program. Throughout the 1970s and 1980s, the Peace Corps often lacked a clear direction in Washington, and the profile continued to shrink. When I joined in 1996, many people responded by saying, "Is there really still a Peace Corps?" I didn't know anybody else from my university who signed up.

But I found that the Peace Corps could still be remarkably effective on the ground. I was sent to China, a new program that was blessed with first-rate staff, both American and local. The volunteers were excellent—to this day, they remain some of my closest friends. And there was no question that the work we did was important. Most of us lived in remote cities, and we taught college students who were going to become teachers of English, part of China's attempt to reengage with the world after decades of isolation. As part of our training, the volunteers received excellent instruction in Chinese, and many of us became fluent. For me, the Peace Corps proved to be a far more intense and useful learning experience than the two years I had spent in graduate school at Oxford.

This experience has been shared by volunteers all over the world, including, of course, Rajeev Goyal in Nepal. And yet relatively few Americans are aware of what the Peace Corps is doing. This is largely an issue of distance—the true value of the Peace Corps can be found in remote places, whereas the more accessible bureaucracy in Washington is without question the weakest aspect of the organization. Unfortunately, this is all that most members of the Senate and the House ever see of the Peace Corps, which is one reason why funding remains low. Most former volunteers will agree with what Rajeev says in this book: The DC part of the organization should be reduced and made as efficient as possible. The Peace Corps needs more volunteers and fewer lawyers.

But it's also difficult to quantify the value of the Peace Corps. Most Americans have a poor understanding of development work, which they imagine primarily as construction: new schools, new hospitals, new roads. The goal is to build things and then move on; the typical analysis involves little more than basic accounting. But the role of a Peace Corps volunteer is subtle. We live in a community for two years, and usually we continue to stay in touch for years afterwards. Most volunteers never build anything. Often we teach, and the value lies in human connections that can't be measured. And there's a strong tendency for Peace Corps volunteers to be humble about what we've done. Rajeev never would have told me about his work in Namje if I hadn't asked; other people described the remarkable water project he undertook as a volunteer.

And Rajeev, like many former volunteers, likes to talk about his failures. This is something else that Americans don't understand, although in truth it's one of the great benefits of the program. Volunteers are humbled repeatedly, and they realize that even the simplest village task—growing a garden, teaching a math class, giving basic health instruction—can become infinitely complicated. A volunteer learns resilience and perseverance, and he also learns to laugh at himself. One of the most valuable things about this book is the way that Rajeev writes honestly and vividly about his mistakes. It was a bad idea to promise things to villagers without thinking hard about the consequences, and it was a bad idea to encourage the women of Namje to knit wool caps to be sold on the streets of New York City. (Tanka Sir eventually put an end to the hat making, announcing, "This is not sustainable.") It was a bad idea for Rajeev to hold a competition in Namje that awarded a ten thousand rupee prize to whoever could grow the largest onion. (The winner produced a bulb the size of a small baby, thanks to a wicked cocktail of pesticides and fertilizer.)

Fortunately, there were also many great ideas. But even the best of them had unintended consequences. Rajeev describes the epic water project that he and the Namje villagers undertook—surely one of the greatest successes ever achieved by a Peace Corps volunteer anywhere in the world. But over the following decade, as Rajeev continued to visit Namje and organize school-building projects in the region, he came to understand that even the fully sustainable water project had some negative effects. With access to more water, villagers began to overbuild with cement. Land prices skyrocketed, largely because of outside speculators, and these economic changes threatened local cohesion. Some of the most important lessons in this book come from Rajeev's observations and analysis of long-term effects of successful projects.

In the autumn of 2010, I accompanied Rajeev to Namje, where I visited the water project and talked to villagers about their community. I met Tanka Sir and Karna ji, the craftsman who became known as the "local engineer" because of his brilliant work on the water project and the schools. (One of the defining characteristics of Rajeev's work is the level of local participation and leadership.) I learned that the communal ownership of the water project had been structured so effectively that not only did it support itself but it also allowed the local school to hire additional teachers. And I also learned some things that Rajeev does not mention in this book, out of modesty. In Namje, older people often refer to him as Shiva, the god who is the source of the Ganges River. Sometimes they weep when his name is mentioned. More than anything, he inspired people. Kishan Agrawal, a businessman from the city of Dharan, had originally sold pipe to Rajeev but ended up taking a more active role as a donor and participant in Namje's projects. He told me that Rajeev had transformed his life. "I realized that every person should be involved," Kishan told me. "You need to do something for other people."

Kishan pointed out that Rajeev had continued working even when there were violent clashes between government soldiers and Maoist revolutionaries. In Namje, people were so busy with their projects that they never got involved in this war. When I visited, Nepal had entered a time of peace, and they were in the process of forming a new government. One day Rajeev and I stopped in the neighboring town of Bhedetar, where we were approached by Mani Tamang, who had been the underground leader of the local Maoists during the years that they had been banned. Since then, the Maoists had been legalized, but Mani still had a wary, hardened look. He stared at Rajeev with such intensity that the American finally said, "Are you upset with me for some reason?"

"I've said thank you so many times that thank you can't describe how I feel," Mani said. "All over the district, we have no buildings like the school you built."

Rajeev dipped his head in polite appreciation, but his response was characteristic. He said, "Do you have any criticisms?"

—Peter Hessler

PART I

CHAPTER I

Royal Massacre

In the weeks leading up to the fateful night of June 1, 2001, the twenty-nine-year-old Crown Prince of Nepal, Prince Dipendra Bir Bikram Shah Dev, had grown distant from his parents. Nursing bouts of depression with drugs and alcohol, he had put on weight and grown his beard out. The source of his discontent was that his mother, Queen Aishwarya, opposed his choice of bride, Devyani Rana, the beautiful scion of a rival clan. Frustrated by the queen's objections, Prince Dipendra was planning to broach the subject with his father.

Once a month, the king hosted close family for a soiree in the palace billiards room. It was a way to make the grounds more open and accessible—a necessary means of washing away any petty family disputes through drink and merriment. Prince Dipendra had been charged with organizing the party that took place on Friday, June 1, 2001. He was not in the best mood, as earlier that day he had accompanied his parents to visit the family astrologer, who counseled strongly against marrying Devyani Rana. By the time the guests started arriving, Dipendra was allegedly acting strangely, slouching against the wall next to a billiards table, appearing drunk. Not wanting the king to see him in such a state, his cousins took him to his room, where a guard later reported seeing the young prince lying on the floor asleep.

When the king arrived, everyone was drinking and having a good time. The king ordered his favorite cigar and barely noticed the absence of his son. After a short while though, Dipendra reappeared, now dressed in military fatigues and carrying an MP5K submachine gun, a Colt M16 assault rifle, and a Franchi 12-bore pump-action shotgun. Everyone, including the king, assumed he was simply showing off his latest toys and playing dress-up, as he was known to do.

As a smiling king stepped toward him, according to several eyewitnesses who survived the attack, Dipendra opened fire with the submachine gun. As he fell to the ground bleeding, the king said, "*Ke gardeko?*" ("What have you done?") Dipendra then unleashed a deafening spray of bullets at nearly everyone in the room, with bullets ricocheting from the walls. Stone-faced, he kicked bodies afterward to make sure they were lifeless. When the guards finally rushed in, shattered bangles, parts of the king's glasses, and jewelry, all smeared in blood, were strewn everywhere. In total, thirteen royals including Prince Dipendra's father, his mother, his brother, Prince Nirajan, and his sister, Princess Shruti, were lying dead or wounded on the floor. Finally, he placed the pistol on his temple and shot himself.

Meanwhile, late into the night, a helicopter was dispatched to Pokhara in western Nepal to find the regent Prince Gyanendra, the king's younger brother, who had not heard the news. At the military hospital, the doctors and nurses in complete shock watched the bodies of the royal family members being wheeled in. King Birendra died on the operating table. The queen's face had been shot so many times that, during the cremation ceremony the next day, it had to be covered with a white porcelain china-doll mask. Miraculously, after an emergency operation, Dipendra lived but was in a critical state on a respirator.

By 11:00 p.m. rumors began racing through the streets of Kathmandu that something had happened in the palace. The local television stations went offline, and radio stations played religious dirges, not reporting anything. Nepalis were tuning in to CNN and the BBC, which were reporting that the king was dead. Late into the night, royal courtiers had no choice under Nepalese tradition but to declare Dipendra, the prime suspect in the massacre, the twelfth King of Nepal.

The next morning the nation erupted in protest, with India and even the CIA suspected of orchestrating the murder. The two-word formal explanation by the state authorities of "Weapon misfire" further incensed an already outraged public. Snipers were ordered in front of the palace with shoot-on-sight daytime curfews being defied all over the city. King Birendra was believed to be an incarnation of the god Vishnu and so if the reports were true, Prince Dipendra had not only committed patricide, regicide, matricide, and fratricide but also *deicide*. An estimated five hundred thousand people crowded the streets to strew flowers on the bodies, as the king's remains were carried by white-clad pallbearers to Pashupatinath on the banks of the Bagmati River to be cremated. Many adult men were shaving their heads in mourning—a Hindu ritual normally reserved for the death of one's own father. Three days after the massacre, Prince Dipendra's heart stopped beating. With his brother and two nephews dead, Prince Gyanendra was now the heir to the throne.

In a carriage drawn by six somber grey horses, the unlikely new monarch, a businessman, sat. A crown of bird-of-paradise feathers rested on his shaved head. Almost immediately, the public accused him of engineering the murders in a bid to grab power. His wife and unpopular son had survived the massacre, and this only fueled the theory. The state soon issued a 196-page report, concluding that Dipendra was the culprit, but practically no one believed it. Devyani Rana fled to London.

While what actually happened on June 1, 2001, will never be known, it was the bloodiest and most complete royal murder in recent history. With eleven royals dead, the massacre was more severe than even the killing of Czar Nicholas II and his family, which ended the Russian Romanov dynasty in 1918. One thing was certain: a Maoist rebellion, which had been growing in the midwestern countryside, gained a major strategic edge.

Just fifty-two days after this brutal massacre, on July 23, 2001, I first arrived in Nepal as a twenty-two-year-old trainee in the Peace Corps. I knew little about the country, beyond its majestic mountains, sure-stepped Sherpas, and the popular "going to Kathmandu" song. As the cradle of Buddhism, Nepal had often been depicted as a white poppy of peace, but this image had blurred.

There were few books or articles I could find that weren't memoirs about mountain climbing, and so I had packed two years' worth of North Face gear. I expected Kathmandu to be an alpine wilderness of roaming yaks and monks, but in actuality it was a hot industrialized city with beeping cars. The Peace Corps representatives arrived with long, white garlands and red tika powder folded in newspaper. "Welcome to Nepal. Your arrival is auspicious. Just today the Maoists set down their arms—for the third time this year. Let's hope three is a charm!" The other trainees and I had little idea who the Maoists were or that they had taken up arms in the first place. We packed into three Land Cruisers and drove off with our oversized trekking packs on the roof rack.

Driving through the narrow streets, I could see Kathmandu was a city with village-like characteristics. We passed women bathing in *dhunga dharas,* water streaming from opulent grey stone spouts fashioned in the shape of elephant trunks. A man who looked like he had traveled for days was carrying a sack of tightly packed cabbages.

Nepal was the roof of the world, home to eight of the ten tallest peaks on Earth, including Everest, and 240 mountains over twenty thousand feet high. Sandwiched between India and China, it was smaller than the state of Arkansas. Though known for its snowcapped mountains, the country was divided into three zones: the Himalayas, the Middle Hills, and a flatland Terai belt, which contained steamy jungles.

The mountains stood above the rim of the Kathmandu Valley as a constant reminder of how the small country was defined and directed more by its complex borders than anything else. A previous monarch had aptly described it as "a yam caught between boulders." But this precarious positioning had served to safeguard its existence. If India prodded or intervened too much in Nepal's internal affairs, Beijing pushed back, and vice versa. Its strategic positioning also contributed to its status as the darling of international donors. As a consequence, Nepal was pushed and pulled, poked and prodded, but never absorbed.

We felt excited to be spending two years in a country whose export to the world was Zen religions. As we drove through the chaotic streets, everything, even the mundane, seemed steeped in spirituality and symbolism. We passed an old woman igniting a fistful of black incense within a phone-booth-sized pagoda right in the middle of traffic. In fact, every *chowk* (intersection) seemed to have a temple, some as small as toaster ovens, with bronze bells that pedestrians would ring as they passed. Fingers reached in to scratch out red powder from the crevices of the statues; they put it on their foreheads or the part in their hair. The driver in our white, air-conditioned Toyota Land Cruiser, ritualistically touched his chest and then his forehead three times as we traversed a river.

Because of the fame of the Dalai Lama, I had always thought of Tibet as the origin of Buddhism, but the Buddha was born in Lumbini, Nepal, in 576 BC.* A thousand years later, a Nepali princess would marry the King of Tibet and bring Buddhism to Lhasa.

Hinduism and Buddhism, which I had always thought of us as distinct and contradictory, were seamlessly blended in Kathmandu. Swayambhunath, a stupa in the northern outskirts of the valley, was worshiped by Hindus once a year as an incarnation of Shiva. Conversely, Tamang lamas, devotees of Mahayana Buddhism, made animal sacrifices to Vishnu. Other subreligions also blended into the two major ones. Nepal seemed to lack the fanaticism sometimes found in other parts of South Asia.

The dissipation of lines and borders wasn't limited to the religious threads. While much of the city was now made of brick and concrete, agricultural patches were mixed in and emerald rice paddies sloped into the valley from all directions. Internet shops and stores with iron shutters filled the interstices left by shrines. So many people seemed to be outside—on their roofs, out in the streets, under the water taps—that inside and outside were hard to distinguish.

When we reached our first stop in the center of town, turning to go through blast-proof gates, I thought we were entering Narayanhiti Palace. Only the steely eyes of the soldiers and the barrels of their propped rifles could be seen above the sandbag bunkers that lined the perimeter. "Is this the palace?" I asked our driver. "Look behind you," he said pointing to the distinctive pink and mauve pagoda, which I immediately recognized from the images I had seen fifty-two days before on CNN. The tips of the long bamboos inside the palace walls barely touched the leaves of the walnut trees of Phora Durbar, an 18-acre US Embassy playground.

Stepping onto a bluegrass baseball diamond, except for the wide roof and slender water tower of the palace, I could no longer see, hear, or smell Nepal. Most of us were dressed in trekking wear and hadn't showered in several days. We all felt quite out of place and confused standing on the manicured grass.

"I'm Michael Malinowski," a gruff, bearded man, who was the US ambassador to Nepal, announced. The white tennis shorts he was wearing were hanging on for dear life. We didn't know yet the complications

---

*There is controversy about the exact date of Buddha's birth. *Merriam-Webster's Collegiate Dictionary* (11th ed.) gives the year as 563 BC; other sources give other dates.

this man would create in our lives as Americans out in the rural villages. We didn't really like this place. It didn't fit our notion of the Peace Corps.

Our country director, David O'Connor, who was responsible for the 120 volunteers in-country, had himself been a Peace Corps volunteer in Ilam district in far eastern Nepal in the early 1960s. Hearing David speak fluent Nepali to the trainers and staff, we felt a rush of excitement and desire to start learning the language. We were introduced to our doctor, who studied medicine in Scotland and was also the personal physician to the prime minister. One of the female language trainers was a famous Nepali folksinger. Observing the eager language staff, the handsome fleet of Land Cruisers, the dinner table prepared in our honor, and the dapper Dr. Ghimire, we felt more like diplomats than volunteers.

The grizzly American ambassador had a well-earned reputation of making inflammatory statements. In the days after 9/11, as the word *Maobadi* (Maoist) was replaced immediately with *aatankakari* (terrorist), Malinowski would be quoted as saying, "We have a foreign policy that people who use terrorism should not succeed. But we also have concerns about the failed-state idea and the danger that all kinds of bad guys could use Nepal as a base, like in Afghanistan." We would all cringe at the term *bad guys* and the comparisons of Nepal to Afghanistan by the highest American in the country. By 2004 he would be the shadow general in a US mission in Nepal that supplied twenty thousand M16s, night vision gear, and counterinsurgency training to the Royal Nepal Army to decimate the Maoists, while they kept getting stronger as this same equipment fell into their hands after successful raids. At the time, it seemed peculiar to us that the United States, which wasn't by any means a significant trading partner with Nepal, would have such a pronounced presence in Kathmandu. Later we would apprehend how this interest had more to do with the strategic location between two Asian tigers and the fact that the small country was the second richest nation in the world in terms of hydropower potential. Perhaps more valuable than oil, the blue glaciers of the fifteen-hundred-mile Himalayan arc fed several billion people.

The Maoists formally declared the beginning of their "People's War" years before the palace massacre, on February 13, 1996. Their demands, which were outlined in a "Forty Point Plan," included abrogating unfair water and trade-related treaties with India; ending class, racial, and gender discrimination; and reforming feudal land ownership patterns. They centered their vision on moving the nation away from a Hindu monarchy toward a secular democratic republic. The immense popularity of the late king Birendra was the main impasse preventing them from achieving their core objective—toppling the two-hundred-year-old Hindu monarchy—but the broken confidence resulting from the royal massacre presented an opening.

Through social shaming campaigns in which men who committed sexual abuses or behaved like drunkards in the villages were punished and humiliated, the Maoists built considerable popular support. With guerilla-style raids on vulnerable police posts in midwestern Nepal, they began dismantling the existing police force while simultaneously amassing an abundant supply of weapons and ammunition. Secluded terrain and a lack of rural infrastructure allowed this guerilla strategy to thrive. In the absence of effective government resistance, the rebels were beginning to devastate the government's security systems and take control of much of the western countryside surrounding the district headquarters.

With armed control came vast political influence. By the time we arrived in 2001, it was believed the Maoists controlled twenty-two of the seventy-five districts in Nepal. They had installed their own "People's Governments" that assumed parallel state functions. Maoist judges were hearing cases and passing out sentences. They were amassing wealth through shadow taxation systems. Beyond these governance institutions, the Maoists assembled an impressive "People's Militia," comprising thousands of armed fighters, and established their central base in the midwestern districts of Rukum and Rolpa, where the movement had first started. The charismatic leader of the Maoist movement was Pushpa Kamal Dahal, who went by the alias, Prachanda, which means "abundance."

Things took a dramatic turn on November 23, 2001, when Maoists, in a single coordinated attack, managed to kill more than eighty members of the security forces in forty-two districts. In the days that followed, more than 250 people were killed on both sides in raid after raid.

Three days later, on November 26, 2001, a state of emergency was declared and basic rights and freedoms were suspended. Nighttime shoot-on-sight curfews were initiated in many district headquarters. The state characterized the struggle with the Maoist rebels as part of the global "war on terror." Prior to November 2001, primarily the police fought the Maoists. Following the November offensive, the government mobilized 54,000 soldiers from the Royal Nepal Army to fight them. This was the Nepal we had entered.

We expected Peace Corps to have nothing to do with the more formal presence of the United States in the country, but in places like Phora Durbar we came in contact with our alter egos. After a short welcome ceremony, some of us went to the Phora café, where the menu listed the tariff for Coronas and Heath candy bars, which were hard to find even back in the United States. A man in a white polo shirt with an embassy badge was sitting next to us. "Are you with Peace Corps?"

"Yes," we answered.

"We love Peace Corps. You guys are the eyes and ears on the ground," he said. It was the word *corps* that made military types view us as their brethren, even though we had no association with the State Department or the Pentagon. I decided I would ask him about the Maoists and what his thoughts were on what was happening. It seemed important to know.

"Well, I have my own theory about all of this. You won't hear the ambassador say anything like this, but I believe . . ." he said, leaning in closer, "that the king and the Maoists are in bed together." The idea that two entities desiring the extermination of the other would somehow be allies seemed twisted, but we continued listening. "I have this theory that Gyanendra struck a deal with the Maoists: in exchange for immunity, he gave them his brother's head. All this army running around the city training for a major assault is just staged drama," he continued. "Well, that'll give you something to think about!" I had little idea what he was talking about or how it could possibly affect me as an English teacher out in the villages.

After five days, we set out for the training site four hours south in Gaindakot, a sleepy agricultural village on the banks of the Narayani River. I liked the idea that the odd collection of individuals in our Peace Corps group, which was the 193rd to enter Nepal since the program was initiated in 1962, represented the United States. There was a Chinese American volunteer who was a champion fencer at Brown, a potato farmer and chemistry expert from North Carolina whose luggage consisted of a deck of UNO cards, and a gay Cuban exile who fled the

Castro regime in the 1980s to become a teacher in New York City. This was the America we had imported to Nepal.

A thumbtack was pinned onto the northwestern corner of the map. I wasn't sure if it was there to pin up the paper or as a marker for one of the seventeen sites we were to choose from.

"What about this village here? Is that a site?" I inquired, curious about it.

"Yes, but we're not completely sure about this one. It's a school in Baitadi, in the far west, right near Tibet and India," the program officer said. "If you don't think it's too isolated, it would be a great post. We're just worried about safety and security over there." After three months of learning Nepali, we were picking our new homes. I figured that since I had already come so far, why not go to a location as remote as possible?

The day before I left to see the village marked by the tip of the thumbtack, I walked to the Narayani River, which was four kilometers from my host family's home, at the confluence of nine major Himalayan rivers. I sat for a long time on the embankment watching the fast-flowing tiers of chocolate-colored water. It was October and much cooler now. It had rained heavily the night before, and branches and cracked trunks from uprooted trees bobbed up and down in the water. I wondered if I was ready to finally go into the village and make a difference. As I watched the debris-filled river, a large creature leaped out and then back in, without a splash. I was ready to enter the mysterious current and see where it led.

CHAPTER 2

⤳

Baitadi on Fire

Overhead a falcon hovered in a tight circle, peering at the strange new visitor below. The only sound I could hear was a faint whistling from the gentle Himalayan winds brushing against the sharp pine needles. A meaty smell filled my nostrils, which I would later learn was the odor of leopards, known to occasionally devour infants in Silanga village.

On a map Nepal was barely large enough to contain the letters of its name, but from Kathmandu it took us three full days to get to Baitadi, and now the driver was gone and I felt very alone. Holding my dented steel suitcase with both hands as if carrying a body, I followed the faded trail through the forest, hoping it would lead to my new home.

It seemed that before I could put my things down, they were being carried into the spare stone abode of Premraj Pant, the former village council head, who was known to all simply as Pradhan ji (*ji* was a commonly used suffix of respect in Nepal), or "the chief." Silanga village was two lines of mud homes facing each other, with a walking trail in the middle, situated on a bright sunny ridge and surrounded on all sides by fading farming terraces.

Pradhan ji was a wiry, energetic man with a sharp nose and warm black eyes. He always wore a pressed white shirt and a vest, even when working in his cornfield, as if any moment a phone call might summon him back into political office. He had the personality of a pushy salesman, but I nonetheless took an instant liking to him and to his house.

One of my favorite pastimes became peering at the white Himalayas through the bright crimson leaves of the rhododendron tree just outside my window. The house had a second story where various agricultural tools, including a hoe, and a tall pile of desiccated blue corn seeds were stored. There was a spot in the roof where the clay tiles didn't quite meet and a beam of glittery light often shot through the length of the whole house. The cramped second story, which had a slanted roof, was where I liked to sit and read. I usually had my morning tea there.

I thought that in Baitadi I would have a solitary life, but people were always around. In fact, my house had a porous quality. Adjacent to the front door, one of the stones in the wall had been dislodged, and often I would see Pradhan ji's hand holding a cup of steaming tea. One night when I sneezed and rolled over in my bed, someone pushed a rag through the floorboards.

A few steps from my house was a *chia pasal* (tea shop), which had an unusually loud radio set that always faced in the direction of my room. Every morning I woke to the familiar patriotic Radio Nepal theme song and the sound of hot tea being poured as a sieve was tapped against a steel cup. Usually when I opened the door, a few old men were seated in the courtyard having tea and talking politics, and sometimes I sat in and listened. It was as if the courtyard of my house was an extension of the tea shop. But when I went for walks, I often found myself standing completely alone on a trail, no trace of life in any direction for miles.

Sri Siddhinath Middle School had approximately two hundred students in. My routine was teaching four English classes a day, in grades four through seven. The classrooms were made of stone and quite simple, without any teaching materials to speak of, but I found it wonderful to teach in this quiet setting. During the breaks, when I wasn't planning lessons, I sat in on the other teachers' classes so that I could listen to Nepali and improve my language skills.

Physically, the school was a small L-shaped, whitewashed building that sat on a large field and exuded a feeling of peacefulness. Along one of the edges of the field, a precipitous fifty-foot drop accentuated the serene telephoto view of the succession of mountains. I often took my class outside. Sometimes I felt like I was teaching everyone in the school, as eyes would be peering at us from all the classrooms. In training, we had learned a simple game of hanging a long string and letting the students use folded index cards to make sentences. It was a great way to teach word order and also the flexibilities of language. There was no library and the modest science equipment we had was locked up behind the headmaster's desk. Our teachers' room had a poster of Nepal's monarchs next to a rather graphic skeletal drawing of the human body, which marked the names of the different muscles and nerves.

The dynamics of a small village school are such that the teaching staff gets very close. The other teachers constantly invited me to their homes for meals, and visiting them was a way for me to learn more about the village. There were two teachers whom I grew particularly close to. The first, Fagendra Pant, was my counterpart and spoke English in a gruff, almost Germanic style. He seemed to view the language as a way to punish and humiliate his students. The other teacher was Krishna Air, who had a dazzling knowledge of the language and was always surprising me with the vocabulary he knew. Whenever I was in the teachers' room during breaks, they would compete for my attention to practice their English.

After teaching all day at Sri Siddhinath School, in the evenings when I came home I would usually find Pradhan ji gently dusting my belongings with a pink feather duster that he had acquired on a business trip to India.

"Rajeev Sir, if I call Lokendra Bahadur Chand," he boasted one evening while seated on a chair next to my bed, "he has to take my call!" He looked at me expecting a reaction but I had no idea who he was speaking about. "If you ever need anything done in Kathmandu, you let me know, and I'll have Lokendra take care of it for you."

"Who is that?" I asked.

"*Three times* he was prime minister! He is from Baitadi. You just wait and see: it won't be long before he's back in the *kursi* for the fourth time. He's the only one who can handle this mess with the Maoists," he opined. The word *kursi,* which means "chair," denotes the seat of power, a reflection of how deeply the notion of kings and thrones had pervaded even the more democratic organs of government.

I was rather surprised to learn that this village in the far western corner of Nepal had access to Singha Durbar (the site of the Nepalese parliament and government ministries). From Pradhan ji I learned how the highest echelons of power needed to plant roots in places like Silanga. It wasn't all that different from the way in which US blue-blood presidential candidates needed support in rural midwestern states.

Pradhan ji turned out to be simultaneously correct and incorrect about his powerful friend. In 2002 Chand would again be installed as prime minister by the king, though he would last only a few months before being pulled from the *kursi* for failing to quell the mounting insurgency.

Pradhan ji's financial fortunes seemed to waver from making him one of the richest men in the village to utterly bankrupting him. If he could manage to send a truck full of the valuable local pinewood down to the Terai border (where it was usually purchased by Indian merchants) without it being looted en route, his fortunes were up, but this only happened a few times a year. Moreover, Pradhan ji confided in me that one of his brothers was in legal trouble and that the cost of the lawyers had put him in substantial debt. Even in Baitadi, lawyers were loathed.

In Pradhan ji's mind there was only one reason he wasn't sitting in Lokendra Bahadur Chand's *kursi,* and that was his son, Shivy, who suffered from a mental disability. Though eighteen years of age, Shivy, was only in the second grade. He was the laughingstock of the entire village because of how he spoke and walked. Other young children often imitated his wide, staring eyes and uneasy gait. Of all the bullies, the one Shivy feared the most was his four-year-old sister, Gomati, who went by the nickname Dalli (little fat one). Each day when Shivy came home from school, the sight of Dalli, who always wore a ragged pink frock, waiting in the courtyard of their home struck terror in his heart.

"Look at my son! What can I do?" he said one evening pointing at Shivy, who had just finished eating a plate of clumped rice with buttermilk with his hand. "This is the son God gave me," he said shaking his head despondently.

"I think you should be happy. He's such a nice person. He never harms anybody," I said.

"He's lazy," Pradhan ji grumbled. "He never does any work!"

Shivy was hard not to like. He always wore a jet black blazer with a single, large gold button on it and dress shoes—as if he was attending a party. He also always seemed to have a wide grin on his face, which instinctively made me smile back. He was probably as clever and cunning as his father, if not more so, though it took time with him to realize this. When people made fun of him in the tea shops or the school, he would laugh the loudest, slapping his knee, and confusing those that were ridiculing him. He had the clearest sense of who was good and who wasn't, based on how people treated him. By observing him, I came to know a lot about Silanga.

I always found it odd that the Pant family had such a unique wardrobe, which almost felt European, whereas everyone else in the village seemed to wear tattered rags for work in the field. These were signs of the family's now-lost prominence and wealth. But my arrival seemed to give Pradhan ji a sense that it was time to make his comeback.

On the day the scholarship forms came in the mail, I walked up to the school and told the teachers about the opportunity. A Kathmandu-based organization had requested nominations for two local students to attend college. The cash prize was enough to change someone's life in Silanga—20,000 rupees, roughly $300.

I initially believed it would quite be easy to determine who the poorest student was, based on obvious factors such as their living conditions, but when I and two other teachers embarked on a fact-finding mission to select the two neediest girls in the village, I realized how wrong I was.

Venturing out into the surrounding hills, I was struck by the simple beauty of Baitadi. We walked through forests that were part of long corridors of rare species of rhododendrons not found anywhere else on Earth. At one point the two teachers and I came to a forty-foot log no more than ten inches wide that was the bridge over a knee-deep brook ten feet below. When it came my turn to pass, one of the teachers, sensing my trepidation, gave me advice that I didn't expect: "Look down first so you know the consequences of falling."

The first house we visited, about an hour's walk down the hill from Silanga, was a single room with six family members living in it.

"Rajeev Sir, she must be the poorest girl in the village," Fagendra Sir, my English-teaching counterpart at the school, said. He pointed to a girl who had just walked in with a heavy bundle of firewood. "Look at her family. They have nothing!"

As he said this, we were served a plate of oranges by the mother. Krishna Air was the economics teacher at the school. He seemed more skeptical. "How many cows do you have?" Krishna Sir asked the father. "How many goats and pigs do you have?"

"Three cows, two pigs, and seventeen goats," the father replied.

His wife corrected him. "Not seventeen, we have twenty-one goats," she said proudly, slicing more oranges by passing them through a sickle that she balanced on the floor with her toes.

"How much do you earn from just the milk?" Krishna Sir asked, sucking on an orange and writing notes on a pad of paper.

"Enough to send all my kids to school. I don't know how much exactly but enough to run the family," the father said.

But Fagendra Sir seemed convinced that this girl was the poorest one. "Look at this house. It's falling apart!" he exclaimed, scratching at the mud on the inside wall. "I need to fix that with some wet mud," the mother said, embarrassed. She wiped her hands with a rag and came over to inspect the wall. To make his point, Fagendra Sir was pulling a stone that protruded from the wall when several rocks tumbled down. "See? She's the poorest one."

But Krishna Sir was not convinced at all. As we left, he walked to the back of the house, determined to find traces of hidden wealth. "Who owns all this land back here?" he asked suspiciously. "Is this yours?" There were acres and acres of orange trees, bamboos, and very valuable *sala* trees. "Is that *sala* wood?"

"It belongs to me and my five brothers. We haven't yet divided it up," he said. "It's all *sala*."

Krishna Sir gave me and Fagendra Sir a coy smile and said, "These folks have more wealth than you think. That's probably 500,000 rupees of just wood. We better keep going!"

We kept walking until we came upon the next candidate. This time Fagendra Sir was sure she would pass muster, even though the family's house was a mansion by Silanga standards, a two-story house with many rooms. We saw several healthy cows in the shed being milked by one of the daughters. It didn't seem to add up that someone living in such a prosperous household would need a scholarship, but when the family came out to greet us, I understood why Fagendra Sir had led us here.

There were eight daughters, one of whom had a slight limp. "Come here," Fagendra Sir commanded. She limped toward us and sat down nervously on a stool, looking at the floor. "Look at her. She cannot even walk properly!" Fagendra Sir said. "And look at how many girls they have to educate and marry."

Krishna Sir was skeptical again. "How much land do you have?" he asked the father, flipping to a new page in his pad.

"Just a little over eighty *ropanis*," the father replied. Six *ropanis* was the equivalent of one acre.

"That's about thirteen acres, ten times the amount I have," Krishna Sir said. Then the daughters one by one brought over a succession of large steel plates. There were cucumbers, apples, boiled potatoes with spices, pomegranates, popcorn, fried eggs, and tea. After eating all the food, Krishna Sir turned to Fagendra Sir, who was rubbing his belly, and asked, "So do you *still* think this is a poor family?"

"I've never tasted potatoes so good . . ." Fagendra Sir said contemplatively. "And these cucumbers are some of the best I've had. *But* the girl is handicapped—she can't even walk properly." He asked her to walk to demonstrate her disability, which she did with her head lowered.

We visited a few more candidates, but everywhere we found the same complex situation. The deeper we looked, the more assets the family seemed to have—livestock hidden in other parts of the village, gold jewelry locked away, more *sala* trees across the river, a child overseas sending home money each month. *How do you compare three cows to fifteen goats?* I wondered. *Who was wealthier, the family that earned 10,000 rupees from selling wood or the family that had the potential to earn 100,000 rupees if they just used their land properly?* "Wouldn't it be better to teach people how to make more money than to simply give it away?" Krishna Sir asked me. I let Fagendra Sir and Krishna Sir decide who should get the scholarships, but I could see how little it would actually accomplish. I also wondered how scholarship programs were administered in a country like Nepal where need seemed impossible to measure.

Krishna Air was one of the wisest and most analytical people I had ever met. He rarely wanted to talk about practical things. Even the political discussions we had were more about philosophical ideology and historical interpretation than current events. He learned English by reading the dictionary cover to cover as well as two *Encyclopedia Britannica* volumes, for topics beginning with the letters *c* and *d*, he had somehow acquired.

Every day after school he and I would have tea at the small shop just below school gate and engage in long conversation about all sorts of things before he would rush home. Always our discussion topics began with the letter *c* or *d*. "Rajeev Sir, today I want to ask you about dialectical materialism," he announced one day as he set his cloth bag down on the floor. "What are your feelings about chaos theory?" he asked me another time. I generally had no knowledge about the topics he wanted to consider, which I was embarrassed to reveal. I started suspecting he spent the previous day picking the esoteric subject we would talk about after school rather than planning the lessons he was to teach.

Krishna Sir bore an uncanny resemblance to the actor Robin Williams. Even their speaking voices were similar. Because of this and his generally very passionate nature, when I sat in on his economics class one day, I couldn't help but recall a scene from the 1989 movie *Dead Poets Society* and amused myself by imagining the students mounting their desks and reciting poetry.

But Krishna Sir actually fell asleep in his own class one day while I was observing. He assigned a reading, walking around sluggishly to look at notebooks, and then returned to his chair next to a window in the front of the room and muttered, "Nepali education system," before falling asleep. The students stared at me, wondering what I would do. I pretended not to notice and, fortunately, the bell sounded and Krishna Sir woke up.

One day I bothered to ask about a peculiar detail that would drastically change my view of the village. Every day at 1:15 p.m. all the teachers walked down to the small *chia pasal* near the school for afternoon tea as the children ran into the playground, where they played marbles and a game called *chungi*, which involves using their feet to bounce a ball of rubber shards up and down .

To warm up, all the teachers sat huddled together on a worn wooden bench facing the long golden beams of sunlight. Shivy, who didn't enjoy games, and feared recess because of the contact with bullies, liked to sit with us, and since he was always so well dressed, no one seemed to notice. But Ram Bishwakarma, the math teacher, always sat on a separate chair in the frigid shadows. Whereas the shopkeeper always handed us our tea, for some reason he set Ram Sir's on the floor.

Upon finishing, the quiet math teacher, who always wore a blazer with oversized shoulder pads, would walk to the side of the shop where he washed his own cup and set it down. The restaurateur would then pour a bit of water into his right palm and sprinkle some on Ram Sir and then the cup, muttering something that sounded like a religious incantation. At first I thought it was just Ram Sir's own personal idiosyncrasy, and even wondered if maybe he was a Brahmin and had to sit apart from us because of how pure he was.

Rolling the teacup to warm my cold hands, I asked, "Why does Ram Sir do that?"

I could tell I had asked something that was not publically discussed. Fagendra Sir ventured to explain in English. "This is system. We invite him to sit with us but he doesn't want. He just follows system." I could see that Ram Sir was uncomfortable with my question and even more uncomfortable upon hearing Fagendra Sir's answer. Shivy laughed riotously, though I couldn't understand why.

Krishna Sir looked at me with a sad and almost apologetic expression, knowing that this one question would change my relationship to Silanga forever.

"He's 'BK,' or 'Bishwakarma,'" Pradhan ji explained when I asked him the same question that evening. "BKs are Dalits." Pradhan ji went on to tell me how most of the villagers in Silanga, including himself, were Brahmin, but the Dalits lived in their own villages around the fringes of Silanga. *Bishwakarma* translates as "fate of the world," perhaps a reference to the unchangeable nature of the caste system.

I never expected the caste system to be practiced in the twenty-first century, but its origins lie in a two-thousand-year-old Hindu Vedic text called *Manu Smriti* in which all human beings were said to descend from the head, chest, loins, and feet of a single primogenitor, Manu. It was from this text that the four castes originated: the Brahmins (priests and teachers) derived from the head, the Chhetris (warriors and soldiers) from the chest, Vaishyas (merchants and traders) from the loins, and Dalits (cobblers, ironsmiths, sweepers, and manual scavengers) from the soles of the feet. I learned in Silanga that, belonging to the Marwari caste of Rajasthan, I was derived from Manu's loins.

Only the Dalits, created from the soles of feet, were deemed ritually impure and polluted, not permitted to physically touch any of the other castes or share their food or drink. Physically identical to Brahmins and Chhetris, the designation was not based on race but simply on last name.

Beneath the seemingly homogeneous mantle of poverty in Silanga, there lurked a violent caste system. It was a very *physical* ordering, not an abstract idea, affecting how people interacted with space, objects, food, and other people—the water they could drink, the doors they could open, the people they could touch, the temples they could bow to.

One afternoon I asked the principal at the Silanga school, Narayan Pant, who was a Sanskrit teacher and a local priest, what he thought of this system. Narayan Pant maintained a handlebar mustache and wore slightly tinted glasses, just as King Birendra had. In fact, he looked very much like a darker version of the king, and I amused myself wondering if perhaps he wasn't King Birendra on one of his incognito missions to discover the true plight of his people. I was surprised by Pant Sir's candid response.

"It's wrong," he stated. "But these things are hard to change because the Dalits practice it themselves. They have their own caste system—high-caste Dalits and low-caste Dalits," he explained. "And if you ask them to sit with you or come into your house, they won't do it. I've tried."

I found it foolish that Ram Sir could teach mathematics to seventh- and eighth-grade Brahmin students but not enter their houses. I felt angry, and I started speaking up more about it in my classes, asking the students what they thought. When I suggested to the other teachers that Ram Sir should sit with us and shifted to make room on the bench, he just smiled awkwardly and walked back up to the school, leaving his unfinished glass near the tap. The shopkeeper picked up the cup and washed it himself, which created an awkward silence.

One evening the tailor came to my house with my new teaching uniform wrapped in newspaper. When I tried to hand him the rupees, he lowered his cupped hands. When I lowered the faded rupees toward his hands, he lowered them even more so that they were almost touching my doorstep. Aggravated, I said I would only give him the money if he took it from my hands, but I could tell this only served to humiliate him, particularly as several others were looking on. On another occasion, I asked my Dalit neighbor to reach into a bag of Doritos my mother had sent me and remove a chip. He did so very nervously.

It finally dawned on me why national-level political events had such a direct bearing in a village like Silanga. There was simply no way to oppose the caste system without violent confrontation. Every Dalit in Silanga was a potential Maoist, and all the Brahmins had to know this. The daily humiliations of having to wash one's own glass, of having to worship the same god but in a special temple—this was enough to make someone pick up a gun. Witnessing Ram Sir washing his teacup, I understood why the Maoist war had happened. Previous to that it all seemed so confusing.

One chilly evening after school I walked to the tailor's small shop, which was five minutes down the trail from Pradhan ji's house. Under a dim red light, the tailor operated his sewing machine with an iron foot pedal, rocking back and forth as he did his work and controlling a fine spool of thread with his teeth. A small boy who appeared to be his son was sorting buttons and placed them according to size and color in different plastic bottles on a cotton mattress on the floor.

"I wanted to ask you why you take this humiliation from the Brahmins," I said. "It just doesn't seem right to me, and none of you speak up against it."

He seemed to lean in closer to the cloth he was sewing, pushing his toes tighter on the iron foot pedal.

"Do you think it's right to be treated like this?" I asked, now getting irritated.

He didn't answer, but as I was about to leave, he stopped working, flipping a switch on the side of his machine that lifted the needle up from the cloth, and looking down at his son, who had sorted the buttons into different piles, and said, "You are right. It's not right, but we have to keep living." The phrase *bachnai parcha* ("we have to keep living") was a term I had heard before. After that, as much as I wanted to speak up, I realized that if I continued, it could lead to even more uncomfortable situations and very possibly violence. Most of all, I was making the Dalits uncomfortable. I needed a new way to try to fight the caste system. *Bachnai parcha*. The words echoed in my ears for a long time.

When the shuttlecock sailed in her direction, none of the other teachers or students expected Bimala to flinch. But the torque from her supersonic shot nearly knocked the Brahmin *tuppi* (a small ponytail worn by Brahmins) off Fagendra Sir's head. "You almost knocked off my antenna!" Fagendra Sir joked in English. Bimala was a little heavyset, and while I don't think I ever saw her face in class, since she sat with a permanently bowed head, when we started the badminton club everyone wanted the mighty Bimala on their team. She had an unusual style as she seemed to wait till the very last moment, almost till the shuttlecock was below her shoulder, before pulling back the racket and punishing the birdie so fiercely that a few dead feathers would wither out of it.

But no sooner was the girls' badminton club started than parents filed complaints that their daughters weren't coming home in time to do housework. Corn needed shucking, *achaar* needed mashing, firewood had to be fetched and chopped. *Manu Smriti* was becoming the bane of my existence in Silanga, because in addition to the chapter establishing the caste system, another one justified the subjugation of women.

In time the badminton paddles were locked into the iron cabinets of Sri Siddhinath School, the birdies lodged back into the long tubes they came in, but, after that, in English class I saw Bimala's face and so did everyone else. When I assigned an essay on whether the caste system was a desirable thing, almost everyone wrote against it. I asked how it could be fought, and one of the Brahmin girls raised her hand and offered a most poignant answer: *Samai le* ("With time").

Narayan Sir called a special teacher conference. He sat contemplatively in the wooden teachers' office room. I wondered what was so urgent that it had to be discussed immediately, but the other teachers seemed to know.

"I require your advice on an important decision that I cannot make on my own," he confided. "We need to decide whether we will replace the portrait of the old royal family with the new one. What do you feel we should we do?"

It was indeed a tricky question.

"If we change it and put up the portrait of King Gyanendra, the Maoists will think we're monarchists," Fagendra Sir observed. "If we don't, the army will think we're Maoists. I don't know what we should do . . ." he said, looking confused.

"How about we put up the picture of the new king, but move this big shelf in front of it so no one can see it?" another teacher suggested. "If the Maoists come, they won't see any picture of the new king and if the security forces come, we can move the shelf and show them we have it up!"

In the end they went with a different solution that was no less brilliant. They removed the portrait of King Birendra's family, placing it on the floor next to Gyanendra's portrait. With both portraits on the floor, if the Maoists came, they would say they had taken the pictures down. If the security forces came, they would say they were preparing to put the picture of the new king up.

I looked up at the graphic chart of the exposed nerves and muscles of the human body that hung on the wall and wondered if that wasn't an apt portrait of Nepal's monarchy in light of current events.

It was common knowledge in Silanga that I had a medical kit from the Peace Corps, as I had on occasion dispensed Band-Aids and painkillers. At the school, when kids got hurt I sometimes dressed wounds since we didn't have any first aid supplies. The nearest hospital was three hours on the road to Dadeldhura, but during the long summer monsoon, there was no motorized transport, due to landslides. Sick people had to walk nine hours through the wilderness to reach the hospital. Those who were too sick to walk were often carried that distance. An image I will never forget is an elderly husband carrying his wife on his back to Dadeldhura. The woman's eyes were only half open, her head going left and right like an object as the barefoot man, with complete determination in his dark eyes, trotted as fast as he could on the uneven terrain to save her life. After being exposed to wrenching scenes like these, it was impossible not to try to help.

I had brought along a book from the Peace Corps library called *Doctor Nabhayemaa* (*Where There Is No Doctor: A Village Health Care Handbook*) and had anticipated using it to learn health-related words, but it ended up being much more valuable.

After one particular treatment I developed an unmerited and certainly unwanted reputation of being the village miracle worker. A teenage girl had a large wart on her foot that had not gone away for years.

Her parents worried it was cancerous, but when I looked up *wart* in the index I found some useful information. It appeared that sometimes in the villages dermatological issues were related to allergies to rubber *chappals* (flip-flops), which almost everyone wore.

"Have you tried wearing cloth or leather shoes?" I asked.

"Would that make a difference?" the father asked.

"Try it for a week and see what happens," I said, realizing it sounded a bit like, "Take two and call me in the morning."

When news traveled that this girl had been cured, it opened the floodgates, and I would wake up to lines of patients outside in my courtyard each morning. Ill people started appearing at the school, waiting in the teachers' room, walking by the window of my classroom. Shivy, who spent a lot of time in my room, became my assistant, fetching water, opening and closing doors or windows, doing whatever else needed to be done. One day a boy with horrible strep throat came to us. The book suggested a dose of "village cough syrup" made from the following recipe:

1 tablespoon honey
1 tablespoon lemon juice
½ tablespoon whisky

Shivy came back with a honeycomb dripping from his hand, and I had plucked a hard lemon from a tree near the house. The Maoists had banned alcohol in the countryside, but one of the teachers kept a bottle of local whisky under his bed and we secured a swig of it. I could only imagine what the Peace Corps would think if they saw me administering local whisky to a child (with Shivy helping mix the concoction). After a while, recognizing the need to intervene, Pradhan ji put his foot down and told everyone to go home and leave me alone.

But one stormy night, Shivy burst into the room, soaking wet, with a small, middle-aged man trailing behind him. The man stood in the doorway dripping until we told him to come in. The little girl the man was carrying was so tiny I didn't realize he was holding her under the purple shawl he was wearing. When he set the girl, who was his niece, on the bed, I instantly felt woozy seeing the large four-inch bulge in her stomach. Pradhan ji heard the commotion and came in. The uncle explained to us, almost in tears, how his niece had been screaming in horrible pain since she came home that day from school. I recognized the man as one of the Dalit metalsmiths from Kami Tol and the girl as one of the first graders in school. As he didn't speak Nepali but Dotelli, the local dialect, Pradhan ji talked to him and translated for me. The girl was obviously in a lot of pain, and I panicked that somehow it was my responsibility to take care of it.

I felt terrible and desperate. Pradhan ji and I ran out into the rain to call the Peace Corps doctor since this seemed to be a real medical emergency. We banged on the door to wake up the phone operator, who didn't hear us because of the lashing rain. Pradhan ji went around to the back and craned his head in through a window, startling the family.

When I called, no one picked up, but a recorded message gave another number for emergencies. Though it was a Nepal cell phone, it rang on an aircraft carrier in the middle of the Indian Ocean.

"US Marines Medical Services. How can I help you?"

"Sorry? Oh—I'm a Peace Corps volunteer and I have a medical emergency."

"Are you in immediate life-threatening danger, sir?"

"No, I'm fine. It's not me, but a girl in the village . . ." I said, starting to realize that it would be unlikely the marines could help in this situation. "She has a large bulge in her stomach and is in pain. I don't know what to do, whether she's in life-threatening danger or not."

Rather than begging off, this doctor likely saved the girl's life by saying, "You need to get her to a hospital *immediately.*"

"Okay, but the nearest one is probably ten or twelve hours away. We probably won't get there till the morning."

"It'll probably be okay. Just get her there as soon as possible."

"What is wrong with her?"

"She probably has a hernia." He then explained how the muscles lining the stomach, which normally keep the intestines in place, can atrophy from too much strain, causing part of the intestine to jut outward. Apparently, it is common in places where young kids perform heavy labor. The life-threatening danger was the possibility of internal bleeding, and so he cautioned that she be carried very carefully. I thanked him, and we went back to the house where the girl had been covered in a heavier blanket by Pradhan ji's wife, Muna. Pradhan ji sent Shivy to find several more blankets and an umbrella.

BAITADI ON FIRE   27

"It's not safe to go tonight, sir; you should go tomorrow," Pradhan ji cautioned. "Also, there's a state of emergency in the country. If anything happens, I'm responsible for you!" I told him we would be fine, and he could come the next day to meet us in Dadeldhura.

As the uncle picked up the girl, she screamed in excruciating pain. The three of us, huddled under the flimsy umbrella, walked on the pathway to the road. I looked back at Pradhan ji, Muna didi, and Shivy framed by the doorway, heartened to know that sometimes the rules of the caste system dissolved away.

When we got to the road, we expected to have to walk nine hours to the hospital in Dadeldhura, but luckily a bus came by. We got on and made our way to the back. We sat in the last row so that she could be laid down. The next day, the operation was successfully performed by a Canadian Japanese doctor, and the girl recovered. Pradhan ji came to the hospital with a bag full of oranges from Silanga for the girl.

When I returned to Silanga, I resolved to not stray too far from teaching. But this wouldn't last very long. I noticed Ram Sir hadn't been in school for several weeks. When I asked his son where his father had gone, he said, tearing up, "We don't know. He just disappeared one day."

"Does anyone know where he is?" I asked.

"Some say he's in Gothalapani. My mother is worried they will hurt him." Gothalapani was the Baitadi district headquarters three hours north of Silanga. I was able to find out from Pradhan ji that he had probably been abducted on charges of being the Maoist area commander. Part of me felt incredibly happy to hear that Ram Sir was sacrificing his life for the other Dalits in the village, that he was fighting this awful system, but seeing his fearful son in school every day made me feel I should try to do something.

When I arrived at the district center, I wasn't sure if it would be wise to bring up the question of Ram Sir with the chief district officer (CDO) Laxman Shahi. I decided I would see how the meeting went and then decide whether to bring it up. The seventy-five CDOs of Nepal were the equivalents of governors—each one in charge of their entire district's administrative affairs. In Baitadi the CDO held control over two hundred thousand people in sixty-one remote VDCs (village development committees), including Silanga. I had instructions from the Peace Corps to introduce myself to him, but four months had elapsed and I had neglected to do so.

A sitting target for Maoists, the CDO office in Gothalapani was heavily guarded. After carefully walking through several checkpoints, I was directed into an empty room to wait for the CDO. Finally, one of the clerks entered and told me that the CDO was ready to see me. I was taken to the rear of the building where the CDO was playing badminton with someone wearing an undershirt who appeared to be a soldier. "Goyal Sir! I am very happy to meet you," he said, coming over to shake my hand. "These days we cannot do any work. Maoist problem, as you know," he said motioning for two plastic lawn chairs to be brought over.

"I was supposed to give you this introduction letter from the Peace Corps a long time ago," I said handing him the letter. I made small talk, asking if he thought the safety and security would improve or get worse.

"The country is *khatam*" he said, a disgusted look on his face as he leaned back in his plastic *kursi*. The Nepali word *khatam,* which I would hear over and over again in reference to the conflict, means "hopeless" or "finished."

As he ordered tea, it occurred to me that I was part of the caste system. The only reason I was able to meet this man was because I was an American. I could pretend that wasn't a caste, but I knew it was a super-Brahmin standing. I decided I had to bring up the question of Ram Sir.

"I wanted to ask you something, if you don't mind. It's about Ram Bishwakarma" I said, studying his face for a reaction. "He is the math teacher, and we need him back. He's not a bad person," I said. "I know his family."

I expected the CDO to be angry that I would broach such a sensitive subject, but he just nodded his head as he looked off in the distance. This reaction confirmed for me that Ram Sir was in state captivity. I left it at that, thanked the CDO, and went back to Silanga.

When I returned to the village, the terror in the air was palpable. "There are new faces around," Krishna Sir said solemnly. "We've never seen some of these people." The teachers had held a meeting and suggested that for my safety I go to Dadeldhura until things cooled down.

"Are they Maoists?" I inquired.

"Maoists and security forces, both in disguise, only we don't know who is who. Silanga is not safe for you now. We are responsible for you. We're afraid there will be an attack soon," Krishna Sir said. "I hope you come back."

When I told Pradhan ji about what the teachers had advised, he brushed it off. "Maoists?! They are children. Look, I know all the Maoist leaders in this district, and many of them come here to ask for my advice and support, so you needn't worry," he said, almost laughing.

"But everyone is saying there are new faces. The teachers seem to feel there's some danger."

"I take responsibility for you. Don't worry," he said.

The day I left Silanga, knowing I would likely never return, Shivy had run away and Pradhan ji was out searching for his son. I learned from Krishna Sir that he was being forced into marriage with a girl from a neighboring village who didn't know about his condition and who was much younger than him. Terrified for himself and the girl, he had fled. It was hard for me to leave the village not being able to say goodbye to Pradhan ji or Shivy. I methodically packed my belongings as I tried not to think too much about Shivy. As I had done only five months before, I carried the dented steel trunk back to the road head. I walked for a few miles until a truck stopped and I hopped in.

The next morning in Dadeldhura, Radio Nepal was blaring, "*Baitadima aago!*" ("Baitadi on fire!") Three hundred masked Maoists including the "sari soldiers," or female cadres, which by that point were believed to comprise more than a third of the People's Liberation Army, had detonated thirteen government offices using socket bombs and ignited jeeps and motorcycles, though no one had been killed.

I have never been back to Silanga. Most of all, I wonder what happened to Shivy, who proved the wisest villager of all. A week later, sitting in Kathmandu wondering what I should do next, it finally dawned on me why Shivy had laughed when I asked about the caste system. He was the only person in the village who could see how absurd it was. As for my own life, I had no vision and no plan. I feared similar unrest if I went to another village. I wondered if I should simply pack up and return home.

CHAPTER 3

❧

Gagris

I kept searching the papers hoping to discover a headline reporting that Shivy had been found. After a fortnight of confusion in Kathmandu, I realized I had to pick up the pieces and start again, as daunting as that felt. A school in a village called Namje in the eastern hills needed a volunteer. The headmaster, Harka Lama, who was a highly respected figure in Dhankuta district, had vexed the operators at Peace Corps with his persistent phone calls. The more my program officer told me about Namje, the more interesting it seemed. Two Peace Corps volunteers had taught there before but neither was able to finish. Both fell seriously ill from the lack of water in the village.

On a cold February morning in 2002, I packed my things into my steel trunk and set off, curious about why this headmaster was calling so much. Somewhere in the Char Koshe Jhadi, an eight-mile belt of forest in the eastern Koshi plains, the small Maruti minivan started climbing, almost imperceptibly. "There it is! That's Namje," the driver said, pointing to a dark green mountain in the distance that seemed to shoot straight up out of the plains. Floating above the massif, I could make out a blinking light, which appeared pink through the fog. Once out of the jungle, we slowed and drove over a narrow wooden bridge traversing a river with no water in it, bouncing as we passed over the slats.

The sun was starting to dip behind the hills as the minivan began coiling up the mountain road. I rolled down the window to lay eyes on this amazing new setting, but soon the fog was so dense that it was inside the van. The windowpanes of the minivan were pure white. I half-expected we were going to drive over the cliff.

Making the last turn that took us along a ridge, we arrived in a town in the clouds, which was called Bhedetar. A dusty blue sign indicated we were at 1,420 meters above sea level. I had heard so much about Bhedetar and was expecting a scenic mountain town, but it was nothing more than a line of tea shops and dingy watering holes. This was the strategic entry point into the eastern Himalayas, guarded by a nearby battalion of several hundred soldiers. The town had earned the nickname Charles Point in the early 1980s when the Prince of Wales graced the inauguration of the famous highway we were now driving on. A rough road forked in the direction of Namje and we veered onto it, thankfully.

After fifteen minutes of rocking left and right over the rocks, the Maruti slowed as we curved around a dramatic bend that led us into Namje village. After the beer billboards of Bhedetar, the site of a mud home with an old man seated on the ground shucking corn felt oddly familiar. Nestled between two protruding mountains, each with a steel tower with a red blinking light at its tip, Namje was laid out in the shape of a crescent. To the left was a succession of bottle green terraces fading into the dark blue river valleys below. It was almost dusk, but I could see that the village was part of a much larger arc of mountains that stretched far into the distance, each ridge delineated softly with fog. Aside from the two-story school building, which was visible just above the road, little of the "development" in Bhedetar had seemed to touch Namje.

We continued past a row of small stone houses painted white. Horizontal saffron stripes across the bottom of the houses accentuated entrances made of blue wooden slats. From inside the doorways, glowing eyes peered into the van. Perhaps it was the time of day, but the place suddenly felt somber and uninviting, and for a moment I regretted coming.

When I finally stepped onto the new ground, I noticed a man with a well-groomed moustache look up from the notebook in which he was writing. He brought his thumbs together in a stiff triangular Namaste and walked over.

"Where are you coming from?"

"Baitadi," I answered, which seemed to make him nervous. "But I'm American. I'm a Peace Corps volunteer here to teach in Gramin Janata Secondary School." For many years to come Tanka Bhujel, the vice principal of Namje high school, would tell the story of how the first time we met, he thought I was a Maoist spy. "Welcome, sir. I am Tanka Bhujel, economics teacher and vice principal of this school. Welcome to my village," he said shaking my hand and already carrying my things into his house as he shouted for his wife, Goma, to prepare tea.

The next day when Tanka Sir took me around to find a place to live, I kept repeating that I was from Baitadi. "Rajeev Sir, please say you are an American and not from Baitadi. Everyone will think you are a Maoist!" he explained. Finally Tanka Sir just asked his neighbor Chandra Magar to clear the two upstairs rooms for me, and I had found my new home.

Other than Brazil, Nepal is the richest country in the world in terms of hydropower potential, but in Namje this was a crude joke. The milky glacial melts from the Himalayas supply water to billions of people, but in Namje at four o'clock each morning, long before the roosters were up, I woke to the dull metallic sound of sixteen-liter aluminum cans, called *gagris,* banging into each other as the villagers prepared for the morning trek to Saacho Khola, a small, gurgling stream that was the village's only source of water for seven months of the year. The journey back up the slippery rocks with the filled *gagris,* which weighed about forty pounds, was a far greater strain than getting down to the river.

The common sight of women fetching water was both disturbing and comforting. They descended in clusters with arms folded under colorful shawls. Sometimes, herds of obedient goats trailed behind, also going to the river for a drink. I quickly learned a new lexicon related to water carrying: *gagri* (urn), *doko* (bamboo basket), *namlo* (jute head strap), *batuko* (bowl), and a word I heard very frequently, *baadyata,* which means "no choice." It was mind boggling that most women made this two-hour trip four to five times a day.

Even at the river there were usually long lines, and people tended to mark their place by putting down a *gagris*. The silver-colored, wide-mouthed *gagris* all looked the same to me, but not to the locals, who knew every dent and bend. Between February and April, the zenith of the dry season, so little water was available that many villagers who lived close to the road picked up and moved to a place called Dhade where they slept in one-room wood shelters close to a stream. Attendance at Gramin Janata High School tapered to less than 50 percent in those painful months just before the high school diploma test known as the School Leaving Certificate (SLC) exam.

But what amazed me about the village was how the local people had a sixth sense for the precious substance. After rains, I would see children using *batukos*—pint-sized silver bowls—to scoop it up from puddles. My landlord kept a towel hanging on a string outside the door to collect the cool mist, which made the perfect face-wiping rag. Washing was a careful ceremony for which only the slightest bits of soap were used to cleanse dishes that were first coated in black ash from the fire pit before being set in sunlight. "Soap eats water, that's the key thing to remember," my landlord, Chandra Magar, would teach me. "The sunbeams are just as good as soap."

On Saturday mornings, I made the journey as well to wash my uniform and bathe. It was an arresting scene of yellow and purple shawls stretched out in the bright sun. The water always felt so relaxing, especially after a week of not bathing. I bathed seven or eight times, irrationally thinking it could somehow make up for the lack of baths during the rest of the week. Men usually sat on the rocks and talked village politics. Women sat under the banana trees complaining about their husbands while layering coconut oil in each other's hair. I found the scene very tranquil, and I viewed the water-carrying ritual as an important layer of the culture. Sometimes people sang Magar songs, which resounded against the granite walls of the riverbed. Young people were known to fall in love during the long walks down. Men behaved like children at the river, searching for a creature known as *paaha,* the local salamander, which lived under medium-sized rocks. The technique for finding *paaha* was flicking a flashlight on and off, which drew the salamanders from between the white stones. When one drew close enough, it was stabbed and then, while still writhing, roasted over a small fire next to the river.

But I always came back to my house irritated, with bloody leech bites on my feet, my hands numb from clutching stinging nettles to break my fall along the way. "Namje's leeches must like that sweet American blood!" my neighbors liked to joke. In fact, by the time I had bathed in the freezing water, washed all my clothes, and trekked back up the mountain, I was already sweaty again, making it all seem pointless. After a while I stopped going down to the river and adopted what I thought was a brilliant system of washing a different body part every day of the week with a single cup of water, so that at the end of a seven-day cycle I had essentially bathed my whole body. I got lazy and started drinking soda when I was thirsty, which was available in Tanka Sir's convenience shop, but this made me more dehydrated.

Because of drought, Namje lacked any of the typical microbusinesses, such as *chia pasals* (tea shops) or *daal bhat* (rice and lentil) restaurants. The only reliable livelihood was farming a spicy white radish that grew naturally without any water. Though it emerged from the ground covered in mud, when washed, this radish was the brightest shade of white I had ever seen. Millet also grew without any attention, but most of it went toward making the local home brew, which was consumed in the pint-sized *batukos* as if it was food. Raising larger quantities of goats, chickens, pigs, and cows—the driving economic engine of most rural villages in the Middle Hills—was out of the question because of water scarcity.

I wondered how this village, so close to Dharan, a city of 107,000 people, which even had a nine-hole golf course, could be even less established than a place like Silanga, where no such water issues existed. When I asked other teachers in the school why the government hadn't helped the people of Namje, the math teacher, Narayan Bhattrai, quoted a Nepalese saying I had also heard in the villages near Kathmandu: "*Battimuni andhyaaro*" ("Below the lightbulb it is darkest.").

During my first few weeks in Namje, I diligently concentrated on teaching, though I didn't care for the English textbook at all. Each chapter contained a new episode in the life of a pesky Brahmin monkey named Chankhe. The Nepali word *chankhe* means "sneaky" or "cunning," but the simian had a slight gut from all the rice he ate, and so it was a play on the English word *chunky*. The students liked Chankhe, who was always outwitting his human masters, but I found him quite annoying. Mostly, I had the students enact dramatic situations, which they enjoyed doing. I tried to use English-language scenarios that might actually arise in their future lives, so often I put them in airports in Abu Dhabi or at the visa counter of the Malaysian consulate in Kathmandu. Most of the English I inadvertently taught them had to do with leaving Nepal.

In Silanga, I had learned my limits. I tried my hardest to look at the water problem through anthropological spectacles. I knew the dangers of trying to alter a culture and I wasn't about to put myself in that position again. I was enjoying what I had come to Nepal to do: teach. But the water crisis kept discharging into my classrooms. Toddlers would tug on my shirt asking for a glass of water, and I usually had no choice but to send them home or out into the bazaar where a small cup of water cost five rupees. The first time I asked the school peon, Birkha Sir, where the water tank was, Birkha tittered cynically and pointed me to a dirty, half-filled plastic bucket with "Water Tank" written on it. Some days, huge colonies of bullfrogs would show up on the school grounds, and Birkha would run out to stop the children from stabbing them with pencils and twigs. Apparently, the new school building was built on an in-filled pond that was once the frogs' home.

Many of the students had dime-sized, bloody open sores around their mouths and on their forearms. Others had odd lumps in their cheeks or more often on the back of their necks. I could tell that everything was treated with some kind of iodine tincture, as students would come to class with purple smudges all over their faces. "*Pani boknu paryo sir*" ("I was fetching water, sir") was the equivalent of "My dog ate it." Some days I would look out at my class and wonder if I was in the pediatric ward of a hospital.

The school had a toilet, but it was more a nest for flies than anything else. Poor Birkha Sir had the undesirable task of trying to clean it without any water. Some days I would see him preparing to go in, his feet covered with knee-high rubber boots and his face masked tightly with a shawl as he held his breath and entered, to the delight of the students who looked on and counted how many seconds he would survive inside.

"*Rajeev Sir uthnus! Paani aayo!*" ("Rajeev Sir, wake up! The water is here!") Each morning I woke up to the same sound of my landlord Chandra Magar kicking open the thick, wooden front door. Panting, he would flick off his rubber slippers and slowly step inside as he crouched down, his fingers bracing the wall until the base of his wilting bamboo *doko* met the ground. I had rented the two rooms on the second story of his beautiful stone house, which was just twenty feet below the road. I usually felt angry at Chandra ji for waking me up when it was still dark, but then the guilt would set in as I listened to the sound of water loudly crashing into the plastic pail next to my cot.

Talking to Chandra ji always seemed to help put everything in perspective. "Rajeev Sir, I wanted to ask you a question," he said one morning. "How come you are so tall? Is it because you eat three times a day instead of twice a day like Nepalis do?" I had been called many things in my life but, at five feet four, never tall. Another time he asked me my salary. When I told him it was 8,000 rupees per month (about $105) he gasped and said, "You live the good life, sir!"

Some nights when it rained heavily I would hear the sound of Chandra ji's feet on the roof above me as he fastened and adjusted the gutters to channel the water into a rusty drum. The pile of firewood next to his attached kitchen was pitched ten degrees so that water could flow over the logs into a small plastic jug. In fact it seemed that anywhere water would fall Chandra ji had put a cup or a jug to collect it.

I renovated the rooms by removing the wall between them and installing large north-facing windows. I suppose the villagers were used to the sight of the Himalayas, but I never quite got used to it. Waking up to the sight of Kanchenjunga, the third tallest peak in the world, never ceased to fill me with awe. I loved everything about his house—except the toilet.

Out of flattened, rusty metal kerosene tins, Chandra ji had constructed a trapezoidal structure that was intended to provide privacy and shelter from the elements but had large, gaping holes in it and was situated right next to the pig sty. Sometimes when I was in the toilet I would have long, uncomfortable eye contact with the eighty-kilogram pig snorting in the pen next to me. Chandra ji tried to cover the holes with shreds of plastic and other materials, but some days the wind would blow so hard that half of the coverings would fly off. Then he would come running with new discarded materials to cover the holes.

Chandra ji's entire livelihood came from carrying three *gagris* of water daily for the soldiers who guarded the local towers. His finances allowed only one vice: smoking hand-rolled, unfiltered cigarettes. Almost every evening he would appear in the doorway with a faded black plastic bag of loose tobacco, shyly asking if he could enter. Seated next to the door, he would tear off a three-inch slip from a roll of coarse white paper into which he would carefully pack the tobacco leaves. Before lighting up, he would fetch me a steel cup from his kitchen filled to the brim with *jaad,* the sour, milky, homemade millet beer. I think he did this to make himself feel less guilty about his smoking.

"Rajeev Sir, this village is hell," he said one night as he moistened the cigarette paper. "I don't mind fetching water, but it's my children, Deepak and Chanamati. They fight every morning over who gets to sleep in and who has to go to Saacho Khola. This morning they fought for an hour. Maybe if I can get this job in the chicken factory in Malaysia, I can buy land down in the Terai . . ." he said sealing the roll-up. A lot of people talked about moving to the river plains but no one ever did. Perhaps the clearest symbol of the pain in Namje was how this man found clipping chicken wings in a hot, foul-smelling Malaysian sweatshop more desirable than living here.

"Chandra ji, you out of everyone must at least be happy, no? If there was water in Namje, you'd be out of a job, right?" I naively suggested.

"I'd rather be unemployed," he said. "You know, the Maoists are going to blow up those towers. It could come very soon. The army don't even sleep there anymore at night, but I have to go in and wash their dishes. I just don't want to be there when that happens!" he said, exhaling a small dark cloud. I was starting to see how eastern Nepal was no less dangerous than the western part of the country.

Watching the smoke curl up toward the bare bulb that hung from a beam holding up the pitched tin roof of the house, I realized I had to do something about this water crisis. I couldn't bear it anymore. *How could people live like this?* After an uneasy sleep, the next morning I walked to Bhedetar, found a phone, and ordered a book from the Peace Corps library on how to build a water project.

Three radiant sunflowers lined the edge of Gunjaman Magar's courtyard, which was a ten-minute walk down an uneven path from the road. Flowering mustard crops, which looked almost neon as the sun faded, rolled below. I had asked Tanka Sir to organize a village meeting here so that I could ask questions about the water problems.

As we took our seats, Gunjaman dai's wife, Laxmi, who wore a beautiful gold *bulaaki* in the bridge of her nose, handed Tanka Sir and me a bronze plate with four cups each containing a different milk product:

cream, buttermilk, yogurt, and pure ghee. "This is why he's the most powerful person in the village," Tanka Sir whispered. "No one else would dare raise this many cattle in a place like Namje. One cow drinks as much water as an entire family."

Though he had only a third grade education and often signed his name with his inked thumbprint, Gunjaman dai, who was known for his strong, powerful grip, was the unchallenged leader of the village. He was not only the village mayor but also school board president, the local agricultural cooperative director, and even the local judge. Recently, he had very reluctantly accepted the position of Women's Cow Savings Group president until they could agree on a permanent female representative. His home functioned as the village administrative center.

The dozen or so men insisted on sitting on bamboo mats on the floor under thick cotton blankets to keep warm, some with cigarettes dangling from their lips. Tanka Sir, Gunjaman dai, and I sat on the veranda along the facade of Gunjaman dai's house. Tanka Sir explained how I had some questions I wanted to ask them directly about the water problem. Then, unsure of my appropriate role at the meeting, I said, "I'm supposed to teach English in this school but I don't see the point as long as the students are out fetching water all day," I said. "Is there any way to fix this problem? Is there some higher water source that can be tapped?"

"We've looked far and wide," Tanka Sir said, pointing at the hills all around us. "We couldn't find a higher stream or lake anywhere. Namje Hill is the highest point twenty miles in any direction."

"What about rainwater?" I suggested.

"There's no rain for almost nine months of the year," Gunjaman dai's daughter Kalpana explained. My very naive question about rainwater made one of the old men laugh so hard he started coughing violently and had to get up to spit out the phlegm caught in his throat.

"What about the fog?" I asked. Namje was almost always enveloped in curling clouds, as the steamy air from the Terai rose to six thousand feet.

"They tried it already in Dada Bazaar but it failed," a boy named Raate, who worked as a technician in the local Kantipur FM tower, explained. Dada Bazaar was about an hour from Namje and had an identical problem and a much larger population. A large net was installed on the top of Bhanu Dada, the tallest hill, and water ran down the fibers of the rope into a collecting pond, but it amounted to only a few *gagris.*

"Well, is there any water source higher than Saacho Khola where the water could be pumped from?" I asked finally. At the mentioning of the word *pump* some of the men seemed to perk up in their blankets.

"Saacho Khola is the only option," Kalpana explained. "If that river dries up, we have to move the village to Dhade permanently."

I took stock of what I was hearing. There was literally no other option, it appeared, aside from pumping the water from that river, but having walked down to it, I knew how far it was. There was also the problem of the conflict. Building a project would invariably involve work within the forests, where it was possible to get caught in crossfire between Maoists and security forces at any time. When I asked my next question, several of the women who I didn't realize were listening in came over and stood behind the men. "Has anyone ever surveyed whether it is possible to pump the water from Saacho Khola?" I asked.

"There was a British NGO [nongovernmental organization] that came about eight years ago to survey the possibility," Tanka Sir recalled. "The engineers said it was definitely feasible but would cost millions of rupees. They feared that a poor village like Namje could never maintain it." To hear that it was at least possible was a promising sign. Then I interjected suddenly, "Would you be interested in building a water project like that? If we could somehow construct it, would you dig the trenches and carry the materials?"

"How can a river run backwards?" one of the old men asked, a quizzical look on his face.

A young woman with a *doko* on her back was standing out of the light as she listened in on the meeting. Setting down the *doko,* she walked purposefully into the courtyard and almost yelled in a booming voice, "Rajeev Sir, I'll work for ten years if that's how long it takes! I'll build that water tank with my own bare hands if I have to!" she said, lifting up her sleeve.

There was animated conversation in the Magar language as more women trickled in. Tanka Sir, who was not Magar, was now huddling within the cotton blanket, speaking in the local tongue, and pointing down at Saacho Khola and then up at the towers. I wasn't sure what was being said, but people seemed excited. Suddenly a seventy-year-old man pushed on Tanka Sir's shoulder to get himself to a standing position. Raising his fist, he yelled, "*Pani thanau!*" ("Let's pull the water up!")

Others joined him chanting, "*Pani thanau!*" The chorus of voices grew louder. "*Pani thanau! Pani thanau!*" More women from nearby homes came and joined, exuberantly chanting, "*Pani thanau! Pani thanau!*"

That night I lay in my bed awake, a thousand questions swirling around my head. I had taken some physics in college during my brief flirtation with premed, though I had no idea what was involved in a water project. I worried that the workers would possess all the likenesses of Maoists, their pockets lined with maps and sharp cutting tools. The Royal Army was smoking out Maoists from the villages based on circumstantial clues. My concern was that the people working on the water project would be constantly moving through the jungles and could easily be confused with Maoists or get caught in a crossfire. It was a legitimate concern. But I was energized by the villagers, and with the sound of their voices fresh in my ears, I turned on the light and worked feverishly the next two hours making a list of the next steps.

CHAPTER 4

✑

Saacho Khola

We had no idea how to proceed—we hadn't done a single survey of the land, and if we were being honest, none of us really knew anything about pumping water.

We invited the district engineers in Dhankuta to help us with the initial survey. About twenty villagers and I spent an entire week waiting for them at the road head with plastic buckets, stopwatches, measuring tape, and packets of instant noodles. When they never showed, we decided to do the survey ourselves. With only a flimsy measuring tape, it took the band of men several days to measure the distance from the river to the top of the hill, which ended up being 989 meters. From the river, the red slow-blinking light of the tower felt ominous like a warning signal. As we descended into the granite ravine, I wondered how people could even work in this setting. How would pipe be buried and fastened under these boulders?

Karna Magar was a soft-spoken thirty-year-old builder from Thumki, a small village five minutes from Namje. Though he had only a ninth grade education, Karna ji had built more than thirty houses. His own house was the only one in Namje or Thumki that had hot water, because he had connected a *gagri* to the chimney of his fire pit. He was a skilled electrician who also knew how to cut, thread, and fasten galvanized iron pipe because of a year he spent in Dubai working in a pipe fittings factory. "He's our local engineer," Tanka Sir boasted. "He's doesn't have the papers, but he can build anything. Those clothes he's wearing—he sewed them himself."

During those walks down to the river, I learned a lot of things. I observed where my students lived and who their parents were, and in class the next day I felt closer to them. I also realized how the villagers possessed a vast arsenal of technical and scientific knowledge. I had never thought about where water came from, but at Saacho Khola the men lifted up heavy rocks to reveal places where freezing, pure *pani* literally bubbled up from the ground. Just before we entered the ravine, one of the old men pulled off a piece of dark bark from a tree and told me to suck it, which I reluctantly did, discovering it to be *daalchini,* or cinnamon. Another man handed me a crushed flower, the seeds of which were an analgesic that numbed my mouth. It was a salve for tooth pain. There was a tree called *ritha,* which produced the Nepali soap, and another bamboo-like shrub called *amliso* planted all over the land adjacent to the river, which not only prevented soil erosion but also was used to make the Nepali brooms. Whereas everything looked green to me, the villagers saw many practical shades.

The book on water pumping finally arrived from the Peace Corps library in a thick brown envelope. There were chapters on pumps, sand filters, groundwater sources, and grey water recycling. My home became a kind of office as Tanka Sir and Karna ji sat at the wood table working on various logistics while I read the book and tried to convey what it said. Most nights we ate dinner at Tanka Sir's house as we continued talking. I couldn't believe how many different kinds of pumps there were. Some pulled the water, while others pushed it; some could be submerged whereas others were dry pumps that required separate chambers. Certain pumps ran on kerosene and diesel whereas others needed a three-phase electric line, and a few pumps, miraculously, were powered by the flow of the river itself. I had no idea if any of these pumps would be available in Nepal or suitable to the specific conditions of Namje.

The book described a common-sense method to measure the flow of the river called the "bucket method." All we had to do was count how many seconds it would take to fill a twenty-liter plastic bucket. Dividing twenty by the number of seconds it took, we would know the rate. On the day we descended to Saacho Khola to calculate the river flow, nearly thirty people gathered in front of Tanka Sir's house, including the VDC chairman, Anil Rana Magar. Using dark green banana fronds, the men concentrated the water in one area. Anil ji held the bucket as the cold water came crashing into it, and we counted seven seconds. "I can't hold it anymore!" the diminutive VDC chairman cried, as the water splashed in his eyes. From this we calculated the flow to be 3.5 liters per second at its nadir in the dry season. It seemed like a drizzle to me but, according to the book, it was more than sufficient for the 535 farmers, 450 students, and 100 staff and soldiers in the tower. In fact it was even enough water to irrigate the whole mountain. Before we walked back up, I took a picture of everyone there. The mayor flipped the bucket over and sat on it, posing with a sickle. In the background, standing behind the others, Karna raised the measuring tape in the air.

We found a scope that belonged to the road department to measure slope. It was fastened to a tripod and resembled a 1920s Polaroid camera. After three days of readings, we tallied all the measurements. The final vertical height from the river to the highest home in Namje was 1,271 feet—21 feet taller than the Empire State Building.

"This doesn't look good at all! You must go to Kathmandu," Tanka Sir said, studying the trail of red and yellow puss-filled rashes climbing up my right arm. The infection had started around my wrists but was now up to my shoulders and I was getting feverish. It was the kind of rash my students got. I started to think about those other volunteers before me who couldn't stay in Namje and hoped I would be okay. My reaction to the rash was a sign of how obsessed I was becoming. Even as I worried about my health, I felt it was fortuitous timing because I could spend the hours between checkups researching water pumps and meeting with water engineers in Kathmandu. "Rajeev Sir, don't worry about the water project. Just take care of yourself," Tanka Sir said through the window of the minivan, patting my shoulder and looking concerned.

It took almost a week of rest at the Hotel Mountain to get rid of the rash. I had to squeeze a red liquid antibiotic into nearly boiling water and soak in it three times daily for two hours each time. After four months in Namje, even though I had contracted scabies, I was grateful to take a hot bath every day and used the time lying in the tub to brainstorm the next steps in the process. In spite of the baths, one of the larger infections on my upper forearm wouldn't go away and had to be removed by incision, which left a one-inch scar.

At first all I could find by way of water hardware were shops selling brass bathroom fixtures in Teku, in the southern outskirts of Kathmandu.

The only water pumps available were household units for pumping a few hundred liters one or two stories. After more searching I learned of an Indian manufacturer called Kirloskar, which built powerful industrial pump sets. I hailed *a tempo* to their office in Naxal.

A faded map with various hand-scrawled markings and calculations on it was a visual history of how the water project idea had germinated. We had spontaneously started drawing on a piece of paper, marking the location of the river, some of the homes, and the towers. As the survey continued, we kept adding to it, and no one bothered to make a new map. It was completely out of proportion, with Tanka Sir's cave-like house bigger than the towers and Saacho Khola the size of the Mississippi. In the center was a large golden beer stain that looked like a rising sun. As I unfolded the torn, beer-stained map for Mr. Patil, the Kirloskar company's engineer, I could tell from his expression that he knew this was going to be an unusual assignment. We talked for six straight hours as I asked him every question I could conceive of and he patiently answered. To explain, he drew on Tanka Sir's map, which now looked as if it had been sketched by Chankhe Monkey. Sensing my fears, Patil kept reassuring me we need not worry about the force of the pumps. He suggested having two stations, one at the river and one midway, where there was a large tea field. Centrifugal pumps were the easiest to maintain but would require a three-phase electric line. I didn't know quite how we would get electricity down to the river, but I was also starting to see this was the least of our problems.

The large vertical distance, or "head," complicated things since the weight of the water within the pipeline was itself enough to rip the pipe out of the ground. The thought of exploding pipes terrified me because Maoists were making bombs from pipe sockets at that moment in Nepal. Expensive nonreturn valves and clamping systems would have to be engineered. The geography was very rocky and I had no idea how we would blast through, but I just made notes, hoping that Karna ji would be able to solve all these things. I put in an order for three pump sets, one of which would serve as a spare. Mr. Patil, noticing some calculations Tanka Sir had made on the back of the paper, asked, "Who wrote these numbers?"

"Oh, it's nothing, just some estimates," I said, feeling embarrassed.

"Actually, this number, $45,000, seems right to me. This is what the project should cost you."

When I returned to Namje, Tanka Sir, wearing an undershirt marked SINGAPORE POLICE, was standing on a tuft of dirt as he commanded more than fifty people, including students from the school, who were carrying excavated rock in the same bamboo *dokos* used to carry water. They were already digging the three circular reserve tanks at the top of the hill. "We're going to use this for rainwater catchment if the pump doesn't work," Karna ji said. "That's why we're building it first." Gunjaman dai was crushing *giti* (aggregate) with a hammer. Crushing *giti* was the lowliest occupation, even in the rural countryside, but Gunjaman dai was doing it proudly. I ran back to my room to get my camera.

"Rajeev Sir, we're going to need money to buy cement, pipe, and other materials. Do we have any money?" Karna asked me, rather concerned that we hadn't really discussed any of the finances yet. Every time I was asked about money, I had brushed it off because I felt convinced that the money was secondary and someone would surely fund the effort. I booked a plane ticket just before Christmas to New York. "Keep digging the trenches," I reassured Karna ji as I left for JFK Airport, not sure exactly where to find $45,000.

"You expect us to donate this huge sum of money for a village in Nepal? Don't you think the Nepalese government should do this kind of infrastructure project?"

"The problem is Nepal is undergoing a civil war, so the government is rather defunct," I countered, recognizing too late it was a horrible idea to bring up the Maoist war.

My parents had organized a holiday party in our home in Manhasset Hills, Long Island, and as the spiked eggnog was flowing, I broke out the slide projector to show images of women and children in Namje carrying water. The moaning was audible when I showed slides of the bloody sores and infants with scabies. Most of my father's friends were, like him, Indian physicians who had grown up in the Thar Desert of Rajasthan with memories of carrying water as children, so I had hoped they would be sympathetic. An endocrinologist was incredulous that he was being hit up for money, his pituitary gland throbbing at the sight of the images.

"Rajeev, why are you doing development work when there's a war going on?" he pointedly asked, looking around at the others to see if they found it as absurd as he did. "Shouldn't you wait till the country is more peaceful?" The others nodded in agreement. It wasn't looking good.

"Rajeev, tell me something. You will build this water project and who will take care of it after you leave?" another doctor asked. I glanced at my parents, who were probably regretting this fund-raising idea. I wanted to tell them I wasn't building it, that the local people were, but I was too defeated to continue speaking.

Just as I was feeling it might be hopeless, my older brother Rishi stood up and said, "Look, there are twenty BMWs parked in the street outside, each of which could bring water to this village in Nepal. I'm writing a check and you probably should too," he said, handing me a folded check, which I would later observe was in the amount of twenty dollars. Then an ophthalmologist raised his hand and said, "You've got a thousand from me."

"And me," another echoed.

"I'll give you two thousand!" a cardiologist said.

In about ten minutes, I was holding $20,000 in checks representing every subspecialization of the medical profession, a sum that was eventually matched by the Peace Corps.

When I got back to Namje, I casually dropped the news that we had all the money in a bank in Itahari. From that point on, for the next six months, the people in faraway Dada Bazaar would see a long, colorful line of villagers digging the 989-meter pipeline from Saacho Khola to the foot of the towers. Lama Sir rearranged our teaching schedules so that Tanka Sir and I had the last two periods off to work on the water project. He emptied a classroom and made it a pipe cutting station so that we could check on things during breaks.

Karna ji's rule was that the three-inch galvanized iron pipe had to be interned at least one meter under the rock, which sometimes annoyed the villagers since certain spots were solid, dense rock. Women smashed at this rock all day with pointed iron rods called *jhampals* until they would finally crack in two. Conveniently, the distance from the neck to the feet of one of Karna's workers was exactly one meter, so this man would be lowered into the trench as a living ruler to confirm the height before the pipe was fastened and buried. Karna and his assistant, Mahesh Bhujel, connected each of the two hundred pieces by layering the threading with jute strings painted over with black paint before being carefully fastened. I didn't realized how complex it was to create a leak-proof pipeline.

One afternoon, when twenty-six electric poles were plunked in front of Tanka Sir's house by the Nepal Electric Authority, I had no idea how these long, heavy objects would be transported, but Gunjaman dai simply cradled one and slid it down the hill till it landed exactly where it needed to be, and the other men ran down to erect it. Seeing the poles fly down the hill, I cringed, thinking someone was going to be hurt.

The last one hundred meters of the pipeline near the river was the hardest to construct. The terrain consisted of steep drops. But the villagers had built tall stone precipices to buttress it. When a black pit viper sprang out of a bush near the river, Gunjaman dai sliced it in half with his *khukuri*.

More than 350 bags of cement and thousands of kilograms of heavy iron rebar were carried from the road head all the way down to the river. People were getting fatigued. A one-armed water carrier for one of the towers, Purna Bahadur Magar, who was a singer, had written a beautiful and inspiring song about the water project. His undulating voice and the sad and wistful look in his eyes when he sang evoked so much emotion that villagers often cried. He slowly bent forward and backward at the waist as his powerful voice moved up and down octaves, gesturing slightly with his left arm, which ended at the elbow. When the villagers were completely spent from the arduous labor, Tanka Sir would have Purna dai pop out of the bushes and sing the water song. "*Tanna Rassile*" ("Pull It Up with a Lasso"), which became an anthem for the project, was about a village trying to pull water up a mountain with a giant blue lasso. It was a mysterious song to me, as it ended with the villagers slipping and falling down the hill. When I asked Tanka Sir about it he said it was just a poetic trope weaved into Nepalese songs.

After more than a year of labor, the pickup truck finally arrived from the customs checkpoint at the India-Nepal border. The seven-foot aquamarine water pumps, which each weighed more than eight hundred pounds, were made of cast iron, and I again wondered how these would be transported. But the men were already slinging long, green bamboos under the steel mounts. They carried the dangling motor down to Saa-cho Khola as if it were an empty *gagri*.

Karna ji's most brilliant engineering was the reserve tank he had con-structed onto the base of a massive eight-meter-wide boulder recessed from the river. Because of this, the tank was protected from landslides, and we saved a great deal of money not having to build a concrete base. The day the holding tank was completed, the usually staid and quiet Karna stripped down to his shorts and declared, "Now we must check if it is leak proof!" cannon-balling into the twelve-foot tank as others followed. Not a great swimmer, I also jumped into the freezing water. As I looked at my friends and what we had achieved, I was struck by how completely at home I felt. How would I ever be able to leave this village I had grown to love?

On the day of the water inauguration in May of 2003, after sixteen months of labor and more than $50,000 of expenses, more than four hundred people from Namje and the surrounding villages crowded into the river and adjacent areas. Purna dai sang a new version of the water song in which the villagers had succeeded in pulling the water up. A he-goat that was almost as tall as a person was slaughtered by one of the local priests, who used an unusually long *khukuri* knife, and its blood was sprinkled on the pump propellers. It seemed everyone wanted to put their fingers on the red button to fire up the water pump for the very first time. "One–two–three!" Karna yelled as the mound of hands pushed down, but nothing happened.

"I don't think it worked," one of the villagers observed. "After all that work," another grumbled. My heart sank as I watched the men trying desperately to figure out what had gone wrong. The decapitated goat head lay there in the river with the water flowing over its opened eye.

We had no choice but to request the district engineer to help us. Gyawali Sir was overweight and wore his pants above his navel. He had a pocket protector that contained a nearly foot-long scientific calculator that almost covered his right eye. We tried to take the portly engineer, who seemed always to be looking over his shoulder anxiously for Mao-ists in the jungles, down to the river to see if he could inspect the pump, but when we were just a hundred feet below the road he said, "That's fine, I get the picture . . ." Flipping open his scientific calculator, he began punching calculations and shaking his head as we all looked on anxiously.

After a few minutes he sighed and said, "Fools! Of course the motor didn't turn on! Look here," he said pointing to a spot where the pipe was exposed above ground as it traversed a ravine. "You fools used plastic pipe for the main line! Do you know how much pressure there will be in the pipeline from the weight of the water traveling up this mountain? Whose idea was it to use plastic pipe?"

It was customary to paint the galvanized iron pipe black to prevent rusting, but the engineer mistook this for the high density polythene pipe, which was also black and used for low-pressure distribution lines. Karna ji tried to correct him, but Gyawali Sir cut him off, saying, "Do you actually think it is possible to pump water up this distance? Have you ever seen any village in Nepal try to do something like this? I warned Tanka Sir when he first came to ask for my help *not* to build this project without an engineer," he barked, snapping closed his calculator. "This isn't a project for a local village carpenter," he said gesturing toward Karna. When I noticed Karna nervously rubbing his *chappal* on a stone, I felt deeply irritated. I was aware of this pattern of district officials humiliating the local people.

"We don't need an engineer. Most engineers only make drawings but Karna actually builds things. Most engineers can't even walk down this mountain," I said. "In fact, Karna knows more than you do about water pumping."

Insulted, Gyawali Sir trudged up the mountain, signaling to his peon to get the car started. Before leaving, he rolled down the window and said, "Rajeev Sir, even if that pump does turn on somehow, which I don't think it can because you have foolishly used plastic pipe, when you go back to America, ask yourself: do you think these Magars can keep it running?" We were happy to see him leave.

"There is a new problem," Karna ji shared just when it seemed like things couldn't get any worse. "We found a big turd in the water tank at the river today." I assumed it was a benign practical joke but Tanka Sir was disturbed. "Who do you think did this?" he asked.

"Maybe someone from Gahiri Tol? The villagers there have been upset about the water project from the beginning, and their village is the closest to the tank. Also, I should mention—it looks like more than one person was involved," he said, showing us with his hands how vast the turd was. Gahiri Tol was an agricultural village just below Namje, adjacent to Saacho Khola. They had erroneously come to believe that even though we were pumping water from below their water source, it would somehow lessen their yield. There was apparently a great deal of jealousy about Namje in Gahiri Tol since Namje was closer to the road.

"We must go now to talk to them," Tanka Sir said as he grabbed his woolen cap and scarf. "Today it is a shit; tomorrow it could be a bomb." Then he said an expression, which he would repeat over and over again, always in English: "Politics is the *dur-tee* game."

When we arrived in Gahiri Tol, a dozen men were sitting in the courtyard of Mani Rana's house, their arms folded, looking very guilty. Mani began the meeting awkwardly, in a formal manner. A man was even taking minutes.

"Thank you all for coming," he began, going through the formalities of an official village meeting. "I wish to welcome our friends from Namje today to Gahiri Tol. Unfortunately, we have to discuss an incident that involves something that is embarrassing for me to even say . . ." he said, unsure of how to continue.

Tanka Sir motioned that he would take over. Standing in the center of the circle, Tanka Sir began his speech solemnly. "The condition in Nepal and in our village is not good. If the people of Namje and Gahiri Tol are one, then no one can come into our village," he said making a fist with his right hand, which he raised in the sky as the others looked on with confused expressions. "But if the fist loosens, then we can get hurt," he said, poking his left index finger through the loosened fist. I wasn't sure exactly what he meant but it seemed the vice principal was saying that if the unity between these two villages diminished, the Maoists would be able to infiltrate through the cracks.

One of the men, Laxman Magar, shifted a bit and said, "Well, you know, if we had a toilet . . . we wouldn't have to look for other places to take a shit." This resulted in muffled laughter until everyone including Tanka Sir and Karna ji couldn't help but find it comical. We had gotten to the bottom of the problem. Tanka Sir promised a toilet would be built for Gahiri Tol, to which the men applauded. Peace had been brokered. "Rajeev Sir, if you want to work in villages, you cannot neglect even one person," Tanka Sir said as we walked back up the hill to Namje. Politics was quite literally a dirty game, I reflected.

A few days after the defiling of the water tank, six loud gunshots were heard from across the hill in Fakship VDC. At the road, a crowd of people had gathered next to a truck. The police had put a thorny bush in front of it, suspecting the driver, who was from Bhedetar, of being a Maoist. The subinspector, who had been caught in the crossfire in Fakship earlier that day, had his gun out of the holster and appeared intoxicated and out of control. When he tried to drag the man out of the truck, a local woman, Sarita Rana, stood between them and said, "If you take him, you take us all." Everyone knew those words were true in more than one way. Sarita didi, though her lip was quivering, didn't back down. The truck driver was allowed to go and quickly drove off. The subinspector angrily marched up to the Kantipur tower. The villagers scurried home in all directions, and soon it was almost dark.

"Please lock up tonight," Chandra ji said, handing me a new, heavier wooden bar made of *sekhuwa* wood to lodge against my front door. "The situation is not good." I opened my pail and realized I had run out of water, as everyone was too afraid to go down to the river. A police post in Ochre village, which was just four kilometers from Namje, had been detonated, and soldiers were out looking for the Maoists who did it. We had been so busy on the water project we didn't realize Maoists were stepping up plans to bomb the towers, infiltrating many of the surrounding VDCs. It was believed that the Maoists now controlled more than forty-five of Nepal's seventy-five districts. If there was an attack in nearby Bhedetar I knew it would be massive, because the large battalion there guarded the strategic gateway into the eastern Himalayas.

That night I slept on the floor under my cot, terrified that the Kantipur FM tower was going to be blown up. I couldn't stop thinking about the elbows, joints, couplings, and other hardware in the pump stations, and whether Maoists would steal them and make bombs out of them. I put up a barrier of pillows, as if that would deflect any stray bullets. Part of me hoped it would just happen already, since living in fear with my fingers in my ears was a dreadful feeling. But the explosion never did come.

Looking at my steel trunk, which had fewer and fewer physical belongings and more dents in it, I started to wonder if my time in Namje hadn't been an utter waste for everyone involved. I felt guilty that I had wasted almost two years of the villagers' time. I felt totally depressed. I was only a few weeks away from leaving Nepal. During the days that remained, I stopped going down to the river, spending more time alone in my room behind the wooden *sekhuwa* bar.

A few nights later, Raate, the young man who worked at the Kantipur FM tower, came to my door. Even though Raate held the rank of peon, he had learned a few things about how electrical equipment operated by watching the sound technicians.

"Rajeev Sir, I can turn the pump on," he said, standing there under the bare bulb, his two silver earrings shining brightly. "What I think is that the pump is fine. The problem isn't the pumps, which are powerful enough: twenty horsepower. The pipeline isn't the problem either— Karna uncle built a strong pipeline. The problem is *voltage.*" I stared at him not sure where he was going with this. "Nepal's electricity comes from India. Those bastards in India use so much electricity that the voltage in Nepal dips down during the day. I see it every day in the tower, and that's why we have to use our generator so much. I think if we could somehow increase the voltage, the motor will turn on."

I was feeling so hopeless I didn't even have the motivation to try, but I reluctantly went with Raate and a local electrician, Bam Bahadur Magar, to Biratnagar, where we purchased a huge tin box that looked like a medieval torture device with heavy knobs on it, and brought it back to Namje. This device was an automatic voltage regulator (AVR), which was used to increase voltage. We put it in a Maruti van and brought it up to Namje.

That evening Karna ji, Bam Bahadur, Raate, and a group of other villagers went to the river at midnight to install the AVR. They brought flashlights and matches to hunt and roast a few *paahas* for dinner. I stayed in my room and went to sleep. Late at night as I was having an uneasy dream, I heard what I thought was my landlord bringing water to my room, "*Rajeev Sir uthnus! Pani aayo!*" ("Rajeev Sir, wake up! The water has come!")

When I opened the door expecting to let him in, it was Govinda Samal, one of my neighbors. Govinda dai was holding a live chicken upside down with its legs tied and a bottle of *raksi* (the local hard alcohol) with a bare corncob lodged in the top. "The water is coming up the hill! I've come to find a chicken to slaughter and wake everyone up! *Pani aayo Rajeev Sir!* Raate turned it on!" he said, running down the road yelling "*Pani Aayo!*"

I threw on a sweater and ran down the hill with Tanka Sir and Chandra ji. As we got closer to the second pump station, we heard a gurgling sound echoing in the pipes. We followed the sound slowly up the hill, listening carefully, until finally the first drops of water crashed into the middle tank with incredible force. Karna and Raate fired up the second pump, which created a high-pitched whirring noise that caused the wrenches and pipe fittings on the newly plastered floor to rattle. "Stand back, friends!" Tanka Sir warned. "Here comes the water!"

On July 9 at 6:34 a.m., when water poured into the three reserve tanks at the top the top of Namje hill, people living near the reserve tanks stepped out of their homes confused, thinking that rain was falling from a cloudless sky. As we stood around the tanks and listened to the water from Saacho Khola filling them, I don't think anyone knew how much Namje and Thumki villages would change over the next ten years and how complex the nature of those evolutions would be. Not knowing how to celebrate, we spontaneously picked up our local engineer and triumphantly carried Karna ji down the hill.

I was amazed I had survived two years in the Peace Corps in one piece. As I drove around the bend, out of the fog, I wondered if I was going home or leaving it behind.

CHAPTER 5

∽

The Hats

When President John F. Kennedy created the Peace Corps in 1961, I don't think he really considered that the true culture shock for the volunteers would be upon coming home. I was a case in point. The dirt from Namje's hills was barely gone from my fingernails when I became a "1L" at New York University law school in August of 2003—just eleven days after coming back from Nepal. Every day I took my seat in the last row, behind a sea of three hundred laptop screens, hoping not to be called on. Even when I had done the reading, my answers came out in broken English.

"Mr. Goyal, can you summarize for the class Justice Brennan's dissent in this case?"

Like a Nepali schoolboy I would stand up and gaze at the floor until Larry Kramer, my Civil Procedure professor, knew to move on to the next student. I was like this for most of my classes. In three years of law school, the only A I received was in Jewish and Talmudic Law. Nothing would stick, for some reason.

At first, I tried to force myself to be interested—I knew that the professors were brilliant thinkers and that law school would have some application no matter what I did in life. Still, I felt no passion. Knowing that I had opportunities to succeed that the students in the village could never dream of left me feeling guilty, but I still couldn't get motivated. My head was still in Namje and I worried about the villagers. How would Namje change now that there was water? In so many ways the water project seemed to me a beginning rather than a conclusion, and I knew that the success of the water system depended on much more than whether or not the 107 families in Namje and Thumki could keep the pump on.

Nepal itself was slipping steadily into civil war, and I kept one eye on the BBC Nepal news portal, which was always open on my laptop. Every time the king's bulletproof Mercedes left Narayanhiti Palace, it seemed the fate of the entire country could flip. In 2004 and 2005, Gyanendra was gambling on the fact that he could count on support from the international community in fighting the Maoists, but the man who would eventually become the last king of Nepal found himself increasingly alone. During that first fall term, I spent a lot of time roaming the streets of New York searching for any traces of Nepal I could find. *How in the world was I going to get through three years like this?* I wondered.

Before leaving Namje, I had mentioned to some of the local women that if they could knit some woolen hats I could probably sell them in New York City for fifteen dollars and could wire them the money. I was worried about what the women would do now that they had all this free time from not having to carry water. My casual suggestion would wreak havoc on the village economy and teach painful lessons about rural development. On the day I left, a long line of plastic bags crammed full of colorful hats was waiting for me on the road head. I could have opened a small store with all the merchandise. I packed two bags with me to Kathmandu, and Tanka Sir freighted the rest to New York. In total, there were four hundred hats in that first round that would make their way to the West Village, where I stored them in the living room of my older brother Rishi's 800-square-foot co-op on the corner of Bleecker and West Tenth streets.

The hats presented the perfect antidote to the tedium of law school, and, more important, a reason to stay connected to the people of Namje. It wasn't so much that the people there needed me but I needed them.

"Rajeev Sir, I cannot stop it," Tanka Sir hollered into the phone. "More and more hats are coming in each day! What should I do with them?"

"Send them to New York. I'll take care of it," I said reassuringly.

The new cardboard boxes that arrived at Rishi's apartment looked like they had weathered a journey around the girdle of the Earth. They stood more than four feet tall. When I opened the boxes, the distinctive smells of the village—the smoky fragrance from the mud homes, the sour scent of fermented millet wine, eucalyptus from the forests—brought back many emotions. I felt happy to know the village was still there and exactly as I remembered it to be. I was amazed to find new merchandise contained within the box—baby booties, leg warmers, oversized sweaters, and matted shawls. From the slip of paper enclosed, I learned eighty-nine women were now involved in the woolen wares business, and they had incorporated a cooperative called WADE, or Women's Association for Development Efforts. There was even a logo of a Nepali woman wading through a field of grass. I found this all immensely exciting, if unnerving, realizing I had better start moving hats fast! Rishi, who was working one hundred hours a week as a medical intern at Columbia Presbyterian Hospital, was less enamored with the initiative and, I admit, the hats were starting to mildew and took up almost half of the square footage of his apartment.

"These won't sell," Karma Sherpa, a successful Nepali hat entrepreneur declared. I had stopped in his shop on MacDougal Street to get advice about where to sell them. "These bright colors might be popular in villages, but in New York people want earth tones. They want plain, not crazy," he said, holding a particularly odd hat that had a percentage sign, ampersand, and dollar sign across the front of it. To my eyes, Karma's hats, which had earflaps and pointy tops, were more like those one might find in a J. Crew catalogue, but the Namje hats had character. Some had random letters of the alphabet repeated over and over again or mysterious words like "Mathematics" sewn into them.

"Rajeev ji, you should get these professionally washed to remove that village smell along with any bacteria. If you don't line the insides, they will cause dandruff," he warned, but I didn't have any money or time to do this, given my long hours in the law library.

Walking through Soho one cold sunny Saturday morning in October, I came across a street market in front of the Church of St. Anthony of Padua on Houston Street. A tall Italian woman selling designer sunglasses was in charge of issuing the vendor permits, and when I told her about the hats, she offered to let me to set up a stall. It was fifty dollars for a few square meters in front of a Nativity scene.

The next morning, I realized just how amateurish my operation was. The other vendors had sophisticated merchandise and attractive display systems, but mine was nothing more than a folding table with a mountain of hats on it.

I sold only two on that first day, bringing in just thirty dollars. I found a sixty-five dollar parking ticket on the windshield of my father's

Volkswagen Beetle, which I was using to transport the table. To make matters worse, in the middle of the afternoon, it rained, and the Namje hats got soggy as I ran to the car to retrieve an umbrella. I tried drying them in the dry cleaning store across from my brother's apartment, but some of them shrunk and had to be sold as children's hats.

"Rajeev Sir, we have just sent another five hundred. The women from the first batch are asking when they can get their money. What should I tell them?" Tanka Sir asked, panic in his voice.

"Five hundred?" Now I panicked. "That's a lot. . . . I don't think you should send me anymore . . . for *now* at least."

"The women have already started making more. I'll tell them to slow down."

"Okay, that's good. Tell them I need more time. I'm still doing market research." Every time Tanka Sir called, I couldn't bring myself to say stop.

But by Thanksgiving, I realized the trick was maybe to sell the *story*, not the hats themselves. It was when I put up a big poster with photographs of the women of the village that people actually started to stop and engage with me. Some bought hats even though I think they probably never wore them. I was surprised to learn that people were hungry to talk about treks they had taken in the Himalayas as well as their lifelong dream of doing the Peace Corps. I often found myself in discussions with interesting people about rural development. It was the inspiration they were buying.

As Christmas drew closer, I started getting bulk orders for ten or fifteen hats at a time, and so I called the village to confirm that the rate of hat production would continue to be brisk. Later I would start selling hats on the law school campus itself, especially in the classes where I knew students were bored to tears and craving diversions. The first time I mustered up the courage to stand up and make an announcement about the hats after Professor Mallman's tax law class, she looked at me with her sharp eyes in a manner so focused I thought I might be expelled. But after a brief pause she turned toward the wall where her jacket was hanging and from a shiny red pocketbook removed a crisp twenty-dollar bill, which she handed me, for a hat. In fact, for the next few classes she would turn to me at the end of class and make the announcement for me. After a while I didn't even need an announcement because people knew my accompanying green duffel bag always contained hats.

There was only one instruction the women of Namje could not follow. When an executive from one of the largest pet apparel companies in New York City stopped at the stall and asked if the women could make dog sweaters and booties, I called Tanka Sir.

"Dogs wear sweaters in America?" he asked very puzzled. The women in the village simply found it ridiculous that animals wore clothing in the United States, and thankfully, despite my passionate imploring, they never did knit them.

By the end of the semester, I had somehow sold $4,000 in hats, which I wired to the village, to be divided among the eighty-nine women. I felt guilty that there were nearly a thousand caps that had to be stored in the basement of my parents' home on Long Island as a constant reminder of how good intentions don't always lead to positive results.

As egregiously managed and ill-conceived as the hat project was, it kept me going psychologically. What I didn't realize at the time was that I was learning how to sell a cause I was passionate about. Wisely, the hat operation was eventually declared "unsustainable development" by Tanka Sir and shut down. Just a few hours after my last Civil Procedure final, a week before Christmas in 2004, I hugged the only two friends I had made in law school, John Brown and Steve Ankrom, and hailed a cab to Newark to get on a plane to Kathmandu, not sure exactly of the purpose of my trip but anxious to be back where it seemed I belonged.

In the transit lounge of the Abu Dhabi airport, I was surprised to discover hundreds of Nepali workers waiting at the gates. Many wore baseball caps with Arabic writing on them. Some looked as if they had been teleported there from a remote Himalayan village. One dark-skinned man in flip-flops and a *dhoti* carried nothing more than his travel papers in a plastic bag. I asked him what would happen once he arrived at his destination, and he answered, "*Mero manche linu aunchha*" ("My friend will be there to collect me."). Even the workers in the airport men's room were Nepali, which meant that some of the migrants had literally walked off the airplane straight into the men's room of the Abu Dhabi airport and been handed mops to scrub toilets for five or ten years. At the time, I didn't realize just how much the migration of millions of Nepalis overseas and the billions in foreign remittance they would send home would transform the rural corners and the overall economic structure of the nation. I felt angry that they were treated like chattel, the writing on their caps like bar codes indicating where they were to be deposited, but for some this was the most exciting journey of their lives and a means of earning wealth that would bring previously unknown opportunity. At the Kathmandu airport, UN helicopters sat on the runways and the usually lackadaisical guards actually seemed to be alert and protecting against something.

Curling around the mountain toward Namje felt surreal. I had made the journey hundreds of times before when we were building the water project, but now I wasn't a Peace Corps volunteer, but rather on a thirty-day tourist visa. Stepping out of the minivan into the bright winter sun set against the turquoise Dhankuta sky, I was overwhelmed to find about fifty villagers, including some of my former students, waiting with colorful flower garlands. At first the only change I noticed from the water project was that the glint in the women's golden nose rings was a bit brighter. A barefoot old man wearing what looked to be underwear and a tattered blazer handed me a bunch of roses and shook my hand energetically. A cloth banner had been posted on two feeble bamboo poles. It read, "WELCOME RAJEEV SIR ON YOUR 22ND VISIT TO NAMJE VILLAGE." They had meant to write "2ND," but it became a premonition of the flurry of trips I would make to Nepal over the next eight years.

"You have become fat!" exclaimed my former landlord, Chandra ji. Normally calling someone fat was a compliment in Nepali culture, but it was true; in just a few months I had put on more than twenty pounds from my sedentary lifestyle in law school. Jokes followed from others about how American food was probably tastier than Namje's *dhedo* and *sisnu,* the farmer's breakfast of cornmeal and boiled nettles.

That evening, as I set my things down on my old cot in Chandra ji's house, it felt as if nothing had changed. That feeling was enhanced by the fact that no one ever really asked me what I was doing in the United States. But there was one important change in my old house, which I noticed immediately: the infamous airy toilet in the rear had been replaced by a new cement structure. A concrete pigsty had also been built in exactly the same location as before, next to the new latrine. The next morning, crouching in the loo, through a triangular-shaped air vent I

saw the old sow staring at me again and grunting. I nodded to acknowledge her. It was good to be home, I thought.

Though my landlord Chandra ji rarely spoke in the community, in
his home he confided many of his frustrations with me. Usually it was
something related to money or the erratic health of his wife and children, who frequently became ill. Sometimes he complained about how
many guests they had, how his only son played too much soccer, or his
prematurely greying hair. That first night back he wanted to talk about
his own health.

"Rajeev Sir, I couldn't pass the medical exam for the wing-clipping
job in the chicken factory in Malaysia," Chandra said handing me a ma-
nila envelope containing an X-ray. At first it looked like a scan of his kid-
neys, but upon closer examination I realized I was peering at a magnetic
imprint of his private parts. "There is some problem with me, sir," he said
pointing to his lower abdomen with both of his index fingers. "I learned
a trick from Tumla's father, who also had this problem. He told me I
should eat lots of bananas and drink a glass of milk just before they do
the X-ray and it won't show up when they do the test at the manpower
agency. Rajeev Sir, is that true? The next time you come, pray that I'm
no longer here," he said shaking his head. I noticed his son, Deepak, who
was a heavier and shorter version of his father, shift in place awkwardly.
"Why do you have to go?" Deepak said sadly. "Rajeev Sir will help you
get a job right here . . . in Namje."

I had hardly been in the village a few days when Manish Magar
pushed open the thick wooden door of the house one evening and also
presented me with some kind of medical report. Manish was one of the
head builders on the water project, and we had spent many long days in
the field together.

"Sir, could you tell me what this says? It is in English, and I can't understand it." I scanned the report, realizing it was a pregnancy test.

"I'm sorry, Manish ji, but I think it is negative," I said, thinking he and
his wife were struggling to have a child and that my conclusion would
disappoint him. But from his audible sigh of relief I intuited the results
belonged to a woman other than his wife. I knew the water project
would usher in many changes, including more free time, but a rise in
infidelity wasn't something I had envisioned.

The next morning I woke up early to walk down the hill toward Saacho Khola. I wasn't sure yet why I had come, whether it was just curiosity or something more, but I wanted to see old friends and observe how my students were progressing. Villagers kept inviting me into their homes to have a glass of *raksi* and spicy radish pickle, the traditional fare for guests. I had a vague desire to get involved in agricultural projects, which seemed logical given that now there was water for irrigation, but I also knew I had no expertise to offer.

During the walk, one woman who lived along the trail to Saacho Khola, Padma Kumari, called me into her small home. No sooner had I sat down on a stool than her daughter, who was one of my former students, handed me what looked like four eggs fried into a giant omelet. When I saw a ball of yarn on the windowsill, I instantly knew why she had called me into her house. "My husband has been in Malaysia for four years and he hasn't sent us one rupee," she began, her eyes diverted to the floor. It was common for some men to not be able to save any money. "I need some money for my daughter's marriage, and I was hoping you could send the money from the forty-five hats I sewed." She looked as if she might cry. "I'm so sorry but I haven't been able to sell all of them," I confessed, guiltily trying to cut through the omelet with the spoon. The spoon started to bend, and the mother asked her daughter to give me a new one. I was learning firsthand that the hat project was more than just a lemon of an idea; it had distorted people's hopes.

Lying on my cot the next day I woke up to a squealing sound so terrible that I thought someone had been murdered, but when I opened my door I found it was my friend the old pig being stabbed through the heart. Because of the prosperity from the water project, people were obviously consuming a lot more meat. Villagers still woke at 4:00 a.m. as they had before, but instead of hauling water, they were fetching the markers of a new prosperity: bags of rice, cement, aggregate, and sand. I found it interesting that the water project hadn't really liberated people from physical labor but perhaps changed only the nature of it. Several villagers were building new cement homes. The banging of the mallets each morning started so early it seemed to wake the roosters. Everything about people's appearances was certainly cleaner and crisper, but there were now more messy piles of raw construction materials everywhere and the village resembled a noisy construction lot.

"I'm trying to raise fish," Tanka Sir's portly older brother said to me as I walked above the school one morning. "I'm going to fill this giant hole with rainbow trout and eat well every day! Can you believe it? The first fishery in Namje!" he said, pointing at a four-foot hole in the dirt that was as large as his belly. Unfortunately, some of the fish died from the near-freezing temperatures and the rest perished when the water seeped through the loose ground of the pond, which he had neglected to line with a plastic sheet, but it was encouraging to see people dreaming up new ideas.

No one had been sure if a bunch of radish farmers would be able to run the electric water pump. As far as we knew, this was the first rural village and school in the entire eastern zone to pump water from such an expansive distance. Not only had they been able to keep the pump going, they had even generated $3,000 in profit from selling water to soldiers guarding the towers. With the advent of water, five new radio and television towers would emerge, representing new water clients. By 2006, the village would generate $10,000 from water sales alone, funds that would be used to support a new teacher and repair the control panel when it was blasted from lightning strikes.

While the water project hadn't in an absolute sense ameliorated anyone's quality of life, in my opinion, it did seem to give the students more time to study and play. In 2003, only six out of eighteen passed high school, the following year thirty-two out of thirty-eight passed, which was the third highest percentage out of sixty-five high schools in the district. Harka Lama, the Namje principal, had wisely ordered all the teachers to move into Namje and Thumki so that they could provide tutoring courses before and after school. No longer fearful of sweating, children were now playing volleyball and football after school.

To encourage higher pass rates, I again made an undeliverable and vague promise, offering full college scholarships of $300 per year to anyone who could pass high school. I didn't stipulate how long I would support them, what the selection criteria would be, or other pertinent administrative details. Months later, when I got the call from Namje that thirty-two students had passed in 2004, I panicked and eventually had no choice but to retract the offer, disappointing the students. "Rajeev Sir, please think before you speak," Tanka Sir advised. "When you talk, people really listen!"

One afternoon as I walked by a villager's house and peeked inside, I was surprised to find his children sick in bed. "What happened?" I asked.

"My kids won't stop showering. They got pneumonia."

The new NGO office was no bigger than a broom closet, appended on to the school library. It was built out of rubber tires, discarded tin, and a sheet of plastic that functioned as a beautiful skylight. I found something deep in the simplicity of the organization's tattered setting. When I first saw the signboard for the NGO that read "SOCIAL WELFARE SERVICE CENTER," I thought the threadbare organization itself needed welfare support.

As I squeezed into the shed, I was surprised to see nine people inside, each representing one of the nine wards of Bhedetar VDC. In the narrow office, they were seated on two benches facing each other, their knees just barely touching. I hovered awkwardly in a corner as the villagers began presenting their demands to me. Because of the Maoist conflict, the VDC offices across the country, which were the key centers of administration and local development, were not operational. At the time I didn't realize that Bhedetar Social Welfare Service Center (SWSC) was essentially a shadow VDC office and that, perhaps most alarmingly, I was the ill-suited American chairman. I recognized some of the faces, but I had never met many of the people sitting in the cramped office. The twelve thousand NGOs in Nepal were high-value targets for the Maoists because so much development money over the last fifty years had been embezzled and had gone into the pockets of development workers. From the beginning, I was perhaps overly wary of formal structures because of the Maoist stance, but the SWSC was innocuous. It had no real infrastructure of its own and was purely a volunteer organization.

"Rajeev Sir, you helped Namje get water, but now we need you in Mukten," Indra Maya Magar, a poised woman in a green sari, said. In time she would become the local Maoist commander. "There is a river called Bhanu Khola just one kilometer from the school; all we need is a small tank and some polythene piping." Mukten was nearly two hours from Namje, off the road, and surrounded on all sides by steep, dark blue valleys and low-lying hills that faded into the Seuti River. Its agricultural potential was infinite because of the rich soil quality and a slightly warmer climate than Namje. Aloe vera, avocados, grapes, coffee, asparagus, tomatoes, and even the Nepalese "soap tree" grew plentifully in the wild without any fertilizers. Beautiful orchids grew from branches in the forests and a highly valuable purplish medicinal plant known as *pakhambed* covered the boulders along the eastern edge of the village. When I was a Peace Corps teacher in Namje, I always wondered about Mukten, which I looked at every morning from my window.

One by one, representatives from villages I had never even heard of stood up and asked for a new water project: Patpate, Ekletaar, Kolpatte, Olaantaar, Jimi Gaun, Majuwa, Karkichap, Dharapani 1, Dharapani 2. After everyone finished speaking, I was so excited by the prospect of making more friends and knowing about their villages, I agreed to try to help them all.

Recklessly installing water pipelines was not the answer. The solution to a water problem might not be a larger water supply but changes in how the existing supply was managed. Projects were complex with environmental, social, and economic consequences—I knew this from the Namje water project. However, because I was no longer "on the ground," filling infrastructural voids was really all I could do. In a way, it also felt good to be needed after being unsure about why I was in law school.

For most of January, we walked for miles and miles all across the area encompassing the many villages administered by Bhedetar VDC, surveying and photographing new project sites. I was learning that "VDC" refers not only to the local administrative governing body but also to the large and diverse geographic area administered by this body. Though Bhedetar was just one of 3,913 VDCs in Nepal, I was startled by the caste and geographic diversity within it. "Each VDC is a small country," Tanka Sir liked to say. Tanka Sir, Karna ji, Gunjaman dai, and one of my former students, Hari Ale Magar, accompanied us wherever we went and coached me about these new settings. Tanka Sir proved to be the consummate insider and would point at an old man squatting in the back of the crowd and say, "Only his opinion matters in this community. Whatever he thinks, the village thinks," and I'd go straight over to talk only to him. Sometimes he would warn me in communities where people were concealing wealth saying, "Don't be fooled. They live in huts but own buildings in Dharan city. They wear rags but have gold under their bamboo mattresses." Knowing that information was invaluable to me.

The process was endlessly stimulating. I couldn't believe how big just one VDC was; it took over six hours to walk from Ward 1 to Ward 9, and the landscape transformed from white powdery rock to green ferns and waterfalls. Each place we went, it seemed, the lines of adorable children got longer and longer and the marigold garlands heavier and heavier. I had received so many *malas* and fried omelets that I wondered if any flowers or eggs were left in the villages. At one of the ceremonies a badge that resembled the accolade one might receive at the county dog fair was pinned to my lapel. "CHEAP GUEST," it read. (They had meant to write, "CHIEF GUEST.") As I kept agreeing to new water projects, the question I never stopped to ask myself was, Were these projects really needed?

On my third visit back to Namje in the summer of 2004, I returned with $13,000, which I had raised through a small Seattle-based NGO to fund construction of new water pipelines to be built by Karna ji with oversight from SWSC.

But I was left wondering, Did these new water projects make any difference? They probably did help mildly with off-season irrigation, but there was something unsatisfying about simply lengthening water lines and enlarging water tanks. What was the deeper *goal*? After the water was brought in, what then? I was beginning to see how development work was no less byzantine than the meaning of life itself.

Before leaving, I announced a competition in Namje. To the woman who could grow the largest onion, I would offer a 10,000-rupee prize. When I went back that summer, one by one the women presented their onions. Just when I thought we had found the largest bulb, which was almost the size of a grapefruit, Moti Maya Magar, a small, quiet woman with big, pointy ears, walked to the front of the room carrying something round and large under her shawl with two hands. Initially, I thought she was pregnant. When she lifted her shawl and set the pumpkin-sized, freakish onion on the wood table, one of its legs almost gave way. Later I would learn that she had used a massive quantity of dangerous chemical fertilizers and pesticides.

CHAPTER 6

✑

The Last King of Nepal

"MASSAGE FOR YOU" was the title of the first e-mail I ever received from Namje village. In 2004 Harka Prasad Lama had opened the first e-mail account in the village. Much of what Lama Sir wrote about was rather mundane but interesting to me: the monsoon starting earlier than usual, a former student getting married, or his selection for a $10-million-cash prize. When Nigerian princes wrote Lama Sir with lucrative business propositions, he innocently wrote back about a new scholarship program or library that was vitally needed in the villages, sometimes attaching proposals and photographs of students.

The two years I had been a Peace Corps volunteer in Namje between 2001 and 2003, the village existed in a dark zone, around the bend of a mountain, completely out of touch. There was no instantaneous way the people of Namje could be reached. But by 2005 more than a hundred cell phones were scattered among the people of Namje and Thumki, and each time I returned the ring tones were more diverse: crying babies, vulgar dialogue from Hindi films, and even peacock calls. The ring tones were so wonderful that most people waited a few rings before answering. I was starting to see that Namje was going to develop regardless of any aid worker's efforts. But the important question seemed to be *how* was it going to develop?

That first e-mail from Lama Sir, the first of thousands of subsequent "massages," contained one poignant sentence:

> Dear Rajeev Sir:
>
> We are here.
>
> Yours Truly,
> Harka Prasad Lama

E-mails were treated with more care and importance than official correspondence with the Royal Nepal Government, each one printed out, punched, and placed in a binder. Because of this, sometimes my casual suggestions were taken very seriously. On one occasion I wrote in an e-mail that a dentist friend of mine was interested in installing a dental camp in Namje. When I opened my inbox during class one day, there were hundreds of pictures of people's decaying molars. I detected an expression of horror in the person sitting immediately next to me in my law school class.

Discovering Google (which he pronounced "go-gal-eh") was like learning how to fly an airplane to Lama Sir. He could travel anywhere he wanted. On "Go-gal-eh" he could solve all the mysteries and provide the answers to all his questions. Lama Sir even opened e-mail accounts for Tanka Sir, Hari bhai, SWSC, and Gunjaman Magar. For those who could not type, Lama Sir would carry the messages to Dharan, type them up, and send them himself by logging into that person's account. This kind of communication, undoubtedly, helped me stay in tune with a community that, it seemed, was skipping generations of technological progress with each blink of the eye.

With the successful conclusion of six water pipelines throughout the VDC, requests were coming into SWSC for new schools. Lama Sir sent me a dozen letters from local principals in the area requesting seven-classroom school blocks. In July of 2004, we went on a fact-finding mission, assuming it would be fairly simple to determine which were the neediest. All we would have to do is figure out which school had the fewest classrooms, the most dilapidated infrastructure, I thought.

The first school we visited was in a place called Jimi Gaun, about thirty minutes down the hill from Thumki, amidst a serene, cicada-filled plantation of white and brown barked pear trees. Exhausted from the walk, we stopped to rest in the home of a school board member, Gyan Bahadur Rai, where we were served sliced pears to help us cool down.

Sitting in his humble house, I looked up and saw a large portrait of Jesus Christ hanging in the sitting room. It was a rather graphic image of the holy son tearing open his chest, inside of which was a glowing ember. I found it strange that he hadn't been made to look at least a little bit Nepalese. It seemed so out of place in this village without electricity, nearly an hour from the road. I had assumed that if any village was going to take up Christianity, perhaps it would be closer to an urban center or an airport, but this was not the case.

The school was a crooked two-room stucco building on a triangular wedge of grass with twenty-foot drops on all sides. It seemed odd that anyone would think to build a school in such a precarious location. When I asked the teacher, Narayan Chowdhary, to show us the rest of the educational facilities, I was startled to learn that this two-room shed was the *entire* school. The first room had a small metal placard that read "GRADES 1–3" and the placard for the second room read "GRADES 4 & 5, ETC." Of all the borrowed English words in the Nepali language, *etc.* was a favorite, and here it was, the placeholder for the library, teachers' room, and science lab.

At first, I was horrified to see the state of things. How could a school operate like this? But when I peeked inside the classroom, it actually didn't seem that bad. Students were seated in the corners of the room by grade level, diligently reading their books. The sound of hushed reading was interrupted only by an occasional sniffling nose. One of the older girls was even helping a young child read her lesson. Another was assisting the teacher by writing on the chalkboard. Contrary to what one might suspect in such a situation, the teacher was not overwhelmed but fairly relaxed, walking around the room brandishing a pear branch that he used to periodically smack anyone who misbehaved. In an odd way, it all worked rather well.

The school benches and tables were brought out onto the small precipice as about thirty villagers gathered to discuss the school's situation. As Chowdhary Sir, who had a diffident personality, opened his mouth to speak, a walnut fell from a tree next to the school and clunked him on the head, to the great delight of the villagers, who couldn't repress their laughter. One of the women stood up and, speaking in Rai, scolded everyone to settle down. Chowdhary Sir confessed to us that he didn't know where to begin. "There are a thousand problems in our school," he said. One of the problems he described was odd—the size of the windows was larger than that of the door, and this meant that students rarely used the front door to enter the classroom. Just as he said this, an elderly man inside the classroom poked his bare feet through one of the windows and obliviously walked toward us, eating peanuts as he strolled by, which incited another burst of uncontrollable laughter. I had expected the community to be miserable and was struck by how lighthearted and happy everyone was.

Another problem Chowdhary Sir described was that none of the students could speak Nepali. Although he was from the flatland Terai, after twenty years of living in Jimi Gaun, he taught his own lessons in the Rai language. I couldn't help but wonder if it wasn't a *strength* of the school that these children were trilingual, speaking some English, Nepali, and a complex indigenous Tibetan dialect.

The humble Chowdhary Sir had a problem of not speaking loudly enough. In fact Tanka Sir had told me earlier that day his quiet voice was jeopardizing his job, since many of the students couldn't hear him in class. As Chowdhary Sir was talking, almost in a whisper, a large burly Rai with powerful arms and legs and a wisp of a moustache, Uttar Man Rai, stood up and interrupted him in a booming baritone voice. "Chowdhary Sir, we appreciate your service to this school. However, as the school board chairman I must remind you as I have in the past that you need to speak louder in public settings!" I expected another round of laughter, but this was clearly not a laughing matter in Jimi Gaun.

When it came my turn to speak, which was usually at the very end of the ceremony, I simply promised a school. Even though we hadn't seen any of the others, I couldn't imagine they could be any worse than this shed under a walnut tree.

The next school we visited in a village called Karkichap was right on the Dharan-Dhankuta highway, equidistant from two of the largest cities in eastern Nepal. Seeing the humble school on the patchy hill, I recalled the saying, "*Battimuni andhyaaro* ("Below the lightbulb it is darkest."). This community wasn't remote by any stretch of the imagination, but the school itself was a pile of rubble. Doors and windows had come unhinged and were stacked up inside the dark classrooms where they were used as furniture. In one of the rooms, a boy had been pinned under a plank of wood with rusty nails in it as a girl slid down another that had been set against the window ledge. To me it was a horrifying scene, but the kids, not knowing better, didn't seem to mind.

Two electric poles ran right through the center of the school grounds. The poles were wrapped in thick blue padding. I asked Gajendra Baral, the long-toothed principal of the Karkichap school if they had tried to move the poles, which seemed to disturb the children's play space. Baral

Sir pointed at a lethargic boy with tufts of hair sticking up who was sitting on a mound of dirt.

"You see that boy over there? He got shocked during one of the lightning strikes. The next day a pickup truck from the Nepal Electric Authority came and padded the pole. But they also put up that second pole," he said pointing to a pole that had even more wires running through it and a heavy-looking, rusty transformer at the top.

I was incredulous. Not only had a child been electrocuted but the district's response was to install more high voltage equipment? For seven years I would try to move those poles, even involving journalists in our campaign, but when at one point it seemed a third pole was going to be added just to spite us, we backed off.

I had seen only two out of ten schools, but here, as in Jimi Gaun, we promised a new building. It was simply too painful to witness the conditions.

But the more schools I visited, the more I found myself questioning what really made a good school. I questioned whether a new building would make any difference at all if there was nothing motivating the students to learn, if the teachers weren't trained or properly incentivized to provide quality education. On the other hand, it was so easy to criticize the teachers' methods and attack the rote learning system, but life for the average Nepali teacher was quite difficult. Most Nepali teachers I encountered were men, though many schools usually had at least one female teacher, most often the nursery or kindergarten instructor. The teachers earned less than one hundred dollars a month, lived far from their families, and had only one day a week to wash their clothes or travel to the nearby city to buy things or deposit their paychecks in the bank. There was the added problem that the Maoists were extracting a portion of their salaries.

I hoped that constructing a nice, new school building might result in teachers having a greater measure of dignity. But I never imagined how long it would take to build each of the schools, how many thousands of hours of labor would go into fetching materials and carrying them to the site. In the end, in addition to Jimi Gaun and Karkichap, we promised to build a third school in Indra Maya didi's village, Mukten, where the need wasn't quite as intense but the community was industrious and committed to longer-term educational efforts. I didn't know where we would find the money, but I remembered an uncle who was a card-carrying member of the Rotary Club of Plainsboro, New Jersey, and the wheels started turning.

Every Wednesday evening, the twenty members of the Plainsboro club of New Jersey gathered at a Holiday Inn Express right off the freeway. No two Rotary clubs were alike, as I would learn. The Plainsboro club, for example, had only Indian men in it, for some reason, and each meeting opened with the blowing of a conch shell and the incantation of a Hindu mantra. Tensions ran high between the Plainsboro club and some of the other Jersey clubs.

I knew we had to raise about $75,000–$25,000 for each of the three schools. Rotary International had a generous matching program for international projects that had an in-country partnering club. My friend Kishan Agrawal was a member of the Dharan Rotary Club and had secured its support. The only problem was that rules forbade school construction due to the fear of earthquakes and liability issues, but the Plainsboro Rotarians assured me we needn't focus on anything *new* being built. Many of the materials from the original schools would be recycled and two of them were being built on the same foundation. It seemed to all of us that a pretty strong case could be made that this was simply renovation. Also, who would go to a remote part of Nepal and actually check?

Interestingly enough, the Rotary Club of Dharan was *also* composed only of businessmen of Indian descent. Through this project I learned more about Rotary Clubs than I ever wanted to know. For example, in South Asia, most of the Rotary Clubs were more like the chamber of commerce than charitable organizations. Most members were wealthy industrialists, doctors, and traders. Oddly, in Nepal most of what Rotary Clubs did was build weird-looking bus shelters in Kathmandu with large, painted wheels on them. I was perplexed that a cement bus shelter was okay but not a school. Wouldn't an earthquake kill the bus travelers too?

Luckily, I came into contact with a Vermont-based nonprofit organization called the Phulmaya Foundation that supported education in Nepal. One of its directors was a lawyer named Scott Skinner, who had been one of the early Peace Corps volunteers in Nepal, spending two years teaching in a village north of Namje, a journey of several days by foot. Scott, who would become a great friend and a very helpful mentor to me, had worked for Ralph Nader and been executive director of both the Vermont Public Interest Research Group and the American Civil Liberties Union of Vermont. He had narrowly lost a bid for the US Senate in 1976. I could tell from his legal profile online that he had never lost his Peace Corps roots. It read that in addition to practicing law, Mr. Skinner "grows berries and maintains a small herd of beef cattle" in Middlesex, Vermont. When Scott heard of our initiative, he and the Phulmaya Board promised $30,000 to build the Mukten school.

With the paperwork filed, we now had to raise only about $30,000 for the Rotary Club of Plainsboro. If I could raise that sum, we would get $15,000 from the Rotary International Fund. I knew we couldn't afford an expensive party hall for a fund-raiser, so I tried to hold an event at the NYU School of Law.

"There isn't going to be fund-raising at this event, right?" the events coordinator asked suspiciously.

"No, no. It's just an event to generate awareness about education in Nepal," I said evasively, very obviously lying.

"It says here you need five microphones. Is there going to be music? You know that this event falls during finals period, right? Some of the students will be studying for the bar exam."

"Yes, just some awareness-raising music, but it won't be too loud or anything," I assured her.

"How many people are you expecting to attend?" she asked.

"Anywhere between fifty and . . . five hundred." The lady shrugged and signed the papers.

On the night of *Shikshyako Asha* (Hope for Education), May 7, 2005, I genuinely didn't know if it would be fifty or five hundred people. I had done everything I could, scouring the streets of New York for any traces of Nepal I could find. We had printed three thousand postcard invitations and plastered them all over the West Village. One of the challenges was that the Nepali diaspora in North America was more divided into distinct and antagonistic fronts than back home in Nepal. The Sherpas had their own organization and boycotted events hosted by the Brahmins, and so on. Every time I met with the leadership of one group, they didn't care so much about the cause but about which other groups were sponsoring the event.

One of my Nepali friends, Dr. Tara Niraula, who was the president of the America-Nepal Friendship Society, tipped me off that every unit in an apartment building in Ridgewood Queens, near the Myrtle Avenue stop for the M train, was occupied by a Nepalese family. I took the subway out to meet Mohan Gyawali, the president of the Ridgewood Nepalese Society, who was from eastern Nepal himself. When I entered his home, I felt as if I were back in Kathmandu with plates of cucumber sesame *achaar* and *chia* in my hands. Mohan dai's personal story was very intriguing to me. He had survived financially in the United States by doing manicures and pedicures in nail salons, and eventually he would go on to open his own nail salon, Everest Nails. Mohan dai assured me he would try his best and took about two hundred postcards off my hands.

The night of the event, when seven o'clock rolled around, I was disappointed to find only a smattering of people in Tishman Auditorium. We had ordered enough bamboo curry from the Himalayan Yak Restaurant in Jackson Heights to feed the entire law school. Just as I was beginning to lose hope, people started arriving at the security gate. Soon the lobby of the law school was filled with more than two hundred immigrants, many dressed in elegant *daura suruwal* and saris. On the postcard we had written that people should wear ethnic dress, not expecting anyone to adhere to that. At the back of the crowd I saw Mohan dai and his family, and I realized then that all these people were from Ridgewood. He had brought the entire apartment building.

The main entrance of the law school was adjacent to the library entrance and it was finals period, so people were generally miserable. As people were exiting the building after a long day of studying, many wore scowls—all except for Ricky Revesz, the dean of the law school who was welcoming each and every guest with a Namaste as they entered. He was thrilled to see this unique New York community in his law school. Fearful someone from the administration would figure out we were fund-raising, I rushed back into the auditorium and waved to my friends Sarahana and Kashish Shrestha, who were operating the sound system to start the music.

When the houselights dimmed, I got on the stage and squinted at the eclectic crowd. I tried to give them an orientation about what to expect, but I had invited so many speakers and performers that even I wasn't sure of the program. I fervently hoped that the festive atmosphere would make people drink liberally and loosen their wallets. The first performer took the stage, Mumbai-born musician Falguni Shah, whose stage name was Falu and whom I knew through my brother, Rishi. Before singing, she spoke a little about how she had never been to the country but was happy to have a chance to help the kids of Nepal. She went on to say how all children everywhere represented love, and so she had chosen a song containing the Hindi word for love: *laal*. When she opened her mouth to sing, it was a mellifluous tune called "O Lal Mere," which filled every inch of the auditorium. From the mesmerized look of the audience members, I knew we were off to a decent start.

Knowing he was a Republican but not knowing the depths of his patriotism, I had invited a charismatic family friend who was the former chief information officer for the Peace Corps, Mr. Gopal Khanna, to deliver the keynote address. At the time Gopal Uncle, as I addressed him, was serving as chief information officer for Tim Pawlenty, the governor of Minnesota. There was pin-drop silence for most of his speech, in which he eloquently conveyed his deep affection for the Peace Corps.

"I want to personally thank Peace Corps volunteers for their service to our great country and our brave commander in chief, *President George W. Bush*," he ended, almost yelling President Bush's name. My heart sank as I imagined the throng of mostly immigrants, students, and former volunteers probably stood on the liberal side of the spectrum, but his speech added gravitas, and before I knew it a Nepali girl named Rosie Sherpa was spinning and leaping to the steady clapping of an elated crowd. I had hired a whole bunch of Nepali dancers representing different ethnic regions of Nepal, thinking that continuous speeches would probably be quite boring.

As the night pressed on, the auditorium became fuller. The strategy had been to pack the room with anyone who would come so that the few donors with deep pockets would write the big checks, but in the end most of the donations came in the form of loose change from Nepali immigrants and impoverished students.

At one point, my father's seventy-five-year-old lawyer Jesse Cohen slowly climbed the steps to the stage. He wasn't part of the program, so I wasn't sure what he was going to say. After putting on his glasses, he read from what looked to be an ancient scroll. It turned out that he had managed to reach the borough of Brooklyn president, Marty Markowitz, who had proclaimed the day "Hope for Education in Nepal Day" throughout Brooklyn. The scroll, which contains Latin and gilded print, still hangs in the tattered SWSC office today. As incongruous as the procession of speakers and performers was, I could tell that for the Nepalis it was uplifting to see something other than the usual body counts and reports of broken peace deals.

But it is at events like this where a helpless image of villages can supplant reality in the quest to raise money. When it came my turn to speak, I hammed up the parts about how miserable the schools were, showing unsmiling children, dirty toilet pans, and collapsing schools. I knew what to say to raise money, and while I briefly hesitated, I decided to present a mostly one-sided argument, underscoring why building a new school was simply the best option.

The presentation about the schools got us about $18,000. We were still $12,000 short. It was the next speaker who would bring down the house like an avalanche coming down a Himalayan slope. Lhakpa Gelu Sherpa was born in the remote Himalayan village of Kharikhola, Solukhumbu, in the shadow of Mount Everest and had summited it no fewer than sixteen times. On Lhakpa's tenth ascent his name was etched into the Guinness Book of World Records for the fastest climb, clocked at just ten hours fifty-six minutes and forty-six seconds. A Nepalese friend of mine named LG Sherpa, who was a cab driver in New York City and president of the United Sherpa Association, which had over seventeen thousand members across the United States and Canada at the time, knew Lhakpa and asked him to come to the fund-raiser from Salt Lake City, where Lhakpa had taken odd jobs delivering pizzas and working in coffeehouses just to make a living. An image of Lhakpa hoisting a brass pole with the Nepali flag on Everest had already become an iconic image. Lhakpa dai couldn't speak English fluently, and even his Nepali was shaky, but he had prepared a speech about how he had studied only through grade three and therefore how important it was to give opportunity to other Nepali children.

But when he summited the stage, he was prevented from speaking. As the wide-jawed, broad-chested hero of Nepal climbed the small set of wooden stairs adjacent to the podium, where just four days before Supreme Court Justice Anthony Scalia had stood, the audience erupted in cheers and applause so loud I thought the oversized oil paintings of the hoary former law deans were going to unlatch from the walls. The sound operators instinctively switched the dial to "Eye of the Tiger" from *Rocky*, a hit film in Nepal. The shy, smiling Lhakpa Gelu Sherpa stood at the edge of the stage, trying to quiet the crowd as people were almost throwing their checks at us. In a few minutes, I was standing on stage with my friend Amit Saxena, who was helping me host the program, holding $30,000 in a small, black metal box. The next morning the cover of the *Kathmandu Post* featured a color photograph of us holding the green, glittered money thermometer we had made on poster board with the words PAISAKO ASHA (HOPE FOR MONEY). Under the photograph the headline read: "Raising Hope in Nepal's Villages."

A few weeks after the NYU fund-raising gala, my cell phone rang. It was Chandra ji calling from Namje to share some bad news: "Tanka Sir was abducted by the Maoists. Did you hear about that?"

On the day Tanka Sir was summoned by a Maoist commander for a mysterious meeting in Gahiri Tol village, Goma didi, Tanka Sir's wife, had gone to Dharan to buy supplies for their store. Telling his daughter Srijana not to worry, Tanka Sir nervously pulled down the iron shutter of their small shop, instructing her to stay inside with her brother, Sujan. Taking Karna ji with him, he took small steps down to Gahiri Tol, which was half an hour's walk from Namje, unsure of what fate awaited him.

When the two men arrived in Gahiri Tol, everyone from the village had fled. Outside the home of Mani Rana Magar, where they had been instructed to go, stood two men with handguns. The men were so young that they could have been Tanka Sir's students.

"Why didn't you come alone?" they questioned.

"I never go anywhere alone." After a pause he added, "One can slip and fall."

As they stepped into the room, Tanka Sir and Karna ji were greeted by Comrade Kamal, seated calmly on a wooden chair, a rifle propped against the wall next to him. Smoked pork strips hung from the wood beam above his head. The Maoists all took pseudonyms, and the apex leader for this part of eastern Nepal had taken a more delicate name that means "lotus flower."

"The people in Namje listen to you. Because of your resistance, we don't have any recruits in Namje, not one. Because of you we cannot blow up the tower. We want you to support us."

"I am just a teacher. I don't know anything about politics."

"Then why did you come here?" Lotus Flower asked, getting annoyed.

"You have a gun. I have no gun. You call me here, so I come."

"The schools that are being built with foreign NGO money— why don't you let us build the schools and give us that money?" the captain asked.

Tanka Sir considered carefully the ramifications of refusing, but then said, "We can give you the money, but if you don't build the school with it then you must answer to the children."

"We will blow up your water tanks if you don't help us," he threatened angrily.

"If you do that," Tanka Sir warned, "you will not find a single friend in Namje. No one will forgive you. You say you are for the people but none of the people would support you." The two men stared at each other silently before Comrade Kamal motioned for them to leave. Bringing Karna (though he didn't utter a single word during the meeting), who was Magar, was a way for Tanka Sir to signal that he had the support not only of his own caste but also of the local Magars, who constituted more than 90 percent of the population of Namje and Thumki.

Tanka Sir had been the first person in Namje to pass high school. As a teacher, he would win a national education prize and complete his master's degree in rural development while going on to become headmaster of Namje school in 2008, when Harka Lama retired. When he was a student in the ninth grade studying in nearby Dada Bazaar village, a Peace Corps volunteer named Peter Jaquinta had taken him and another student, Mahendra Ghimire, into his home. Jaquinta tutored them each day and predicted that the sharp, disciplined Mahendra Ghimire would go on to be the headmaster of the school and the more ambitious Tanka Sir would become a political leader. Eventually, the opposite transpired as Mahendra would become the VDC secretary and Tanka Sir the headmaster of Namje school. But Jaquinta's observation about Tanka Sir's pragmatic and political skill was correct. Tanka Sir instinctively knew how to speak to different people in languages and codes that he knew they understood. He was one of the only people in the village who spoke *both* Magar and English fluently. His rule was that one could not be too soft or too hard in dealing with anyone. But above all else, Tanka Sir's mantra was never to talk to the lower cadres and always to go directly to the highest source of power.

Gahiri Tol and Namje had held petty feuds and rivalries for as long as anyone could remember. In the 1980s and '90s drunken fights during the Saturday vegetable market in Namje sent people home with bloody noses. The source of the struggle was perhaps a jealousy on the part of Gahiri Tol because the Namje people were closer to the road and more affluent. Another bone of discontent was that Namje had few toilets and so fecal matter from the fields would flow down into the Gahiri Tol water system, and this was one reason people from Gahiri Tol often retaliated through defecation on Namje land, as they had done with the water project.

But when Maoists occupied Mani Magar's house, he and all the other residents of Gahiri Tol walked up the hill in tears to the tell their brothers and sisters in Namje what had happened. Though Goma didi tried to calm them down and tell them to go home for fear of the army finding out, no one would leave Tanka Sir's courtyard. In just hours, news had traveled as far as Dada Bazaar and Rajarani.

When Tanka Sir and Karna ji finally came back to Namje, government soldiers were already waiting outside their homes to escort them up to the tower for interrogation. The simple act of meeting with Maoists was deemed subversive terrorist activity at this time in Nepal, and anyone who went into an army barrack was lucky to come out. Just before they trekked up the hill, Tanka Sir asked the soldiers if he could change his shirt, but discretely he shuffled into his small bedroom and frantically flipped through the two- by two-inch, flimsy maroon-colored diary in which he kept the names and contact numbers for some of the most powerful people in Nepal. He called one of his in-laws in Dhankuta, a high ranking army official, to save him.

Up at the tower, each time the army captain interrogated them about what Comrade Kamal had said, Tanka Sir again responded that he was just a village teacher and didn't understand politics. "Well, why did you come here then?" the frustrated captain demanded.

"You have the gun," Tanka Sir answered. "If you call me, I will come. They have the gun too. If they call me, I will go to them. Whosoever has the gun, if he or she calls me, I will go to them" was Tanka Sir's brilliant answer to which even the captain had to smirk a little. Here was the lowly vice principal of a school, the name of which—*Gramin Janata Madhyamik Vidhyalaya*—translated to "Village People High School," outwitting both a captain in the Royal Nepal Army and a Maoist chief. The story of Tanka Sir's abduction would become a legendary tale, one that he would frequently recount in his living room, almost always in English to add dramatic effect. Peter Jaquinta would have been proud.

Even though he cleverly escaped, Tanka Sir's abduction made me seriously question if we were putting local people in danger with so much money floating around. Not only that, the school construction was also placing huge burdens on the people: On my tenth visit to Namje, when I visited Mukten I found men and women crushing aggregate under umbrellas as the monsoon rains poured down on them. One woman's hand was bandaged, the result of having slammed a hammer on her middle finger. An elderly woman, whose children were all overseas, carried a basket of bricks. When she dumped the heavy load on the ground, a chipped brick cut her leg.

I knew that building a school was not likely to make a great difference. After all, a good teacher could teach just as well under the shade of a banyan tree. But in the back of my mind I had hoped perhaps we could build special farm schools. Rural Nepal seemed the ideal setting to construct schools with working organic farms that could provide nutritious food for students, provide opportunities for educational demonstration, and bring in income through the sale of crops, poultry, milk, and whatever else could be produced. By incorporating solar power and rainwater harvesting, we could also demonstrate more sustainable energy practices, I thought. I surmised if we just planted some ideas in Karna ji's fertile brain, surely his imagination would run wild with new architectural designs. In the end the only innovation in the new schools would be that one of the rooms would have a slightly bulged face.

King Gyanendra started to realize it might be time to soften his stance towards the protestors. After nineteen days of violent protest, twenty people had been killed and thousands injured in the streets of Kathmandu and in fact all over the country. The seven major political parties, who had never agreed on anything, were standing hand in hand with the Maoists as a noose was tightening under Gyanendra's double chin. Even his own civil servants—teachers, ministry staff, VDC officers—were in the streets chanting for him to abdicate. In the end it took a visit from the Indian special envoy Karan Singh, himself the son of the last King of Kashmir, to convince Gyanendra to reinstate parliament to quell the spreading unrest that was now headline news all over the world. After ten years, the Maoists were emerging from their remote strongholds.

On April 24, 2006, a pale-faced Gyanendra, appeared on television, standing between two red flags, one of Nepal and the other of the royal seal. The camera was oddly positioned very far from him, which only served to accentuate how distant he had grown from his people. His first words were, "My dear countrymen . . ." The king's face had an unfortunate natural scowl, but his voice, which I was hearing for the first time, was remarkably pleasant and reassuring. In the speech he promised to restore parliament and projected free elections. Little did he know at the time that this same parliament would vote to strip him of his absolute privileges and transform Nepal into a secular state, ending 239 years of divine Hindu monarchy. Many Nepalis feel that had he heeded Prime Minister Girija Koirala's advice and abdicated to his grandson, Hridayanendra, skipping over his unpopular son Paras, the monarchy could have weathered the storm. It is a sign of the bizarre lives that kings and queens lead that in the worst hour of his life, when the king was reduced to a citizen under the law and stripped of his absolute privilege, he went from being a king to the richest man in the country.

The question on the public's mind was how much the crown was really worth. It was rumored Gyanendra had inherited Swiss bank accounts worth billions when his brother was killed, but nothing of the sort was found. He owned thousands of acres of land, including Mount Everest and national parks, palaces and summer residences, but much of this was nationalized. Most of his personal wealth, which consisted of about $100 million in business holdings through the Soaltee company in Kathmandu, was untouchable because it had been passed to his daughter Prerana. It would take another two years for the monarchy to be officially abolished, in 2008, but the nineteen-day protests known as Janandolan II, or "People's Revolution II," changed the balance of power forever.

Ironically, in the days after he left the palace, Gyanendra would state in an interview with the Japanese press that abolishing the kingship was "an anti-democratic act," citing a poll that claimed 49 percent of the public supported him. Many still question if the monarchy is gone in Nepal. After all, the king and his wife did not leave the country; they simply moved uptown to another one of their palaces, up the road from Narayanhiti. They even remain protected by the same soldiers they once commanded. Although in 2010 the gates of the royal palace opened to the public for the first time as a museum dedicated to democracy, a royal still lives there: a ninety-four-year-old mistress of the king's grandfather Tribhuvan who stated she had nowhere else to go.

In April of 2006 I landed in Kathmandu to attend the inauguration of the new school building in Jimi Gaun. I was finishing my last semester of law school studying abroad at the National University of Singapore law school, and I had neglected to watch the news, somehow missing that the largest political protest in a generation had gripped the country, with daytime shoot-on-sight curfews in most places. The villagers in Namje had a plan for getting me to the village that initially seemed like a good idea. While the protestors had shut down all road transport, ambulances were still operational. Tanka Sir instructed me to wait at the *chowk* next to a petrol pump outside the Biratnagar Airport and hold an opened umbrella. He had called someone from his special diary and managed to dispatch a Rotary ambulance; its driver would recognize me from the umbrella. I was to lie down in the ambulance and act sick. As the vehicle approached, the driver actually sped up and passed me. A brick had shattered the windshield, and he waved his hand at me as if to convey "bad idea."

The only other option was a cycle rickshaw. The peddler I hired was so small that he could barely transport me and my luggage, so I put him on the passenger cushion and pedaled up toward Namje myself. It was so exhausting that for most of the trip we walked along the road, each of us holding a handle of the rickshaw as we pushed it up the hill. The scenes we passed were part dystopia and part revolution, smoke from burning rubber tires everywhere, security forces firing rubber bullets at teachers and bankers, students and doctors. The chant was the same: "*Gyane chor, desh chod!*" ("Gyane is a thief, leave the country!")

We finally reached Dharan, where I was relieved to see Tanka Sir, Hari, Karna, Chandra ji, and Kumar Sir, the accounting teacher, waving excitedly as they walked quickly in my direction. When I asked Kumar Sir if he had gotten bored waiting for me, he smiled and said, "No, I protested a little against the king!" The next day we walked for six hours via the old walking trail from Dharan to Namje. This was the historic trail villagers had used to transport their vegetables to the markets in Dharan before the advent of the highway financed by Prince Charles in 1985. They would tell the story over and over again of how I rode a rickshaw through Janandolan II, the violent April 2006 uprising that restored parliament, for the school inauguration.

I always had an intuition that one day the Rotarians were going to come after us, but when I got the call from Tanka Sir in New York that the next day a man was coming from Calcutta to audit the project, we panicked.

"What should I do, sir? They will see the new schools."

"We definitely shouldn't lie. We can't hide the new schools. Hopefully they will agree that it was just an extensive renovation?"

I could hear the wheels in Tanka Sir's brain turning. "Actually, I know how to take care of this," and with that he hung up. Though Tanka Sir bore no fault and was not even a Rotarian, as a village leader it fell on him to deal with the problem.

The next morning, the auditor, Mr. Aurora, who was quite heavyset and wearing a starched shirt with a necktie over a loincloth, arrived in the village carrying the Rotary audit files. The line of children to welcome him was so long that it took nearly an hour for the man to walk to the gate of the school. I think part of Tanka Sir's plan was to have so many children with flowers that it would be time for the auditor to leave before he even reached the school gate. Tanka Sir had brought children from neighboring schools and even bused in his own students from Namje. The garlands were made of some of the rarest flowers in the forest, and the ceremony was so grand that when it was the Rotarian's turn to speak, he stood before the crowd of Nepalese children in the shadow of the two-story school building and, almost in tears, stated, "I've never seen a project or community as wonderful as this in my life."

Just when Tanka Sir breathed a sigh of relief, Mr. Aurora continued, "But I'm afraid that the funds were inappropriately used for the building of schools in violation of Rotary International law."

For the next year, passive-aggressive e-mails flew back and forth among the Plainsboro Club, the Dharan Club, and International debating the subtle nuances between new construction and renovation. But we had defined renovation so liberally that nothing at all would seem to constitute new construction. At the end of it, we agreed to resolve the matter by returning a percentage of the matched funds.

A few years later, a friend invited me to be a guest speaker at a Rotary event in Kathmandu. Just before the blowing of the conch shell, from a conversation between two of the Rotarians, I learned just how much damage we had done:

"It's really too bad that Nepal's Rotary status hasn't been granted. You know we had a great project lined up to build an eye hospital. Do you know what the reason is?"

"I hear some club in Dharan didn't follow the rules and now they're punishing all of us for it. Some people just can't follow rules." I felt terribly regretful about the harm we had caused, and these words would echo in my head for many years to come.

Around the time of writing this book, controversy surrounding the American development worker and former mountaineer Greg Mortenson of *Three Cups of Tea* fame surfaced. An investigative report by author Jon Krakauer uncovered severe financial irregularities within the Central Asia Institute (CAI), Mortenson's nonprofit organization that had built schools across rural Afghanistan. According to Krakauer and others, millions of dollars had allegedly been used to finance book tours instead of schools, buildings had been erected in sandy deserts where there were no children, and a myth had been propagated about an American saving Afghanistan. Though I have never met Greg Mortenson or visited any of the CAI-funded schools, my own reaction when the controversy surfaced was that a naive public was being duped into thinking that building schools was somehow saving helpless villagers in rural Afghanistan.

The CAI's publicity seemed overly focused on Mortenson, as if he was building the schools himself with his bare hands. Certainly, for the five schools we built in Bhedetar, local people contributed thousands of hours of their time, the local materials, and the land. I usually just showed up to snip the ribbon at the inauguration. I can't imagine it's that much different in CAI's work.

To be fair, I think anyone who has felt the weight of the flower garlands from the children's hands would know how hard it is to walk away. What do you do when everyone in the villages wants a new school building? But for me at least, it seemed that rather than focusing on the number of schools (or water systems, or other issues), it was more beneficial to create just one very good example, as successful projects usually got replicated, sometimes with an imaginative twist. If we had built just one great ecoschool, I imagine it would have been worth the weight of one hundred schools in eastern Nepal.

I have actually always liked the title *Three Cups of Tea* and the underlying message of it that one must spend a lot of time in a community before intervening, but, ironically, it seems Greg was having the first cup and going on to the next village. If all CAI had done was build a lot of schools all over Afghanistan, I still would be critical because of how that is projected as saving a helpless country, but what I found most disquieting was the money issue. Millions of dollars (including pennies from kindergarteners) were collected in the name of saving people and then used to fund more fund-raising events. A closed loop was created that had nothing to do with children in Afghanistan but with salaries, rents, and travel.

I started out in Nepal as a Peace Corps volunteer, and all around us were Maoists who loathed nothing more than the largess of NGOs. I think maybe for that reason I was always fearful of setting up something fancy and decided we would all continue to be volunteers. It never seemed right to take a salary or have anyone pay for my hotel bills.

Of course, it's not just NGO workers but also donors who can add to the problem by wanting to see signs of professionalism like a nice office or glossy reports, but we found just as many donors who were attracted to the tattered setting of SWSC or the fact that the Phulmaya Foundation had nothing more than a post office box with some very committed volunteers behind it. I wouldn't have known how to fund-raise for office rent.

After the school inauguration in Jimi Gaun, when I got back to New York in 2006, I applied to law firms in Manhattan for a brief time, but no one would hire me because I had no normal experience. However, on my flight home during transit in New Delhi, I had met a young lawyer named Fred Rawski. Fred had also graduated from NYU law school a few years before me and was working in the human rights cell of the United Nations in Kathmandu. He handed me his card and told me to call him if I ever wanted to be a field interpreter with the UN.

When I eventually took the job in October of 2006, a month before the historic peace accord was signed between the Maoists and the major political parties, which officially ended the ten-year People's War, I didn't realize I would meet the prime minister of Nepal and take part in some of the most sensitive missions affecting the country. I was rather exhausted from the Namje projects and all the traveling back and forth, and naively believed that being a translator would let me be a little more on the sidelines.

CHAPTER 7

Gaur

The moment the landing skids hit the ground, we were in a cloud of twirling dust. When the blades finally stopped whirring, it was so quiet that I imagined we were in some desolate location, but outside a thousand dark-skinned men, fresh after the kill, stood motionless, staring at us. Normally the site of a UN helicopter in a village would bring all the schoolchildren out, cheering and howling, but not on this day. We had landed at the site of unspeakable crimes in a Terai town, with the unfortunate name Gaur (pronounced like the English word *gore*), just a few kilometers from the Indian border.

"I hope you're ready for this," Lena Sundh whispered in my direction as her cloth shoe met the warm ground. As the country representative for the United Nations Office of the High Commissioner for Human Rights (OHCHR), she had more than a vague sense of the horrors that lay ahead. The men parted and allowed her to pass as she made the slow walk toward the Gaur hospital. I zipped up my blue and white vest and scurried after Lena.

After five months at OHCHR, I had grown used to having no identity, of just being the lowly interpreter who mechanically transferred information back and forth, sometimes for hours in one sitting, without responding to it on any emotional or analytical level. But when the coroner led us past the main administrative building to a shaded alley behind the building, I nearly vomited. Twenty-seven dead bodies laid side by side, many with flies hovering around the eyelids. Each was marked with a white tag on the big toe. The coroner, a small, bald man with thick lenses in his wire-rimmed glasses, stood silently next to us. Some wore an unbelieving expression that I imagined they carried at the very moment of receiving the final blow that had killed them. Their bodies were twisted and contorted in unnatural positions, hands and feet facing the wrong directions. Perhaps most disturbing, some were children.

I expected Lena to be expressionless. After all she was the seasoned UN diplomat who had served in African war zones. Some in the office seemed to get a rush from the kidnappings and the political gaming inherent in the turbulent peace process in Nepal, but as I would learn on this mission, not Lena. She almost always appeared agonized by these things. As she hunched down to observe the body of one child more carefully, her blue eyes twitched as tears welled up in them. She exclaimed in a voice slightly out of control, "Oh, god." For a moment it appeared she might fall over from the shock. Instinctively my fingers tightened around the small spiral pad in my pocket. "Stay close to me," Lena said as we followed the coroner. From that moment, I barely slept for eight straight days. Seven of us were on the mission and until my colleague Mark Turin arrived three days later, I was the only translator. Information was what we were there for, and all of it, whether I liked it or not, had to flow through me.

"These are the medical reports," the coroner said, almost whispering as he handed us a document with frantic writing on it that I couldn't really make out.

"Have FIRs been filed?" Lena asked. First Information Reports were the first step in the process of registering a crime. "No," he confessed. Lena nodded, knowing that in such situations the police usually froze in inaction, especially since in the border regions of Nepal it wasn't clear who the authorities were. In fact most of what OHCHR did was criticize the inaction of the Nepali law enforcement agencies.

"What does this say?" she asked curtly. I tried scanning the document. It was the kind of translation I hated most—being handed inscrutable writings that contained information of the highest sensitivity and being asked to discern the subtle meaning on the spot. All too frequently in the office back in Chauni in Kathmandu a human rights officer would poke his or her head into our office with some important press release containing Maoist jargon and ask us to summarize it right there and then. The worst part of this was that stylistically the Maoists liked to put pages and pages of information into a single sentence. The style reflected their steady control and appealed to their teleological leanings.

My heart racing, I translated every word I could, acknowledging the words I couldn't make out. Lena asked follow-up questions of the coroner. There was a word repeated over and over that seemed important—*pharata*—and I confessed I had never heard it before. There were other words related to ruptured body parts that the Peace Corps training hadn't taught me. It seemed from the document that many of the victims had perished from some kind of head blow that had sliced through their skulls. Some had signs of first- and second-degree burns, which seemed bizarre and caught Lena's attention immediately. Several of the victims were women—one a seventeen-year-old girl. Lena abruptly said we had to leave, and we walked out of the hospital toward the UN jeep that was waiting for us.

Luc Pier, the tall security officer, was there with three jeeps stocked with food, maps, and water. Indefinite *bunds,* or strikes, all over the region meant that obtaining supplies could present challenges. Luc was a former architect who left his practice in Paris to become a member of the French special forces. Because of his tan skin, he was frequently mistaken for Nepali, but his thick French accent would throw people off instantly. One way in which the UN was radically different from the Peace Corps was in how international it was.

"You," he said pointing at my chest. "I want you up front with me. Roads are blocked everywhere and you will talk us through this." Each time we were stopped, I explained who we were, and the massive felled trees were pulled back to let us pass. Our first stop was the Gaur police station. Just as we approached the entrance, bearded Indian commandos in Sikh turbans and carrying Uzis were exiting the building. This seemed very odd, but as we would learn that week, Gaur was walking distance from India, and sometimes events like this pushed the border back and forth like a shifting ocean tide.

I had woken up that morning knowing it wasn't going to be the usual routine of translating reports and press releases on the fifth floor of the office. The radio was reporting that Maoists and members of something called the Madesh Janadhikar Forum, known simply as "the Forum," had clashed in the field next to a rice mill in Gaur. The details were murky but deaths had been reported and there were rumors of rapes as well. That morning I threw some clothes and toiletries in a duffle bag and went to the office prepared, knowing I was probably going to Gaur.

In an odd twist, in the preceding months people from the Terai, who were more Indian-looking with dark skin, had completely broken away from the Maoists, whom they accused of installing only Pahadis, or "hill people," into positions of power. The splintering of the Madeshis from the Maoists was probably the worst blow the rebels could receive, since so much of their support system, including food rations and weapons, came from the Terai. Most of the media believed the nascent Madeshi movement had royalist support, since the weakened monarchy had the most to gain from the attenuation of the Maoists, but most ordinary Madeshis found this idea insulting.

The officers at the police station greeted us with awkward smiles and frantic boot shuffling. The head of the Gaur police was already waiting, seated at his desk, as the seven of us entered. I took my place between Lena and the inspector. There was no Namaste, only the sound of Lena and the inspector breathing until Lena finally pierced the silence.

"Something horrible has happened here," I translated. "My office is interested in knowing, as you can imagine, what transpired here yesterday. What has happened here in Gaur is affecting the fragile peace process that everyone is working so hard to bring to a fruitful conclusion. But my concern and the concern of my colleagues today is that there are twenty-seven dead bodies in that hospital, and we need to know what could have been done to prevent it." The inspector, who had two stars composed of small, intersecting *khukuri* knives in each of his shoulder lapels, leaned back in his chair, brought his hands together under his chin, and nodded uncomfortably, tightening his lips. Lena continued, "What we want to know is if the state responded adequately and in accordance with Nepalese and international law in dealing with this. Did you have any warnings that there could be a clash between the Maoists and the Madesh Janadhikar Forum?" The inspector raised and lowered his shoulders nervously, squirming in his chair.

When he answered, as happened so often in these situations, the Nepali inspector looked directly in my eyes, trying to find sympathy and camaraderie in the one Nepali in the room. "We did know maybe there could be a clash. The Maoists and the Forum were planning rallies at the same time at the same location, so that was a bad sign. As you know, for the last few months all over the Terai, including in Lahan, there have been bloody clashes between the Maoists and Forum. This is the problem of the day. But I assure you I didn't have enough men to control the situation."

"How many men did you have available that day?"

"One hundred fifty-seven."

"How many did you post at the rice mill?"

"Fourteen," he confessed.

This was exactly the kind of shortcoming that would be strongly condemned by the office. As we left the police station, the inspector walked a little slower than the rest of the group and tried to grab my hand, saying with a note of desperation, "We're not going to get in any kind of trouble, are we?" I shook my head and apologized, saying I was only a translator.

From the beginning, working at the United Nations had not been what I expected. My official position was United Nations Volunteer, or UNV, but it was a far cry from the Peace Corps. As a UNV my monthly salary was almost $3,000 compared with the $105 I earned in Namje. I was given special housing and travel allowances and lived in a nice house. Before I could begin work I had to take an online training in disaster management, which included simulations of what to do when the vehicle you were traveling in was detonated. I traveled mostly in air-conditioned white jeeps and spent my days in a comfortable office in front of a desktop computer. One of the distinctive features of the Peace Corps is that there's no uniform and blending in is part and parcel of the job description, but as a UNV I rarely removed my blue UN vest, even when I was sitting in front of the computer, since it protected me. In the Peace Corps, if someone wanted to get a hold of me, runners had to be sent from Bhedetar, and when I was in Baitadi it was even more complicated and involved radioing the local army outpost. But in the UN, I carried a walkie-talkie at all times, and if I missed my call sign, the safety and security office would send out an alert to find me. In all, it was probably the sexiest job I ever had, except for the fact that UNVs were the bottom-feeders of the institution and sometimes made coffee and fetched chicken sandwiches for the human rights officers. Admittedly, the hardest part for me was to not share my personal opinion and simply be a passive instrument to facilitate the conveyance of language.

The other crucial difference between the UNV program and the Peace Corps program was that anyone from any country could be a UNV, and in developing countries it was considered extremely prestigious to become one. It was seen as a road to a more permanent position in the P-system, which conferred a special diplomatic passport.

The translators stuck together like a tribe. The office was a white concrete five-story fortified box in Chauni, just outside the ring road a few hundred meters from the Vishnumati River. The scent of decaying garbage and animal carcasses in the riverbed reached our nostrils in the office—a humbling reminder of how little the UN could really do for a place like Nepal. We usually ate lunch in the open-air top floor and I always sat with the Nepalis, speaking only in Nepali mostly because I tended to feel more comfortable with them. Working in a human rights organization, you're bound to find all kind of ironies. One of them was that it was a rather segregated and hierarchical work setting.

From practically the first moment, I knew I was going to get along with Lok Sangraula. Lok dai, as he was known to everyone, including Ian Martin (the head of mission for the $90 million United Nations program in Nepal), was a human dictionary. Translation was some of the most ir-ritating, angering, and frustrating work I have ever done largely because, though my English was fluent, my Nepali was a far cry from a native level. What made Lok, who had studied in a government school in Jhapa, so impressive was that he was basically native in Nepali and English and knew all kinds of strange English idioms I had never heard of.

"I feel like a spit on the fry today, Rajeev," he would say, hanging his hat as he entered the door. One evening when he was leaving he said, "That was like water off a duck's back today," but I had no idea what he meant. In fact, he would use other animal idioms that none of us un-derstood. "I think this might just be horse feathers," he once observed.

Lok had worked as a journalist for many years and was a student of Nepali history, so he had a rare understanding of society, politics, and culture that made him not only the indisputable final authority on trans-lation but also a trusted advisor. I felt lucky that my desk was stationed across from his. One of the tricky things about translations from English to Nepali was that often the sentence order was completely reversed, but this didn't faze Lok at all, and I imagined he must have had a mirror in his brain.

Though in the beginning we didn't speak much, when we discovered each other's mutual passion for language and also that we had a similar sense of humor about the absurdity of working in an organization like the United Nations in a country like Nepal, we became mutual distractions to each other. "Translation is an art and a science," Lok would often say.

Much of what he did in the office consisted of decoding a single word, which sometimes took weeks. At first I didn't see why it mattered. When Lok's phone rang it was usually Mark Flummerfelt from downstairs. The two would go on for hours about whether the appropriate word was *should*, *must*, or *ought to*. While it seemed to me it shouldn't matter, I later learned how these nuances were the very essence of human rights law.

There was one instance when the difference of a single letter in the alphabet almost caused a riot in the office. A meeting had been convened in the OHCHR conference hall, which was right next to our office on the fifth floor, between senior members of the Madesh Janadhikar Forum, including their chairman, Upendra Yadav, and Maoist MPs to try to resolve a stalemate. The word *Madishe* was a derogatory term referring to dark-skinned people from the Terai, whereas the word *Madeshi* was the proper nonderogatory term. The translator kept accidentally using *Madishe*, and I could see the members of the Forum fuming in anger to the point that one of the Forum members interrupted the translator and asked him to stop saying that word. In Nepali, some derogatory words were used so commonly that they lost their sense of insult, but given what was happening across the Terai at this time, this was not the case with the word *Madishe*.

"That's the word they use in my village," the translator said defensively. That an *i* switched with an *e* could derail a peace negotiation was to me the best example of how political language can be.

I instinctively went back to my Peace Corps roots when I met Lok, spending hours telling him and the other translator in our room, Nirupama Sharma, about American culture and politics, which fascinated them. My questions about some word I didn't understand would lead to a long, mesmerizing lecture about Sanskritic roots, and one word would skip Lok to another and then to another until he had taught Niru and me twenty new words. I wasn't a very good translator by any means, but among the internationals, other than Mark, who headed the whole unit and focused more on the written reports, my translations were deemed the best. There was a policy against sending Nepalese translators out into the field for reasons of safety, so I often got interesting and unusual assignments.

"Rajeev, we're going to need you tomorrow at the Hotel Himalaya at 3:00 p.m. sharp to translate for a few journalists. Can you do it?"

"Sure."

"It's a little bit formal, so you might want to put on a blazer," he added casually.

For a translator, there was nothing worse than not being prepared. That evening on my way home I picked up a cheap, checkered blazer for 300 rupees (four dollars) from a street vendor in Naxal who was selling coats on a plastic tarp. When I arrived at the Hotel Himalaya the next day it was just a minute or two past three o'clock. I casually walked into the main conference hall to find more than four hundred journalists, including two full rows of photographers. There were four seats at the head table, which was on a raised stage with a bottle of water for each speaker. I instantly recognized the tall, charismatic Ian Martin, already a legend in the country and credited with bringing Prachanda, the leader of the Maoists, out of the forests. Next to him was Lena Sundh, my boss and the head of OHCHR, and next to her was another high ranking UN officer. I nearly fainted when I saw the final placard bearing my name.

"Rajeev! There you are. Now we can begin," the press officer hollered.

As I quickly took my seat I saw Lok dai in the background, looking very nervous because he knew I was being thrown to the dogs.

"I'd like to begin by introducing each of our speakers today," the press officer said, almost inaudible from the clicking of the cameras. "First we have the Head of the Permanent Mission for the United Nations in Nepal." I froze. I couldn't believe it. I had completely blanked on how to say "United Nations" of all things, so I just said it in English but with a thick Nepali accent, the sweat beading on my forehead. The press officer hesitantly went on to the next introduction. "And now we have the Nepal Representative for the Office of the High Commissioner for Human Rights in Nepal, Lena Sundh." Though I had translated the name of the organization I worked for many times on paper, I blanked on how to say it. So I clumsily said with a Nepali head nod, "Oh. Ech. See. Ech. Aarr." I looked back at Lok and Niru, both of whom looked as if they had stopped breathing.

The translation went on for more than an hour. But the problem wasn't just that I didn't know the words; each time the speaker said, "And the United Nations condemns the Royal Nepal Army for the murder of Maina Sunuwar and the cover-up of her death," I kept translating it as, "And the United Nations condemns the Royal Nepal Army *and the Nepal Police* . . ." The UN was frequently condemning this or that action, but always, it seemed to me at least, we condemned *both* the police and the army, but here the police had for once played absolutely no role whatsoever in what was perhaps the most high profile murder case during the entire ten-year Maoist conflict, which the whole press gathering was about. As we finished and I stood up, I felt like I had just been flogged in a ten-round boxing match. Lok, Niru, and Mark came over to me, and Niru reassured me, saying, "You did well. That was not easy and no one could have done better."

A journalist who thought I was Nepali came over and said, "So this is the level of the interpreter for the United Nations? You should have practiced young man!" Upset, I retorted, "I'm an American, not a Nepali!"

The next day the chief inspector for the Nepal police, not surprisingly furious about being implicated in the infamous Maina Sunuwar case, almost had me by the neck, but all the Nepali translators came to my rescue. When the head of the human rights cell asked the other interpreters if I had said the word *police*, they all bluffed, saying they couldn't recall exactly. My tribe had saved me.

In late January of 2007, a former Canadian Supreme Court justice, the High Commissioner for Human Rights, Madam Louise Arbour, arrived in Nepal for a critical seven-day mission. The office had been planning the event for months and during all seven days of her visit every word she uttered and therefore every translation of every word from her mouth would carry consequences. It wasn't an exaggeration to say that people would be castigated, indicted, and imprisoned based on the subtle nuances of what she said. When the translation unit asked me to be her translator, I had no choice but to agree and went into study mode for weeks before her arrival, keeping cheat sheets for all kinds of criminal, heinous, and violent terms like *summary execution, extrajudicial killings, torture, mutilation,* and *premeditated killing.* Words that I didn't know even in English—*impunity,* for example—came up repeatedly, so I went back to Black's legal dictionary.

On a brisk, sunny morning, Madam Arbour, her special assistant, and I climbed into a white Land Cruiser with three police cars trailing behind and three in front. We flew through the streets of Kathmandu, sirens blaring. The traffic police, whistles dangling from their mouths and waving in the crowded streets, frenetically opened up passageways for us. We were on our way to the Baluwatar residence of the prime minister of Nepal for an hour-long parlay. Girija Prasad Koirala had been PM on three previous occasions and guided the country at its most critical junctures. I made some adjustments to my wardrobe this time, looking more professional.

As we pulled into the residence, guards opened the doors and we were seated in the prime minister's empty meeting room, a large den with high ceilings and plush furniture. I wondered what Tanka Sir would say when I told him I was sitting in Girija Babu's house, in the home of the first prime minister of the fledgling peace process. When the gilded doors on the far end of the room opened, as if for the entrance of a rock star in Madison Square Garden, no was one there, only a bright light. Then, solemnly, his head bent downwards with long strides the prime minister of Nepal approached us and we all stood up from the plush sofas to greet him. He was much taller than I expected, over six feet and exceedingly handsome. In fact, as he took his seat, I wondered if he had indulged in plastic surgery. (Later Lok and Nirupama confirmed he recently had a facelift in Thailand.)

Arbour began making her introduction and presented the prime minister with, of all things, a special edition Human Rights Swatch Watch, which she had brought with her from Geneva. As I began translating, Koirala made a gesture as if he was swatting a pesky fly, looked angrily in my eyes, and said with measured emphasis on each word, "DON'T APPEASE ME, MADAM ARBOUR. I AM THE PRIME MINISTER OF NEPAL. WE CAN CARRY

ON IN ENGLISH." For the rest of the meeting I sat awkwardly between the two dignitaries saying nothing and waiting for them to finish. I had been in situations like this before and sometimes been asked to leave, since Nepalis felt uncomfortable around other Nepalis discussing sensitive issues.

As we stood up, a cameraman from the state news service was waiting near the exit to take official pictures. I recognized it was the site where the PM took official photos with foreign dignitaries. As Madam Arbour exited, he took a picture of Koirala and Arbour shaking hands firmly, followed by one with the special assistant, and when it came my turn, I held out my hand but the cameraman was already packing up his equipment. Puzzled, Koirala turned to me and said, "*Babu ko gaun kaha parchha?*" ("Little boy, where is your village?") Not knowing how to respond and perhaps a little stunned, I simply answered, "Namje," and climbed into the jeep.

OHCHR was established in 1993 after the staging of the largest human rights gathering in the world in Vienna. The OHCHR office was established in Nepal in 2005, with the simple mandate of monitoring human rights violations. Many times people appeared in the front lobby because they had experienced some crime, such as domestic abuse, but we often had to turn them away since these matters were officially the province of the police. The office's focus was on emblematic cases that captured a particularly prevalent human rights issue. OHCHR was the precursor to the establishment of the much larger UN Permanent Mission in Nepal authorized by Secretary-General Ban Ki-Moon, which was charged with the herculean task of locking up the Maoists' estimated twenty thousand weapons and containing their combatants (initially estimated at thirty-five thousand) in seven cantonments. This duty was one of the key tenets described in the historic Comprehensive Peace Accord (CPA) signed on November 21, 2006, which formally ended the war.

I truly wondered whether I belonged in an organization like the United Nations and found myself mulling over the notion of human rights and what it exactly meant. I had translated many reports about the right to food, water, and a clean environment but what good were these paper entitlements?

Despite my insecurities about whether I belonged, what was amazing about the place was the access. Like clockwork, someone would be on TV for a high profile, extremely sensitive case or issue and the next morning I'd be in Lena's office translating with him or her. I talked with Maoist commanders whose one-name aliases had at one point struck fear in the hearts of millions in the countryside. On one occasion I almost met with Prachanda himself, the leader of the entire Maoist movement and, until 2006, the most wanted man in Nepal. There were strict policies about confidentiality and it was torturous to not tell my friends in Namje. Each time they asked what I was doing in Kathmandu, I casually said it was consulting work.

There was one day when my impression of the United Nations and its role in Nepal flipped. A Swedish human rights officer, Johan, whom the Nepali staff all liked, asked me to go on a fact-finding mission about a person disappeared by the Maoists and believed to be hidden in Dolakha district somewhere, a few hours north of Kathmandu, near the district center in Charikot. The drive was beautiful, and I was glad to leave the smog of the valley and be passing through rice paddies and villages again. Johan was unlike some of the other officers who scolded me for talking on the phone or doing basically anything other than translating their words. He asked me if I liked the music on the radio and wanted to know about me and what my interests were—I was so used to translating I almost translated his questions to me. It was a small thing, but he treated the driver well and continually asked him if he was okay to drive on. His care and thoughtfulness made such a difference that I was motivated to carefully and accurately translate all his words. On one occasion an officer had bothered me to the point where I just gave very terse translations. Translators were the lowest rung of the ladder, but we knew we possessed our own kind of power since the whole operation rested on accurate information.

After driving for several hours through the mountainous Dolakha region, we stopped near a *uttis* tree where there was a small bamboo gate. Johan had been here before. He radioed in that we had arrived, and then suddenly Johan became very serious and provided me with a detailed briefing of what I was to expect. Apparently the Maoist commander we would meet was going to deny vociferously that he had in his custody a man who had been missing for years, but Johan suspected he was hidden somewhere within a one-hundred-meter radius. This was a common kind of mission in OHCHR where we were trying to untangle the many informal shadow jails that had been set up by Maoists during the People's War.

Johan's style was effective. Even though he didn't speak much Nepali, he understood the importance of simply being nice and respectful. Chit-chat of all sorts went on for almost an hour as we sat on the floor of a low-ceilinged room, and as I was translating Johan would make eye contact with me where he saw openings in the conversation to inquire about the man we were looking for, but he never interrupted him. Then, after a pause, rather suddenly, Johan stood up asked for some time alone to speak to me and asked what I thought. I was totally taken off guard, but I said, "I think he'll give the guy to us if we don't try to press them on any others they might be hiding here." Johan agreed, and when he asked if we could take Krishna K. C. with us, the young cadre took us out of the building to another location. We passed several junior cadres who also knew Johan and genuinely seemed to like him. Then we were asked to stand in a location behind a third building, which could not be viewed from the road, and from which the man, Krishna K. C., was released. Johan looked at me gravely and said urgently, "Now, we move, *fast*."

We tried not to appear hurried as we entered the jeep and drove off leaving a trail of dust, which hadn't settled even as we drove around the bend. For hours in the jeep Johan asked questions of Krishna as an angry bright orange sun set behind Mount Dhaulagiri. Krishna told Johan he hadn't been abused in any way except initially when he had been hung upside down in a cave. Johan tried to find out the location of the cave but Krishna couldn't remember. Apparently he had been abducted for carrying some religious literature related to a fundamentalist Hindu organization called the Shivsenha based in Maharashtra, India. He wanted to know if his family knew he was coming home. Johan informed him they wouldn't be expecting him since we had no idea we would be bringing him home that day.

It was already past dusk when the white Land Cruiser stopped in front of a cement building by a small river. A young girl was washing dishes in the courtyard of the small home, shielding her eyes from the long beams of light from our vehicle. I'll never forget the moment when

Johan exited the vehicle holding Krishna's hand, walking the man to the front gate of his house. The young girl began walking backwards and dropped the plate in her hand, yelling, "*Aama! Aama! Buva aayo! Buva ghar aayo!*" ("Mother! Mother! Father has come home!")

I watched as Krishna's wife and three daughters hugged him, realizing that there were times when something objectively good can happen. I wanted to keep watching this scene of reunion—it was so positive and full of hope, the impossible peace that everyone wanted so desperately was actually transpiring—but Johan respectfully signaled to the driver that it was time to depart. The family tried to stop him and invite him in for tea. I'll never forget his wife holding his sleeve and trying to find the words to thank him, but he just folded his hands in a Namaste and let her know it was time for us to go.

"Some day, huh?" he said as we rolled back to the OHCHR office.

A few days later, a group of men gathered in front of the enclave in front of the OHCHR gate. At first none of us knew who they were, but each day there seemed to be more of them and their shelters were becoming more permanent. They had gone from sleeping in the open air to building several tents. One of the men inside one of the tents appeared to be on a hunger strike. Apparently, this was a group of people who did not have any specific grievance but simply claimed that their human rights in life had been denied. Lok dai, Niru, and I couldn't wait to see how OHCHR would handle this unusual situation.

"Rajeev, you're needed downstairs. Lena wants to talk to the gate huggers." I was surprised that, of all people, the head of office was going to handle what seemed to be some harmless encroachers. But the problem was escalating and it was hard for vehicles to enter or leave the building. I also think OHCHR was worried that this protest might catch on and we'd be encircled by virtually the entire country outside the office gate.

"We want a word-for-word replay of what happens," Nirupama said, laughing as I put on my vest and headed to the stairs. Lena was already waiting quietly on the inside of the gate and trying to listen to what was happening on the outside. The guard unlatched the door.

"Hello. So, my name is Lena Sundh," she began. "*Waha nai ho yahako thulo manche. Oy Bimal, utha!*" ("She is the boss. Bimal, wake up!") one of the squatters announced. Bimal, who was lying in the tent, lethargically got himself upright. He didn't look to be in good shape. I flipped open my spiral pad and started translating for Lena.

"Our job is to safeguard human rights in Nepal, but we can't do that if our vehicles can't enter or exit the building." The men just stared at me, their arms folded in defiance. I looked up out of the corner of my eye and saw Lok dai's bald head and glasses peeking out of our window. Some people from the other offices were also peering at us. "I think you should stop your strike and come into the office and talk to me about what you need."

One of the men who seemed to represent the group explained who they were. "We are just people without any money, without any land, without anything. We don't have human rights, so we came here because we know you would not turn us away."

But in the end, that's exactly what we did. For obvious reasons a vague complaint about being poor or hungry was not good enough. But it spoke to a deeper point about the systemic conditions that made people vulnerable to the specific violations OHCHR did take up. By the time I was upstairs I had rather changed my mind about this group. I was starting to feel some empathy for their plight, but Lok dai, Niru, and the others wouldn't have it. Apparently the hunger strike was a fraud. Bimal was having big breakfasts each morning. To my colleagues at OHCHR, if these folks were human rights victims, then so was everyone in Nepal.

"This is a *pharata*," a man said bringing over two equal halves of a twenty-foot green bamboo that had been sliced in half. I touched the edge to see how sharp it was and realized this was the weapon that had cut through the skull bones. "It doesn't look strong, but the longer the *pharata* is, the more sling there is," I translated. "The day before the rally we knew the Maoists were coming to hold their own rally also at the rice mill. Usually us Madeshis, we are weak stomached, we get scared and back down. But in the days before, we just prepared. Everywhere in Gaur people made *pharatas*. Bicycles were coming around to collect them and take them to the rice mill, hundreds of them."

"Thousands of them!" a man added, raising his fist. After two days of sealed lips, finally people were coming up to us and talking. We were having them speak in Hindi, not Maitheli, a local dialect I didn't know.

"Okay, then what happened?" Andrew McGregor, the Scottish human rights officer in charge of the final report, asked.

"We set up our stage. The Maoists had set up theirs in the morning, but we trashed it. Later in the afternoon, the Maoists came. They were firing their guns as they came running onto the field trying to intimidate us. At first we were really afraid and grabbed our children and ran toward the center of town. But then we realized there were four thousand of us and just a few hundred of them, and so we turned back and picked up our *pharatas*," he said, holding the twenty-foot weapon the air. "And after that . . ."

He couldn't finish the thought, but we would learn it was complete carnage after that. Clusters of people lashed at Maoists with the *pharatas* until they were beaten lifeless. Some were chased through town, as we discovered, for many kilometers and then cornered and killed a half an hour after the initial incident. But most troubling, we discovered that three Maoists had been chased along the banks of a river to a small village called Hajiminiya where there was a small whitewashed school. Initially they were held in one of the classrooms, and then it was alleged that the Maoists were taken to a small Saraswati temple in front of the school and burned as a sacrifice.

When we investigated the rice mill, we were all taken out of our proscribed roles. It turned out that Luc, because of his architecture background, was highly skilled in making three dimensional maps. He worked with one of the other officers, trying to mark the exact locations where people were killed and also marking where sharpshooters had been posted around the rice mill. Andrew interviewed some of the local people who were eyewitnesses and found home video footage of the attack. We all watched the video played from a camcorder on a TV screen. For a split second a small flash of white light appeared to come from one of the Maoists' hands. From that we deduced which side had fired the first shot, a crucial detail. I was part of a team trying to figure out what had happened to a girl whose body had been discovered in a sewer under another dead body. What had happened at the rice mill was proof that Nepal at this time was flirting with civil war between Pahadis

and Madeshis, *khukuris* and *pharatas*. On the face it was just one inves-
tigation, but if we had found that Maoists had been raped or sacrificed
(which we ultimately didn't), it was possible that the peace process could
have unraveled.

On the last day of the mission we drove to the school to speak with
the teacher in Hajiminiya who was there at the time the Maoists had
been chased down and killed. As our vehicle approached, he stood expressionless in the gateway. I was mentally and physically exhausted, and
something about seeing ethnic conflict in Nepal and on a school ground
no less, was too much to handle. While the others inspected the blood
markings on the grass in front of the small shrine, I returned to the jeep
and closed the door, feeling sick to my stomach.

On February 17, 2004, Royal Nepal Army soldiers paid a visit to a home
in Kavrepalanchowk in search of Devi Sunuwar. Earlier that day, a Maoist cadre being interrogated had stated that Devi was also a Maoist cadre.
Finding that she was not at her home, the officers grabbed her fifteen-
year-old daughter, Maina Sunuwar, and took her to the Birendra Peace
Operations Trainings Center in Panchkhal, the site where Nepali soldiers were trained for UN peacekeeping operations overseas.

When the young girl wouldn't answer questions about her mother's
affiliation to the Maoist party, the officers beat her repeatedly. When
she still wouldn't answer, her head was dipped into a cauldron of water
six or seven times until she almost choked. Finally, the captain ordered
that a live wire be brought over from the geyser line. The electric wire
was connected to her wet hands and the soles of her feet as she was repeatedly shocked while seven other officers looked on. To make it stop,
Maina confessed her mother had been involved for a few months with
the Maoists but by then blood was seeping from her wrists. The captain
ordered she be taken to another location within the military grounds
where she was handcuffed and blindfolded. When they found her dead
an hour later, they put a bullet in her back and the soldiers secretly buried her body within the compound.

The next morning Devi Sunuwar came to the camp asking for her
daughter's whereabouts, but the soldiers said they had never seen her

before. The principal of Devi's school and another teacher were also turned away. It was only later that Devi Sunuwar was falsely told her daughter had died while trying to escape captivity.

When I first started working at OHCHR, I didn't understand why so many people in the office were assigned to this one case. Writs had been filed with the Supreme Court, voluminous legal reports had been authored, and high-level press conferences organized. OHCHR and every other human rights group in Kathmandu seemed almost obsessed by the case. In fact, the whole purpose of the High Commissioner Louise Arbour's visit was to press for the proper punishment of the men involved in Maina Sunuwar's death. They had only been given six-month sentences for the crime of "improperly disposing the deceased." There was an attitude within the Nepal government that what was done was done, and why exhume her body and risk rupturing the peace process? They contended that over the course of ten years, between 1996 and 2006, more than sixteen thousand people died from the conflict and countless atrocities were committed—it was time to forget and move on.

But on a cloudy afternoon on March 23, 2007, when the small ivory-colored bones of Maina Sunuwar's remains were finally dug up and laid out in the shape of her body for the whole country and the whole world to see, I realized why this one case mattered so much. The story of a Dalit girl being murdered by the Royal Nepal Army and her remains being concealed contained within it the story of the entire conflict: summary execution, disappearance, issues of caste and gender, the brutal effect of the conflict on children. If this girl, whose mother had fearlessly taken on the highest echelons of power, mattered, then human rights meant something that went beyond guarantees on a piece of paper. *Impunity* was the one word I always forgot during translations, but after Maina Sunuwar's tragic case, the word *Dandahinata* became etched in my mind.

As I thought about Baitadi where I had taught kids not unlike Maina, I started to realize my journey had come full circle. I wondered where they were now and hoped they were okay. At the very least, they could take pride in knowing that fifteen-year-old Maina Sunuwar had brought the General of the Royal Army and perhaps even the King of Nepal himself down on his knees.

I also realized that after seven long months it was time for me to leave OHCHR. I was happy to know that *someone* was doing this difficult work, but I needed a break. I had been offered a more permanent position as a political affairs officer, but I had found the work to be too emotional. I couldn't bring myself to be dispassionate about what I was seeing—and I knew that was a liability. I bought a one-way ticket to New York, resolving that for once I would find a normal job in America.

PART II

∽

CHAPTER 8

American Idealists

In the parched radish fields of Namje, politics seeped into everything. Nepal was in the clutches of a Maoist war, which was one reason why this was so. But it was also because each village project, no matter how small, impinged on land, natural resources, and caste pecking orders. Most of what we did was make an array of minute decisions—where to build the school, where to tap the river, the diameter of the pipe, the depth of the reservoir. These decisions entailed intricate social, economic, and political questions. Like rings around a planet, national, district, and VDC politics hugged us tightly, even if the wispy fog suggested we were somehow divorced from the rest of the country and the rest of the world.

I was one of these rings, one that changed and evolved. Though I began as a lowly Peace Corps volunteer, one day I found myself akin to an international donor and then almost a VDC politician. The ample fried eggs and heaping spoonfuls of *mulako achaar* (radish pickle) were the village equivalent of lobbying. During my many visits to Namje between 2004 and 2008, people came to my door from distant villages with project applications, entreaties to look at a collapsed roof in their school or a dilapidated water system. Sometimes I'd be standing (albeit in scuffed Crocs and a torn T-shirt) on a radish terrace before a hundred people giving a speech. I found myself making public promises, signing my name to pledges, and cutting ribbons during opening ceremonies for new schools and toilets. This had been my only training in politics.

I was the least likely person to lobby the US Congress for anything. Unlike my peers at NYU law school, I didn't graduate with a strong grounding in American law and policy. I had never lived in Washington, DC. My citizenship was in the mountains and rivers of Nepal. But in

January of 2008, when I heard that a campaign was brewing to double the size of the Peace Corps, that sounded like a cause worth advocating. I had mailed letters to more than 300 law firms in Manhattan but not a single firm wrote back, which was probably for the better. The Nepali words for "torture," "rape," and other criminal acts still in my mind, I traded in my spiral translator's pad for a size thirty-six-short suit and the keys to a rented Pontiac and became the national coordinator of "More Peace Corps," a national campaign to double the budget of the Peace Corps. "Is that your real job?" was the innocent retort from a friend when I told him of my new position.

As I try to recount here my strange activities over the past three years, I realize there were at least two Rajeevs. The first Rajeev rented cars, fought off house cats in strange houses, and had a portable office in the back seat of his rental. He ate Fijian cassava pies and drank peanut soup in backyard hoedowns. He sometimes felt like he was organizing for the American Association of Retired Persons. He was the community organizer.

The second Rajeev wore a slick black suit, carried a leather portfolio, and spent a good part of his day scrambling for electric power outlets in the marble halls of the House of Representatives to charge his iPhone. He carried a five-inch plastic comb, which he used to perfect his bowl haircut in front of the vanity mirrors in the Longworth Building restrooms. He took his lunch in the House of Representatives' Longworth Cafeteria, making several extra trips to the salad stations, spending a little extra time next to the bowl of Parmesan cheese in hopes of bumping into key aides. In the course of three years, he met hundreds of members of Congress and some of the most powerful advisors in the Obama administration, without any appointments, through a strategy best described as "strategic loitering." These two Rajeevs worked together, communicated with and motivated each other.

As the elevator floated up to the forty-ninth floor, I cursed the cheap suit and clunky shoes I was wearing. I had hoped to make a better impression at my first job interview. A high-pitched bell clinked and suddenly I was standing in the rococo Madison Avenue office of the Rockefeller Brothers Fund.

"Hi, Rajeev," Donald said, coming out to greet me. I sat down across from him, noting that the only props in his office were a faded knapsack and an opened bag of jellybeans. Scott Skinner, a director of the Phulmaya Foundation, who had introduced him to me, described Donald K. Ross as "the greatest organizer since Martin Luther King Jr." During the 1970s and '80s after returning from the Peace Corps in Nigeria, Ross served as Ralph Nader's key organizer on the ground. Donald built a network of grassroots advocacy associations called Public Interest Research Groups. The PIRGs would become trailblazers in the fight for environmental justice, racial and gender equality, and consumer protection. Even a young Barack Obama had worked for Donald during the 1980s in the New York PIRG office.

"So, Rajeev, how much organizing experience do you have?" Donald asked.

"Well, I organized a village in Nepal to build a water project," I said. Surprisingly, this answer satisfied him.

"What do you know about the Peace Corps?"

I thought it was a trick question. Naturally, I assumed I knew everything there was to know. But as I opened my mouth to answer, a string of incoherent proper nouns sprang forth: "Kennedy . . . Shriver . . . Chris Matthews . . . Paul Tsongas," I said before confessing, "Actually, not much." The Peace Corps was remarkably good at making you think you were out there on your own, cut off from any kind of infrastructure. Like most Returned Peace Corps Volunteers (RPCVs), I didn't know the fifty-year battle in Washington for relevance and survival, the twisted saga of how it was founded, its dramatic beginnings on the steps of a college campus.

"Let me put it to you this way: In 1966, just before I got back from Nigeria, there were more than fifteen thousand volunteers in forty-eight countries around the world. Sargent Shriver, President Kennedy's brother-in-law, was the director then. Today, there are about 7,200 volunteers and the Peace Corps budget is roughly equal to that of the US Army marching band."

It was hard for me not to feel outraged at hearing this. How had we let this happen? I wondered, as I wrote down what Donald was saying like a junior reporter.

"The world's population has almost doubled since 1966. The problems that propelled the creation of the agency, arguably, have worsened, but the Peace Corps is half as big," he said. "You're a fresh face, Rajeev. No one knows you and you have a positive story, so we need to get you out into the grassroots talking to the two hundred thousand RPCVs." Then he smiled and shook my hand, saying, "Congratulations."

We then walked down the hall to meet the president of the Rockefeller Brothers Fund. RBF was providing the initial grant to support the campaign. "This," Stephen Heintz, the RBF president said, "might be the only campaign I've ever seen to *expand* a federal bureaucracy!"

The next day I was given an office on Broad Street, next to the New York Stock Exchange. I started by reading everything I could find on the Peace Corps. I was surprised to learn that the Peace Corps, which had a budget of $331 million in 2008, cost the United States basically one dollar per taxpayer. By way of comparison, the baseline budget for the Pentagon was $540 billion, more than a thousand times greater than the annual Peace Corps budget. In the $40 billion US foreign assistance bill, the Peace Corps was a very small slice of the pie, less than 1 percent. As foreign aid spending itself was 1 percent of the total US budget, the Peace Corps was less than 1 percent of 1 percent. Basically, our campaign was to try to make this *2 percent.* To put it in perspective, the annual budget of the Peace Corps, including the cost of supporting 7,200 volunteers working in seventy-six countries was equal to the sum spent in just five hours in Iraq. It was the cost of two F-22 fighters, half of Senator John Kerry's net worth. These illuminating cost comparisons would become the sound bites of our campaign.

At first I wondered if the problem was demand. Maybe fewer people were interested in volunteer service than in the 1960s. But in 2009, applications had grown to more than fifteen thousand for fewer than four thousand positions. One source indicated that the Peace Corps website was visited by more than one hundred thousand unique visitors each year. In 2007 and 2008, largely because of disenchantment with war and probably also because of an ailing economy, the Peace Corps had seen thousands of additional applications.

Demand overseas had also grown. There was a waiting list of twenty new countries that had formally requested Peace Corps programs. One of these was Indonesia, the largest Muslim polity in the world, certainly a place Americans needed to understand better. Just picturing the first volunteers on fishing skiffs floating through the sixteen thousand islands and atolls was exciting to me. Another country on the waiting list was a much smaller chain of islands off the coast of Mozambique called Comoros. Fragrant vanilla and ylang-ylang vines grew in dense clusters on the shores of this small Muslim, Francophone nation, also known as the Perfume Islands, with a population of less than a million people. Nepal (which had closed in 2005 due to the Maoist conflict), Egypt, and Vietnam were among those waiting for new programs. Being a volunteer program, the Peace Corps was light on infrastructure and staff salaries, and as a result it cost just $4 million to open a new country program. More was spent annually on bottled water in the US Capitol.

Looking at the world map of where volunteers were being sent, I saw one noticeable gap: South Asia. I couldn't believe that India, Bangladesh, Pakistan, Nepal, Sri Lanka, Myanmar, Bhutan, or Nepal didn't have a single volunteer. Part of this was related to tightened safety and security post-9/11, but it was also because of a lack of funding. Many of the existing programs were undersized and in need of more volunteers. For example, a country as large as China had only 138 volunteers. Though Africa still had the largest number of volunteers, the Congo, Sudan, Chad, Nigeria—once among the countries hosting the largest programs in the world—no longer had volunteers.

The more I learned, the more I realized the Peace Corps had become a shriveled relic of its once vibrant self. Until 1983, it was listed in the federal budget under the heading "Miscellaneous." A State Department memo called it the "Peach Corps." Though half its original size, the organization now had four times as many lawyers compared with the midsixties. Though the volunteer experience out in the field was still just as life changing, the Washington side had lost its way. I was rather skeptical that a whole campaign was needed. This seemed to me like a real no-brainer. Who could oppose the goal of expanding the Peace Corps?

I blinked in amazement at the names on my laptop screen. More than twenty US ambassadors, five sitting members of Congress, including Senator Chris Dodd of Connecticut, the governor and first lady of Wisconsin, college presidents, mayors of major cities, even an astronaut had been Peace Corps volunteers. There were more than a thousand RPCV writers, and there was an organization devoted to promoting their writing called PeaceCorpsWriters.org. In the ultimate irony, there were even Peace Corps billionaires. Michael McCaskey, the owner of the

Chicago Bears, for example, had been a volunteer in Ethiopia. NetFlix, Tumi Luggage Company, the Nature Company, Sur La Tables—these were all Fortune 500 companies founded by RPCVs.

"Why don't you just get Bill Gates or Brad and Angelina to write a $400 million check?" a friend suggested when I told him how much it would cost to double the program. But the Peace Corps was a federal agency, and this meant every dollar had to be appropriated by a sub-committee known as the State and Foreign Operations Subcommittee (SFOPS). There was one SFOPS subcommittee in the House and one in the Senate. It was therefore fifteen senators and fifteen House of Representatives members who held the purse strings to the Peace Corps.

It was 1961 all over again. The timing of our campaign seemed flawless. President John F. Kennedy had, during the 1960 presidential campaign, described the 1950s as "the years the locusts ate," and the post-9/11 era could be described the same way. The man about to step into the Oval Office was even more Peace Corps–esque than JFK. The small Luo village his grandmother called home looked, on TV at least, like a volunteer duty station. His globe-trotting mother, though never in the Peace Corps, could have been its poster child. His family tree was a world map, stretching from Indonesia to Kenya to Kansas to Hawaii. The parallels between 2008 and 1960, between Barack Obama and JFK, ran deep. Through their charisma, speaking power, and hopeful message, both men ignited the passion and idealism of young people all over the country and all over the world. Both resonated deeply with a nation beleaguered by pointless wars and searching for a more peaceful rela-tionship with the world. Just as with Kennedy, Obama's very candidacy represented an eschewing of the establishment as well as a challenge to ordinary people to go beyond themselves and do extraordinary things through service and volunteerism. It seemed improbable, given the wars in Iraq and Afghanistan that an US presidential candidate could draw tens of thousands of cheering supporters abroad, but this was exactly what Obama did in his Berlin speech on July 24, 2008 (and what Kennedy had done twenty-five years earlier on June 26, 1963, in his famous "*Ich Bin Ein Berliner*" speech). Both Kennedy and Obama were leaders who sublimated the pragmatic and political concerns to a high level of bold ideals. In her January 27, 2008, *New York Times* op-ed piece endorsing Obama, "A President Like My Father," Caroline Kennedy Schlossberg wrote, "I have never had a president who inspired me the way people tell me that my father inspired them. But for the first time, I believe I have found the man who could be that president."

All this was a perfect storm of sorts for our campaign. I daydreamed of the first volunteers stepping onto the sandy shores of Jakarta on Air Force One, the president himself deplaning to greet the locals in Bahasa. Our campaign was shaped by Obama's own words. During his presidential campaign, on December 5, 2007, at Cornell College in Iowa, he first vowed to double the Peace Corps by the time of its fiftieth anniversary in 2011. Seven months later, in July, at the University of Colorado, with a fiery look in his eyes, he said it again: "We'll also grow our Foreign Service, open consulates that have been shuttered, and double the size of the Peace Corps by 2011 to renew our diplomacy." Then, during the second presidential debate, he again promised doubling the Peace Corps—this time before a television audience of more than fifty million people. He even wrote a piece in *Worldview,* a magazine published by the National Peace Corps Association (NPCA), the Peace Corps' national alumni organization, in which he called for a "bigger, better, bolder Peace Corps." Senator John McCain, the Republican candidate for president at the time, was also bullish on expanding the Peace Corps, as well as its domestic counterpart, AmeriCorps. I felt somewhat guilty that I was being paid to do what the major political candidates had already pledged they would do.

The Blue Nile is a nine-hundred-mile river originating in Lake Tana, Ethiopia. It is also a restaurant and nightclub in St. Paul. I was running late as I stopped at Kinko's to print out my fact sheets and graphs. Though I had met prime ministers, army generals, and CDOs in Nepal, I had never met a member of Congress before and I was nervous, not knowing what to say to her or how to properly address her. I pulled into the parking lot and walked in with my clipboards and sticker sheets, nearly tripping over the carpet. The representative I was meeting that evening was Betty McCollum from Minnesota's fourth district. RPCVs in the area had also been invited to the event, which was an introduction to the campaign.

Congresswoman Betty McCollum's foray into politics had home-grown roots. When her daughter was injured on a playground slide, she wrote the local politicians to fix it. When they didn't, she ran for Congress herself, rising to become one of the brightest stars of the Democratic Party and important for us one of the fifteen members of the House of Representatives on the State and Foreign Operations Appropriations Subcommittee, which decided funding levels for the Peace Corps.

The honey wine was flowing generously into almost eighty goblets. The RPCVs were happily trading stories.

"Hey, you're the guy leading this campaign to double the Peace Corps right?" a middle-aged man seated next to me asked.

"Yes, we're trying to—"

"Look, you seem like a nice enough guy, but you do realize you're going to fail, *right?*" he said. "Every few years, someone comes around and starts a campaign to double the Peace Corps. Don't get me wrong! It *is* a good idea, but war wins elections, not peace." Just as I was getting a little depressed listening to this man, the congresswoman appeared in a dark coat. She quickly scanned the crowd. Members of Congress did this scan not only to understand their audience, seeing if a key donor or supporter would need to be recognized but also to see if any crazed constituents were in the room. Because of their public stature, they often attracted a lot of them.

I handed her a "More Peace Corps" sticker. Not knowing the proper way to address her, I called her "Your Highness."

When it became my turn to present, I explained how the Peace Corps had lost a step. When I said, "There are *warheads* that cost more than the Peace Corps!" I sent a glass of honey wine sailing across the room. "The cost of the Peace Corps is two F-22 fighter jets. It's half the net worth of Senator John Kerry," I said, which upset people. My final line caused an audible groaning: "We can double the Peace Corps with what we spend in *five hours* in Iraq."

The congresswoman then walked purposefully to the head of the long line of tables as if it were a podium. I really wasn't sure what she was going to say. She was wearing the MORE PEACE CORPS sticker. The waiters from Addis Ababa, who were also listening, almost overfilled the glasses of wine they were pouring as Congresswoman McCollum spoke. "What America needs, now more than ever, is more Peace Corps volunteers! I'll fight in Congress, but to win our campaign, I'll need you to raise your voices too!"

"*Our campaign.*" That night, as I lay on a dusty couch in the basement of a former Colombia volunteer, praying the cats didn't come downstairs as I was deathly allergic, I felt elated. The next morning, I powered up the Pontiac and cruised north to see an old friend.

"License and registration please," the officer demanded, not looking very pleased. It was somewhere on I-94 North that I was pulled over for going thirty miles over the speed limit. "Where are you going in such a rush?"

"Officer, I'm on my way to a meeting for the Peace Corps," I said expecting him to rip up the ticket, give me a pat on the back, and issue a county proclamation. He peered through the window at what was basically my office—suits and ties, piles of letter and stationery, and damp swimming trunks for whenever I could stop in the water.

"Peace Corps? Is that still around?" he asked, bending my New York State driving license, very skeptical of the veracity of my answer. After I got the $130 speeding ticket, annoyed by this question, I took the next exit and stopped to adhere some of the Peace Corps signage to the hood and doors.

As the highest-ranking Indian American in the Republican Party and a former chief information officer for the Peace Corps, I knew Gopal Khanna, or "Gopal Uncle," as I called him, would be a crucial ally. I was surprised by how spartan and simple his house in the northern suburbs of St. Paul was. In the open living room area, there was a fleet of photographs of Khanna with George Bush, Governor Jesse Ventura, and a host of other political luminaries. With the porch door open and long-branched trees swooning in the gentle zephyrs outside, we sat at the dining table with Mrs. Khanna having *chai* over sweets and Samosas.

"Rajeev, I think this is a great initiative," Khanna said, scratching the back of his shaved head. "My only advice is that you have to be very careful growing Peace Corps too fast. It has to be done adeptly. Flooding an organization like the Peace Corps with money could destroy what is best about it." I knew this was wise counsel. "You know, in 1961, there weren't any cell phones, and most of the volunteers never spoke to their parents or girlfriends during the two years. The world is vastly different from 1961, but the Peace Corps must keep that original humble essence. Of course, I do agree we need a lot more volunteers."

"Well, if Senator Obama wins, we'll get the funding," I said almost immediately realizing my faux pas. Mrs. Khanna was now studying me through the sugary steam of her *chai.*

"Rajeev, you are a Republican, right?" she asked.

I looked down at the carpet in shame. "Well, Obama seems good for the Peace Corps."

When I looked up, the Samosas had magically shifted to the other end of the table and Mrs. Khanna looked at me disapprovingly.

"Sorry, Auntie," I said in shame. I never cared that much for party differences and had always felt doing away with them would be a good thing. Most volunteers would agree that next to Sargent Shriver, the best Peace Corps director was the heiress to the Miller Brewing Company, Loret Miller Ruppe, a Republican. Ruppe was the wife of a Republican congressman from Michigan, Philip Ruppe. She fiercely guarded its independence and autonomy, thwarting attempts to fold it into the State Department.

In 1983 Ruppe actually saved the Peace Corps from being shut down. At a small White House gathering to honor the prime minister of Fiji, where Ruppe was also present, the prime minister said, "President Reagan, I bring you today the sincere thanks of my government and my people for the men and women of the Peace Corps who go out into our villages."

"What did you pay that man to say that?" Vice President Bush jokingly asked her afterwards. When his cabinet proposed zeroing out the Peace Corps, President Reagan's response was, "Don't cut the Peace Corps. It's the only thing I got thanked for last week!"

As I got in my car, Gopal Uncle came over to the window with a tattered copy of a book. It was called *Action for Change*, an organizing manual that Donald Ross had written with Ralph Nader in 1973. Khanna's copy of the organizer's bible was full of highlights and scribbling in the margins. He had taped up the tattered pages to keep it intact. "Keep up this fight, Rajeev. I'm really proud of you," he said, now serious. As I drove on through the meandering country roads of rural Minnesota, there wasn't a single car on the road. We now had two crucial endorsements from opposite sides of the aisle. I pushed a bit harder on the accelerator.

It seemed an unusual backdrop for a Peace Corps gathering. I nearly walked into a life-sized marble bust of Dr. Martin Luther King Jr. in the lobby of the African American Heritage Museum in Sarasota, Florida. More than 150 people were seated in rows of folding chairs in the dark. "Rajeev! Welcome. We're just about to start the film," Anita Rogers, who was the museum's director, whispered loudly, before hitting play. I found a chair and sat down to watch a documentary film about Sargent Shriver called *An American Idealist.*

Until I met Anita Rogers, I didn't know that the Peace Corps had ever been in Afghanistan. I had grown so accustomed to thinking of it as a country Americans could only visit in a bulletproof vest. But between 1962 and 1979, there had been 1,652 volunteers before the program was finally suspended due to growing unrest from the Mujahedeen conflict.

Most people consider John F. Kennedy to be the creator of the Peace Corps, and while that is true in a political sense, the person that would actually build it in a pragmatic day-to-day sense from the ground up was the subject of this extraordinary film. Watching it, I learned the Peace Corps was born not out of complex legislation or some long-winded policy paper but from in an impromptu speech delivered at two o'clock in the morning on October 14, 1960. The only reason Kennedy was at the University of Michigan was to get a good night's sleep. He was tired from having just debated Richard Nixon earlier that day, but seeing ten thousand students waiting for him, some of whom were dangling from trees, he walked to the steps of the student union and delivered a three-minute speech that would ignite the idealism of a generation:

> How many of you who are going to be doctors, are willing to spend your days in Ghana? Technicians or engineers, how many of you are willing to work in the Foreign Service and spend your lives traveling around the world? On your willingness to do that, not merely to serve one year or two years in the service, but on your willingness to contribute part of your life to this country, I think will depend the answer whether a free society can compete.

Kennedy was acerbic in his criticism of diplomats who did not speak the languages of the countries where they served. Of the forty officials in the US Embassy in Belgrade, only three could speak Serbian. None of the officers in Delhi were versed in Hindi. He was known to have delivered a copy of a 1958 best seller *The Ugly American,* a fictional story about aloof diplomats living apart in walled compounds, to every one of his Senate colleagues. Three weeks later, in San Francisco, on November 2, 1960, before forty thousand people, he first proposed "a Peace Corps, of talented men and women." If Kennedy had his way, it would have become a part of the State Department's international aid bureaucracy, since that was what JFK had in mind, but Shriver would insist on it being an independent agency.

Judith and Al Guskin, two graduate students who were there that night in Michigan and who would be among the first volunteers to serve in Thailand, drafted a petition and secured a thousand signatures of willing volunteers. Without their petition, the Peace Corps idea could easily have evaporated. By Inauguration Day, Kennedy knew he had to act as more than twenty-five thousand letters had poured into the White House. He tapped his talented, charismatic brother-in-law Sargent Shriver to build it. Shriver was the most politically skilled asset on Kennedy's campaign—a sign of just how much importance the president was allotting the new Peace Corps, but Sarge had set his sights higher. He wanted to be the governor of Illinois or the secretary of education in the new cabinet, but Kennedy insisted, joking that if it didn't work out "it would be easier to fire a relative than a friend."

The larger-than-life Shriver approached the task of creating the Peace Corps with the same enthusiasm he had shown during the last stages of the presidential campaign. In his first three weeks on the job, he visited nine countries, meeting everyone from Emperor Haile Selassie to Prime Minister Jawharlal Nehru. The Peace Corps director had more star power than the secretary of state. The Peace Corps' identity was hard to separate from the bold and hard-working personality of the man who built it. A famous *Time* magazine cover in 1961 showed the Peace Corps office with the lights on after midnight on a weekday. According to some accounts, staff waited near the elevators in the mornings just to ride the elevator up with Shriver. A common expression among secretaries working at the Peace Corps office was "Shriverize."

Any letter leaving the Peace Corps office had to be Shriverized, which meant that the ideas in it had to be enlarged, multiplied, and applied with far greater imagination.

The blueprint for the new Peace Corps was found in a unique paper called "A Towering Task." The paper was authored by two federal employees, Warren Wiggins, a thirty-four-year-old deputy in the Far Eastern Operations Division of the State Department, and Bill Josephson, a brilliant twenty-six-year-old attorney. Appealing to Shriver's penchant for size, "A Towering Task" contended that one hundred thousand volunteers a year was not an out-of-reach goal. But beyond numbers, Wiggins and Josephson shrewdly advised that the young BA, "know-nothing" generalist whose only talent was fluency in the English language was in fact the *ideal* Peace Corps candidate. Just a few days after receiving their plan, on March 1, 1961, Kennedy issued Executive Order 10924 to create the Peace Corps "on a temporary pilot basis." Five months later Congress approved it by a voice call. However, initially it was the only agency during the Kennedy era to earn the status of "Emergency Agency."

Leaning forward in my chair in the cool, dark room in Sarasota, I could hardly believe the depths of Shriver's idealism. He had created not only the Peace Corps but also many other domestic social programs that had helped millions of low-income and disadvantaged Americans: Head Start, Legal Aid for the Poor, Job Corps, Upward Bound, and VISTA Biographer Scott Stossel would say about Sarge, "He probably had an effect on more Americans and more people across the world than anyone who hasn't been a president or a world leader, and probably even more than some of them."

It was tempting to credit Shriver's achievements to his lofty family connections, but Shriver was a powerful force in his own right. "What do you say to people who contend there are too many Kennedys in public office?" he was asked in an interview. "I would say my name is Shriver," was his proud answer. In fact, Shriver was sometimes laughed at by JFK and especially Bobby Kennedy who called him "a fucking boy scout" because of his youthful exuberance.

The most moving part of the film told a story of how he and Harris Wofford, a young advisor to Kennedy's presidential campaign and future US senator, helped save Martin Luther King Jr.'s life. Wofford had heard from King's pregnant wife that her husband was imprisoned in

Georgia on false charges. She feared that if he wasn't released soon he could be lynched. Shriver, on Wofford's urging, raced to O'Hare airport to catch the president before his flight took off and convinced Kennedy to call Coretta Scott King from the airport as a show of public support. As it was just a few days before the election, this was a risky political move, and one for which Bobby Kennedy later castigated Shriver, but JFK agreed it was the right thing to do. Some historians have said this single call not only saved King's life but also won Kennedy the tough-fought election of 1960. Learning that the man who created the Peace Corps had a hand in saving Martin Luther King Jr.'s life, made me admire Shriver even more.

Shriver wanted the Peace Corps to be separate from the other alphabet agencies of Washington. He wanted it to thrive on the youthful energy and idealism of the volunteers. On one occasion when a top-down organizational chart of the agency was presented to him, he drew a large box in the center and wrote "VOLUNTEERS," then drew arrows from the other boxes to that box in the center.

The Peace Corps would find a second founding father in President Lyndon B. Johnson, who helped ensure it didn't become an appendage of the International Cooperation Association (the precursor to USAID). The bureaucratic impulse was to place the Peace Corps within a neat organizational chart, pulling all foreign assistance programs into one unified department, but then–vice president LBJ agreed with Sarge that it was too popular a program to attach to the other unpopular programs. President Kennedy grudgingly agreed. This perhaps more than anything influenced the renegade, youthful direction of the new agency.

Everyone else was enraptured too. The film went on to say that during those early days, Sarge met with every single member of Congress and was considered the best lobbyist in Washington. "One night I was leaving about 7:30," the House Rules Committee chairman would recall, "and there was Shriver walking up and down the halls looking into the doors. He came in and talked to me. I still didn't like the program, but I was sold on Shriver—I voted for him."

I remember four moments from marching in President Obama's inaugural parade very vividly. The first occurred at 3:00 p.m. An RPCV had just read on her BlackBerry that something was wrong with Ted Kennedy. The Peace Corps volunteers, carrying majestic ten-foot flags from 139 countries spontaneously huddled together—in part because we were freezing but also because Senator Kennedy's health was heavy on our minds. We stopped complaining about the cold, and our thoughts went to thinking the parade would be canceled. Some wanted to know if we would still be on TV. Then, another RPCV, who was on the phone with his father who was watching CNN, excitedly announced that Barack and Michelle Obama were on Twelfth Street. We started getting into position. From blocks away we heard cheering so loud it shook the ground. The new president and first lady were just minutes from the viewing station. Then, at that moment, Harris Wofford, wearing a Peace Corps baseball cap, appeared with his grandson, who was wearing a bright red AmeriCorps jacket. I looked back and saw some of the older Peace Corps volunteers point at Harris and tear up, and it was because decades ago Wofford, who was the special director to Africa and personal advisor to President Kennedy, had come to their villages, trained them, and shown them the way. And he was here again to show us the way through this bitter cold.

The kids from a middle school marching band in the contingent in front of us picked up their trombones and started playing "When the Saints Go Marching In." As the kids played, Harris, who was carrying the Peace Corps banner, began dancing. Not just moving back and forth— he started spinning around with Peace Corps volunteers.

The second moment came when we actually started marching. As we turned onto Pennsylvania Avenue, people from all over America were there and looking at us. I've never quite experienced anything like that. I started waving back and smiling. You couldn't help it. Then, person after person started raising their fists and cheering, "Go Peace Corps!" and "Thank you!" One woman was jumping up and down and crying. The Peace Corps contingent, walking in unison, was a sea of flags perfectly horizontal in the twenty miles per hour wind. To the crowd this embodied the hope that President Obama had promised. Then, three men in bumblebee yellow jackets and red backpacks came running up to us. I recognized two of them—Tim and Mark Shriver—and the third was much younger. Tim was wearing black sunglasses. I couldn't believe how much his bold, positive smile reminded me of his father, Sargent Shriver.

From the front of the line, locking arms with Harris, they waved to the Peace Corps volunteers.

After walking twenty meters with us, they raced back to take their positions in the Special Olympics contingent. As we turned another corner, I saw Mark Shriver about a hundred meters ahead, looking back at us. The expression on his face was full of so much emotion. Because of my angle, I could see it very clearly. He was overwhelmed by the sea of flags. This look was the third moment I remember so vividly. It appeared as if he wanted to remember the image of the flags in his mind forever. It was an image of how one person had changed the world and the inner world of all the marchers—and this person was his own father.

The Obamas and Bidens were in a giant, heated, white cube with a poster on it that said "PRESIDENT OF THE UNITED STATES" in cursive letters. It was getting a bit darker, and as we approached the viewing station, the crowds were getting larger and larger and much louder with thousands now cheering. Then it happened—the final moment I remember from the parade. This one also had to do with Senator Wofford. As we came closer, I saw the new president and first lady and the Bidens. They looked beautiful and happy, almost glittering. When they saw us, they seemed genuinely warmed. But then President Obama noticed Harris, and he started pointing excitedly and telling the first lady and Joe Biden, and they started pointing too and telling others in the room that Harris was there. The new president looked at him with his characteristic megawatt smile, only the look was very different, more peaceful and nostalgic. Harris kept dancing, stopping only for a second to ceremoniously salute them. I wondered if the president was remembering traveling around the country with Wofford, hearing all the Peace Corps stories. Harris, who was Obama's surrogate for Pennsylvania, was there at perhaps the future president's most important speech of the campaign—the Philadelphia address on race. Whatever it was, the president was tearing up. He was completely fixated on Harris. I wish I could have seen Senator Wofford's face, but I was so focused on the glowing cube and Obama's smile and trying to absorb what it all meant.

Then the president and first lady saw the sea of flags, and they leaned forward and craned their necks a bit. I don't think they were expecting we would have such tall flags or so many of them. I wondered if the new president was searching for the flag of Kenya, where his father was born, or Indonesia, where he had lived and gone to school for four years with his sister, Maya, and stepfather, Lolo. As I looked at the cube of glowing light, I knew that we were now Obama's kids being ushered in by Kennedy's kids. I knew then that President Obama was going to do something great for the Peace Corps.

CHAPTER 9

ℒ

The Hill

The morning of February 17, 2009, barely a month after the parade, the phone rang in my office on Broad Street in New York City with dreadful news.

"Not a *dime?*" I asked, incredulously.

"Nope," an aide on the Hill confirmed. I scoured the president's $787 billion job stimulus again just to be sure, but the words *Peace Corps* were nowhere to be found. The domestic service programs AmeriCorps and Volunteers in Service to America (VISTA) had received a $201 million jolt, but our request for just $50 million to jump-start the promised expansion had received the smarting retort of "Peace Corps is not a *job*" from Rahm Emanuel, the president's chief of staff.

I was very surprised, and it didn't at all sound like the new Obama administration. The relatively small sum could have created a thousand new positions from Mongolia to Thailand, South Africa to China. Including all the administrative expenditures, it cost $42,000 to support one Peace Corps worker per annum, while the stimulus, by some estimates, spent $300,000 on each job. I thought about the president's tears upon seeing the sea of flags and realized it was probably premature to fret. But at the same time, the 2010 Peace Corps budget was just a few months away, and if this was what his chief of staff was saying, it was probably best not to take any chances. Asking myself the question, "What would Shriver do?" I bought a one-way ticket from New York's Penn Station to Union Station in Washington, DC.

ℒ

The red circles flashed at the edge of the platform as the white train rushed into the station. After two dull chimes that sounded like the lowest note on a xylophone, the doors unbolted and I sat down next to a large man flipping through *Politico,* a free newspaper about the latest Capitol Hill gossip. Peaking over his shoulder, the names and faces were alien to me. It was raining heavily when I rode the long escalator out from the metro station.

My skeletal umbrella nearly blew away as I walked through the rows of imposing Georgetown mansions near the NBC studios. I cursed myself for being late to such an important meeting. Every time I asked someone how to reach advisors in the Obama administration or members of Congress, the answer was always "Talk to Maureen." As a special correspondent to *Vanity Fair* magazine, she had profiled everyone from Madonna to Vladimir Putin to Carla Bruni, the first lady of France. Bono was a regular houseguest. The Pulitzer-Prize-winning novel *Lonesome Dove,* considered by many to be the great American novel, had been dedicated to her. Her husband was the late Tim Russert, the famous moderator of *Meet the Press.* I didn't really know any of this when I pushed the glowing doorbell of her home. All I knew was that Maureen Orth was the conduit to the president and vice president of the United States.

The woman who opened the front door was not Maureen but Carolina Barco, Colombian ambassador to the United States. "You must be Rajeev," she said, smiling as she handed me a long-stemmed glass of wine. There was another friendly, bearded man in hide-skin boots, who was a former ambassador to Australia. We sat down in the den, a candle glowing from behind a glass partition.

"We'd love to see volunteers back in Colombia!" Ambassador Barco said excitedly. "You know, Peace Corps is sorely missed in our country."

"You made it!" Maureen said entering the room. "And you've met the ambassadors. Sam should be here soon as well."

By Sam, I didn't realize she meant Congressman Sam Farr. The two had been in the same Peace Corps group in Colombia in the mid-1960s, long before their illustrious careers in journalism and politics. On Capitol Hill, Farr was known as "Mr. Peace Corps." His was one of the most painful stories of all. When he was a volunteer in Colombia, his mother died of cancer in 1963. On the trip in which his father and sister traveled to Medellin to console the young Farr, his sister, Nancy, fell from a horse and injured her head. She died on an operating table in Colombia. Within the span of a week, he had lost his mother and his sister.

The doorbell echoed. Wearing a bright red vest under his silver suit, Mr. Peace Corps was now standing in the antechamber with his wife, Shary. Suddenly everyone was speaking animatedly in Spanish, arms waving up and down, laughing, clapping. I just stood up excitedly from the couch and tried to pat down some of the moisture on my blazer.

Congressman Farr's coat had a rather impressive American eagle lapel pin on it. At the time I didn't understand how vital this pin-wearing custom would prove to me. Members of the House (senators tended not to wear them) wore these pins not just to identify themselves to the public but also to Capitol security. The composition of the House changed so fast even the guards couldn't keep up. Moreover, some members, like the congressman from Peoria, Illinois, Aaron Schock, were younger than their aides, barely twenty-seven or twenty-eight years old.

Just before we sat down for dinner, Maureen showed us copies of the latest issue of *Vanity Fair*. She and the famous portrait photographer Annie Leibovitz had done profiles of each of the members of the new Obama administration, everyone from David Axelrod to Valerie Jarrett to Steven Chu to Reggie Love. This was the tightest inner circle of the president of the United States, and Maureen knew them all. During dinner Maureen told us about the school in Medellin where she had taught as a Peace Corps volunteer. She showed us pictures of a beautiful new school she had helped construct as well as photographs of children in this school using computers donated through a program called One Laptop Per Child. Like me, she had been back to her Peace Corps village many times and maintained strong ties to her Peace Corps country.

After dinner, I felt embarrassed when the congressman bused my plate. Washing the dishes, wearing long, yellow, rubber gloves and an apron, at one point he leaned into the sink and scooped out some salad bits. I looked on as this nine-term member of Congress from the seventeenth district of California, the chairman of the House Agriculture Committee, a powerful member of the House Appropriations Committee, yanked up a morsel and stared at it as the water drained. It gurgled loudly.

I assumed Farr had no idea who I was or why I was there. Looking at these powerful people, I was half-wondering the same thing when he came over and sat in a chair across from me, leaning in, his jaw clenched. "Don't you worry. We'll remind the president," he said almost biting on the words. "Tomorrow I'm dropping the bill in Congress. I was a super delegate. The president came to me asking for my vote. I asked him to triple the Peace Corps. He promised to double it. We shook on it. We're going to fight for a $110 million increase in this year's budget, which will get us up to ten thousand volunteers for the first time since 1968. It'll get us into Colombia, Vietnam, and Indonesia. Remember one thing, Rajeev. As you try to get cosponsors on my bill, 'Squeaky wheel gets the grease!'"

We all got in a cab. The driver looked as if he'd just spotted a celebrity. I thought he noticed the congressman in the back seat, but he was looking me up and down and shaking a finger. "Is that Dr. Sanjay Gupta in my car?" he asked. Though I believed I looked nothing like the CNN chief medical correspondent, I was frequently mistaken for this Indian doctor in Washington.

The next day Congressman Farr pounded on the House podium as he introduced House Resolution 1066, the Peace Corps Expansion Act, authorizing $450 million, $600 million, and finally $750 million in 2010, 2011, and 2012, respectively. That last budget of $750 million would effectively double the number of Peace Corps volunteers.

I didn't know what "the Hill" was or what it looked like the first time I went to Washington in February of 2009. Bearing a physical likeness to the World Trade Center hijackers, I was as cautious about the people within the ivory rotundas as they probably were about me, but it was time to shake off these fears. I had no idea that when you arrived at Union Station and stepped off the Amtrak, you were just a five-minute walk from the Capitol Rotunda. Naturally I assumed that it would be a protected, sealed-off place, but nothing could have been further from the truth.

"My passport, officer," I said, sliding the dusty dark-blue booklet toward him, which contained entirely too many tourist-visa stamps to the former Himalayan kingdom.

"No ID required. Place it in this basket, and pass it through." I started removing my belt and shoes. "What are you doing? No, no. You keep all that on, just place your bag on the conveyor belt and step through, please."

I collected my belongings and scurried off, bewildered that literally anyone could enter the US House of Representatives office buildings without a single piece of identification. My heels clicked loudly as I fluttered down the long, hard marble corridors. Even the insides of the buildings on Capitol Hill were facade-like. The warped glass bay windows looked out onto the nondescript, empty white rooftops of *other* office buildings. The walls were adorned with paintings of the very building I was standing in. There were black-and-white photographs depicting construction of the Capitol Rotunda in 1903 and 1904. I passed all kinds of unmarked doors interrupted by ones with large state flags outside them. I passed one slightly ajar door behind which bottles of champagne wrapped in white cloth were being poured into cups held by army generals and congressmen. *What is this place?* I wondered.

The 435 House of Representatives members had their offices in one of three adjacent Greco-Roman edifices: the Cannon, Longworth, and Rayburn buildings. Each was named after a former Speaker of the House and had its own personality. I didn't really know any of this history about the US Congress. When the great bank robber was asked by the reporter why he robbed banks, his clever answer was, "Because that's where the money is." I suppose if someone had asked me why I was standing in these hoary buildings, I would have delivered the same answer.

The Cannon Building was all white marble containing a rotunda lit naturally by a large oculus. It felt more like a bathhouse in Budapest than a congressional office building. The Longworth Building had low ceilings and smelled like tuna sandwiches, celery sticks, and fish tanks. The Rayburn Building was composed of a bluish-grey granite stone and had corridors that went on for nearly a kilometer. The three buildings were connected by long, complex tunnels and interlinking escalators. Initially I didn't realize this, and every time I needed to visit an office in an adjacent building, I would leave and go through security all over again.

A small elevator marked "MEMBERS ONLY" opened, and I almost walked into Congressman Barney Frank. He was surrounded by noisy reporters, and it looked like he was wearing a *mala* of tape recorders.

When the elevator for the general public opened, three astronauts in puffy orange spacesuits observed me as if I were a Martian. They looked as though they had just landed on the roof of the Longworth Building. I watched them spacewalk down the corridors carrying classified binders stamped with NASA insignias. On the third floor a fleet of paraplegics was racing in the direction of video cameras outside a hearing room. In the other direction, a slow-moving herd of Texans in jewel-encrusted neckties. Everyone had come to Washington with some burning issue in their briefcase. The insignia of the Peace Corps was a wavy US flag with white doves in place of stars, but no one really wore this insignia. The uniform of the Peace Corps was the absence of one.

Capitol Hill was a multibillion-dollar marble brain stem powered by more than eighteen thousand staff, many of whom were in their twenties. US politics was a spoils system, as these staff people were often carryovers from the representatives' local electoral campaigns. They held polyvalent functions, sometimes operating simply as a line of defense that protected the member of Congress from nasty, crazed constituents, sometimes fielding letters and e-mails, often assisting in research and the drafting of legislation. Most of the ones I encountered were blond haired and blue eyed and had the air of an Ivy League varsity sports team. But there were always a few curmudgeonly, older types who were the repositories of all kinds of process and technical knowledge that was indispensible to members. They were the nuts and bolts behind the slick veneer.

Collectively known as "the Hill," three House buildings and three Senate buildings sat facing each other with the famous Capitol Rotunda in the center. As I discovered, this layout was one of many false symmetries. The Senate's Russell, Dirksen, and Hart buildings were much farther east than the House buildings. Even the Capitol Rotunda was misleading. It supposedly marked the center of Washington, equidistant from the Anacostia and Potomac Rivers, but the center of DC was actually closer to the White House. In fact, the whole place had a piecemeal quality, which contradicted the orderly white facades. At times, as I walked through underground tunnels from one building to the next, I passed through thick plastic curtains and walls boarded up with misshapen pieces of plywood, wondering if I had somehow wandered into restricted territory, but these were legitimate pathways open to the public. Perhaps the greatest symbol of this false discipline and general absurdity of the US Capitol was that, on the interior roof of the Capitol, 180 feet above the rotunda floor, hangs a fresco called *The Apotheosis of Washington* in which George Washington is literally wearing a pink dress.

Turning the corner, I walked by an old man with an uneven grin in a striped banker's suit. Miming a fake gun with his arm, he actually fired it at me with a double-clicking sound just as he winked. I some-what instinctively did this back to him, not realizing the absurdity of the interaction. This was how Capitol Hill worked. It absorbed you in ways you didn't recognize until you started engaging in strange rituals to fit in. After a while, I started wearing the same ridiculous bowl haircut that I had perfected in the restrooms. I even sewed an extra pocket into my blazer so I could more easily grasp my business cards.

I finally found the office at the end of a long marble corridor. A silk Texan flag stood at rest beside it. "Do you have a business card?" the sec-retary asked, haughtily tilting her head. I produced a flimsy one and slid it across the counter. "Please have a seat. John will be with you in just a few minutes . . . Hey, John, a guy from Peace Corps is here to see you?" she said into a phone, not taking her eyes off of the Fox News program playing on a TV screen.

These offices were grab bags of cultural artifacts, usually full of ob-scure slivers of American culture from the districts they represented— moose heads, interlinking hockey sticks, Little League baseball pennants. There were bowls of saltwater taffy or gumdrops produced by local companies that created jobs back in their districts. Some of the Iowa offices had buttered popcorn machines. Unfailingly, there was an at-tempt to make the office feel homegrown, but this sometimes made it less inviting for me. A grotesque beast with a soggy, wet tongue hustled around the office of Congresswoman Ileana Ros-Lehtinen, the ranking member of the House Foreign Relations Committee, a fact that kept me far away from her office.

While most were visually cluttered, the most breathtaking office I visited was the office of Hawaii senator Daniel Inouye, the longest serv-ing US senator. Huge oil paintings of Hawaiian kings and queens and books depicting the lush valleys of Kauai completely captured my at-tention as I sat waiting for an aide. The office even had a saltwater fish tank full of live coral and tropical seahorses. It was the one office where I always had trouble focusing on the conversation.

The secretary escorted me into an empty room with a long table surrounded by expensive leather chairs. I sat down and opened my binder. The square-faced foreign affairs aide, Mark, sat down and asked me what he could do for me. As I spoke, he sat studying me without expression from across the table. He had his hands in the shape of a Namaste under his chin, gold elephant cuff links peeking out past his blazer sleeves.

"So how *high* did you get?" he finally asked.

"Sorry?"

"Altitude. Did you make it to base camp? You know, in Nay-pawl?"

"No, actually I've never been trekking."

"Look, I actually think Peace Corps is America's best soft power instrument," he said. "Do we have any volunteers in the West Bank? Iraq? How many do we have winning hearts and minds in Afghanistan, showing the American way?" he asked.

"Soft power" was one of these catch phrases I commonly heard in relation to the Peace Corps, but I rather despised it. Aligning Peace Corps with US strategic interest was at best imprudent and at worst downright dangerous for the volunteers. Kennedy's secretary of state Dean Rusk had wisely cautioned in 1961, "The Peace Corps is not a part of American foreign policy. To make it so would rob it of its contribution *to* American foreign policy." There would be times when the Peace Corps was co-opted by a political objective on the right or the left, though it always ended poorly. "Soft power" sounded to my ears like a euphemism for erectile dysfunction. Another catchy expression I heard a lot was "smart power." This sounded to me like practicing abstinence.

After a pause, looking flushed in frustration for some reason I couldn't understand and passing his hands through his hair, he said, "Before we decide whether or not to cosponsor the bill, tell me something. How do you prevent gays from getting into the Peace Corps?" He didn't even try to lower his voice as he said it.

"I'm sorry?"

"You know. How do you prevent the *weak*, the people that don't represent our country in the best light from serving?" I must have stared at this young aide for a full five seconds without the faintest idea of how to respond.

"Uh . . . sorry? I don't really . . . Could you repeat the question?" I walked out of the congressman's office pretty upset, sweating profusely. I couldn't believe it—this aide wanted to support Peace Corps if it would incorporate what was basically a "Don't Ask, Don't Tell" policy. I leaned over one of the fountains in the marble halls, a little dizzy, and took a swig of water and straightened my tie. How do you prevent idiots from becoming staffers for members of Congress—it was on the tip of my tongue, but I was glad I didn't say it.

In the popular consciousness, the Peace Corps was a humanitarian poverty-reduction development program. If I had learned anything in Namje, it was that poverty was a *construct*. The discourse of *developed* and *underdeveloped* countries fell short in my estimation. To call Nepal a "least developed country" (as influential economists like Paul Collier have done) made little sense. It ignored certain critical facts, such as Nepal being the world's second richest nation in hydropower potential, having one of the most diverse landscapes of fauna and flora of any country, or having more than two hundred mountains over twenty-thousand-feet tall.

The difficult question for us was how to "sell" the Peace Corps without playing into this discourse. What I learned in places like Namje was that informal economies were impossible to measure. Maybe people did earn a dollar a day, but there was substantial hidden wealth. They lived in the shade of long beautiful bamboos, ate organic fruits and vegetables, treated ailments with medicinal plants from the jungles, and woke up to the staggering view of Kanchenjunga each morning. This was to say nothing of the myths, folklore, and indigenous knowledge embedded in each village. Though I have never been to sub-Saharan Africa or seen the most crushing levels of famine and disease, I would guess that villages there too are "poor" only by a particular definition of the term.

Although there were exceptions, most often the discussion went one of two ways—either the one about smart power, soft power, winning hearts and minds or else the discussion on "fighting" poverty, saving people. I did my best to navigate these carefully.

At first, my strategy in these staff meetings was to show a graph of plummeting volunteer numbers juxtaposed against the growing domestic and overseas demand. Usually the pushback would be, "What do we take the money out of? Where do we find the offset?" The challenge was that money had to be taken from *another* account within the State and Foreign Operations bill. When I realized how critical this question was, I began carrying with me a copy of the State and Foreign Operations bill, with highlights for all the accounts that were bloated or wasteful in my opinion. The State and Foreign Operations bill, in addition to funding the State Department, which had a budget of roughly $17 billion, contained huge sums for military capacity building in nations referred to as "front-line states"—Afghanistan, Pakistan, and Iraq. I highlighted and drew red stars around the Pakistan Counterinsurgency Capability Fund (PCCF), which had more than $2 billion. Another line item highlighted on my tattered copy of the SFOPS bill was the Embassy Security Construction and Maintenance (ESCM) fund for the State Department, which was upwards of $7 billion. Post-9/11, expensive new security procedures required building even taller embassy walls farther recessed from public walkways.

The Iraq embassy, which cost more than half a billion dollars, was a fortress of twenty-one buildings on 104 acres, with more than 5,500 Americans and Iraqis working within it. To my thinking at least, the lavish palatial US embassies projected the wrong values and were extremely wasteful. The new US Embassy in Nepal, constructed in 2010, was an $80 million walled fortress. It was perhaps the most environmentally unsustainable building in Kathmandu. Even many of the construction workers were flown in from overseas.

But as the months wore on, I realized so many of these wasteful military accounts were politically immune. I put away the statistics and fact sheets and just started telling the story of the water project in Namje. This would sometimes lead to hour-long discussions about Nepal. Then just as I was leaving, almost as an afterthought, I would mention the Peace Corps bill and the response would be, "Oh, sure, don't worry, we'll get on it." Twelve thousand miles away, the people of Namje had no idea their example was inspiring others to work for more Peace Corps funding.

In the village, Tanka Sir would constantly say to me, "Rajeev Sir, to get anything done, you must go directly to the *highest* power." I soon discovered I could bypass the aides altogether and go directly to the congressmen and congresswomen. Politicians thrived on being approached and recognized. Unlike movie stars, they didn't dress down or cover their faces with newspaper. If you were willing to loiter in the right places, you could meet and talk to anyone. Lawmakers were biological beings. They needed to use the toilet, they got hungry, sometimes they needed to walk outside or get a Coke from the vending machine. I started to lurk in these spaces.

For members of Congress, meeting constituents meant cementing votes. Their political survival required face time with reporters and media, lobbyists, and even their own colleagues whom they would rally onto bills. They were constantly campaigning for the next level, for coveted committee and subcommittee assignments, caucus leadership positions. To be more readily recognized, they wore congressional lapel pins but their entire being was a symbolic brand. Hair was made abnormally white and more powdery, eyebrows bushier, drawls thicker. These attributes helped make them more recognizable, and this recognition itself was a form of power. Had I stopped to consider all this I would have been less surprised that, on the Hill, members of Congress were easier to find than the men's room.

I never had an office on Capitol Hill and I think this was a good thing. My office was the empty table I could find in the Starbucks on Independence Avenue, it was the bathroom stall in the Rayburn basement I knew was sometimes empty for hours consecutively where I could type up e-mails, it was a chair near a power outlet in a committee room.

On the eastern edge of the Capitol lawn, where New Jersey Avenue meets Independence Avenue, members of Congress have to cross the street to get to the House office buildings. I learned that if I lurked around in the willow trees on a wedge of grass right near the crosswalk, I could jump from the trees and meet dozens of House of Representatives members in this way. One lapel pin after another, a flurry of coins spilling out of a slot machine. "Congressman! Congressman!" I jumped out of the grove of trees and chased after them. "Peace Corps? I'll sign that," members would say, giving me the name of the aide to give the bill to in his or her office. "You don't even know my name, do you?" one congressman said to me. "I don't . . ." I confessed, "but you wear a pin!" Pleased with this answer, he sent me to his chief of staff. Sometimes I jumped from the wedge of grass to stop four or five members together and they would all agree to sign. Back at my hotel, I made notes about who I had met, where the gaps were, and sent this detailed information out to the grassroots. As I learned more about how members of Congress were members of committees and subcommittees as well as caucuses (some of which were country caucuses that had Peace Corps volunteers), I started creating new flowcharts of who was connected to other members we needed to reach. We reached out to ambassadors of the countries where Peace Corps would open if the funds were appropriated and they spoke to members they knew. The Nepal ambassador Shankar Sharma, while presenting his credentials, even mentioned to President Obama his desire to see Peace Corps back in Nepal.

A small, spiral congressional face book I carried in my knapsack contained the names, head shots, and salient biographical data for every member of Congress. By far the most important thing to know was a representative's name. It was the entrée to a conversation with anybody. In addition, the book told you where they went to college, where they were born, what they did before coming to Congress—all further entrées to conversations. When I didn't recognize someone, I reached for it and flipped through until I saw his or her face.

Among K Street lobbying firms, what I was doing was known as "bird-dogging." It referred to tactically waiting outside committee hearings to meet with a member of Congress without an appointment. Rather than my three years in law school, it was my experience selling the Nepali hats on Houston Street that had relevance here on the Hill. Lobbying was about getting someone excited and inspired so that they would stop and talk to you. You had just a few seconds to inspire someone and make them stop walking.

I became a mainstay at all kinds of boring hearings on transportation reform, child day-care programs, and nomination ceremonies for agency officials and ambassadors that went on for hour upon hour. The hearings I most dreaded were with the Minnesota senator Al Franken whose voice was absolutely dreadful. Every time he opened his mouth, all I could think about were the sweaters he wore as the character Stuart Smalley in the famous *Saturday Night Live* sketch. I kept waiting for him to add after his prepared remarks, "And I'm good enough, I'm smart enough, and *doggone* it, people like me!"

But these hearings were also a good time to draft newsletters on my iPhone. Keeping the volunteers at the grassroots informed was in many ways more important than chasing down members of Congress. If we knew a certain congressman or congresswoman was refusing to sign, the software in our e-mail system allowed us to send an alert to former volunteers living in that person's district. Sometimes I'd walk by the congressperson's office later and delight in hearing a panicked secretary trying to calm down an angry RPCV: "I know you're upset Ma'am, and I'll certainly convey your feelings that you'd like to see the congressman on the Peace Corps bill." My iPhone often felt like a joystick. If someone was recalcitrant about signing, we hit a few buttons and suddenly the RPCVs were jabbing back. But some RPCVs were getting peeved at the barrage of spam. "Desist from sending me this shit immediately asshole" was one of many messages I got.

I figured out there are certain nodes where members of Congress log-jam in huge numbers. For example, at the underground connection point between the Longworth and Rayburn buildings there is a rotunda with an entrance to a monorail system that transports members to the Capitol. Standing under the sword of an eight-foot Roman gladiator statue, I met dozens of members. Members of Congress themselves stood there to bird-dog peers onto their own bills and letters. Congresswoman Dianne DeGette usually placed herself right near the monorail entrance and we sometimes came into competition. Under the oculus of the Cannon Building is another key location where members of Congress are interviewed on CNN. The camera crew themselves would try to bird-dog members and land interviews, and there too we sometimes competed.

"Excuse me, Ms. Bash," I said recognizing the famous CNN anchor Dana Bash, who was in a blinding, fluorescent white light as an aide applied glittery purple blush to her cheekbones.

"Yes."

"I wanted to ask if you could give these documents to Kiran Chetry." Kiran was the daughter of a US Peace Corps volunteer mother and a Nepalese aid worker father. Important for us, she was the coanchor of the CNN *American Morning* program.

"Will do," she said. (I was relieved she didn't mistake me for her colleague.)

In my zeal, I sometimes bird-dogged people who could be of absolutely no help to us. One afternoon, I spotted a man strolling nonchalantly down Independence Avenue. He didn't have a care in the world, seemingly too aloof, too detached to be a member of Congress, but his face was really familiar. I stopped and paged through the directory. As he neared, I retreated, realizing this was the chief justice of the United States Supreme Court, John Roberts Jr. I briefly considered asking him to talk to the president, but thankfully realized how asinine an idea this was.

The time spent chewing on a rock-hard piece of Armenian Lavash bread in a volunteer's backyard might have seemed depressing at the moment, but when we needed the passionate phone calls and e-mails, those grassroots meetings could make a difference of millions of dollars. An example of this was a former Colombia volunteer, Maureen Shanley, who was the president of the Connecticut chapter of former volunteers. She truly scared the bejesus out of members of Congress, even if the Connecticut chapter had only a few dozen members. Shanley, who had a booming voice and a no-nonsense disposition, started working the phones, organizing friends, knocking on the doors of neighbors. Rather than "Please sign the Peace Corps Expansion Act," the message to the secretaries was "And why exactly hasn't the Congressman signed the Peace Corps Expansion Act yet?" At one point I thought she was going to come to Washington herself and bop each of the members of Congress on the head with the large hand purse she carried.

Beth Gamburd, an RPCV who had served in Korea during the 1970s, was an organizer who struck fear in the Michigan delegation. Anytime I needed anything done in the state of Michigan I called her and within an hour Gamburd was rallying the troops.

It was easy for people in Washington to think only Washington mattered, but that seemed to me a deadly error. Without an organized citizen base buttressing the effort, it was all paper thin. In the brilliant 1972 book *Who Runs Congress? The President, Big Business or You?*, produced by the Ralph Nader Congress Project, it is written:

> Some citizens, peering into the chasm between congressional potential and congressional failure, may understandably shrug their shoulders in indifference. But mixed among all the cases of sloth, political hackery, insensitivity to injustice, and the dual hurdles of bureaucratic intransigence and business lobbying, are remarkable instances of citizen power. Congress has been moved by men and women with no special wealth or influence, little or no political experience, and no uncommon genius, but with the modest combination of

commitment to a cause and the facts to make a case. Not often, but enough to show the way, citizen advocates have taken on industrial giants, bureaucratic inertia, public indifference, antipathy to "trouble-makers"—and they have won, or least made a difference.

Life went on like this for months. Each day, when I got back to my hotel in Woodley Park, I was usually a little crazed and very tired. All I really wanted was to fall asleep to a slow baseball game. There were days I collapsed on the hotel mattress still in my suit, woke up at 7:30 the next morning, and walked out the door to the metro. By Friday I longed to be back in New York.

I scheduled as many thirty-minute meetings with aides as I could get between 8:30 a.m. and 5:30 p.m. This usually meant I had a few minutes to dash from one building to another, but sometimes it meant I had long one- or two-hour windows. Soon I realized the golden ratio was about five or six staff meetings peppered throughout the day in vastly different parts of the Capitol. I really didn't care where the representative stood—Republican, Democrat, anarchist—the only thing that mattered was where you stood on Peace Corps funding.

One afternoon in April of 2009, I walked over to 1128 Longworth where Congressman Sam Farr's office was located. I went in to see Marc Hanson, Congressman Farr's foreign affairs aide who was an RPCV in Honduras from 2003 to 2005. Marc was running his own campaign to increase Peace Corps funding. Among the eighteen thousand staff on the Hill were hundreds of RPCVs filling coffee, answering phones, filing papers. A handful were among the most powerful people in Washington: Brendan Daly, a former Peace Corps communications liaison, was Speaker Pelosi's communications director. The chief of staff to the all-powerful chairman of the Senate Appropriations Committee, Senator Inouye, was one of the earliest Peace Corps trainers in Hawaii, Patrick DeLeon. Marc was organizing meetings with them to expand the internal staff network.

"Rajeev, we did it!" Marc said, slapping my hand. "We got 132 co-sponsors on the bill!"

"Is that good?" I asked.

"The highest level of congressional support in Peace Corps history. Now we just need the president to include the $110 million increase in his budget."

❦

One sunny afternoon in May of 2009 I was on the phone as I stood outside the entrance of the Cannon Building when an SUV with tinted windows parked at the bottom of the steps. Guards in dark cargo pants with pistols strapped to their belts stepped out and opened the doors to perfect forty-five-degree angles. They had massive black attack dogs. "Looks like someone important just showed up!" I said. The dogs posed at the foot of the steps, like imperial stone lions, and then I saw who it was. "I have to go."

A lean, bespectacled man trotted up the steps toward me. He was smiling like a politician, looking left and right as if to acknowledge cheering crowds (the streets were empty), holding under his arm a leather-bound document of some kind. Behind him, moving more slowly up the steps, was a stubby, self-assured fellow with an almost olive complexion, carrying no papers and appearing very out of place and rubbing the back of his layered neck.

One of the things that can happen when you work on a campaign is that the names and pictures in *Politico*, the *Hill*, and other beltway dailies become relevant to your professional life. I instantly recognized the bony man to be Peter Orszag, the director of the Office of Management and Budget (OMB)—in other words, the man responsible for the federal budget—including the Peace Corps. I nearly passed out realizing the leather book under his arm was the president's 2010 budget itself. He was, at that very moment, delivering it to the House leadership, the ink still setting from the president's loopy signature.

"Mr. Orszag, I'm very happy to meet you," I said, half-expecting the dogs to take me down, but they remained frozen.

"Hi there," he chirped.

"I hope it is $450 million today for the Peace Corps!"

He pulled back his lanky arm and slung it around in an arc till it clapped with mine. "We're right there with the Peace Corps, young man." *We're right there with the Peace Corps*—what did that mean? Was it 450? I suddenly felt a little concerned and wanted to grab the budget from him and change the numbers if we needed to. There was still time.

I recognized the other shorter man only when we were face to face. It was Larry Summers, Obama's national economic advisor and the former president of Harvard. He had the oddest expression, an almost bored look tinged with a focus so deep he looked half-asleep. I repeated to him what I had said to Orszag, but he just stared at me in silence in a way that made me feel very small and rather ill. As I watched these two men enter the Cannon Building I suddenly realized who Summers reminded me of: it was the arrogant scowl of King Gyanendra. I felt a sense of dread.

As representatives from the National Peace Corps Association and I approached the New Executive Office Building, I still believed it must have been a misunderstanding. Obama's budget had come in with an anemic $34 million, or a 10 percent increase for the Peace Corps that would bring its budget to $374 million. It was $76 million less than what was in the Farr bill, the sum endorsed by more than 130 members of the House and now forty senators, who had signed a letter of support from Senator Chris Dodd, a Dominican Republic RPCV. The administration's $374 million budget would barely stabilize the decline in volunteer numbers due to inflation and rising global costs. Moreover, the press release boasted that this budget would "Keep the Peace Corps on the path to 11,000 volunteers by 2016," as if a promise of 16,000 volunteers by 2011 had never been made. Did they think they could switch the "16" in 16,000 with the "11" in 2011 and no one would notice? I imagined it was just an oversight and we could amend the budget somehow. I hoped it would all be straightened out at this meeting with the head of what was known as the "150 Account," a budget account that contained fifty billion dollars' worth of US foreign affairs programs.

As we approached the building, out of the corner of my eye, I saw a young man who looked quite familiar. He was surrounded by other young people, laughing and joking. I stared at him more carefully until his name sprung to my vocal chords: "Jon Favreau!" I remembered him now from Maureen's profile in *Vanity Fair* magazine. This was the young twenty-eight-year-old presidential speechwriter who wrote all of Obama's speeches, flew around with him on Air Force One, and was dating a Maxim model. I ran up to him and said, "You wrote those words." A little startled, he looked at me, and his friends were also studying me. "You wrote those words about doubling the Peace Corps. Didn't you mean it? Was it *just words?*" I asked, my lip quivering a little from nerves and also anger.

"Sorry?" he said. I tried to hand him a copy of Congressman Farr's bill and my fact sheets, and he threw up his hands and stepped back from me. "Sorry, I'm not allowed to accept any unauthorized papers," a very serious look in his eye. "I can pass the message along," he said.

"We need you to write one more speech," I said.

As he walked with his friends, a girl mocked him, "Yeah, Jon! *You wrote those words! You wrote those words!*"

I collected myself, took a deep breath, straightened my coat, and followed the National Peace Corps Association representatives, who were looking at me like I was insane. As we entered the large, solemn room, seated across a long wooden table with an open binder in front of him was Steven Kosiak, the head of the 150 Account, flanked by Christa Capozzola, his deputy, and two other corpulent bureaucrats.

"So, tell us why you're here," Kosiak began. The NPCA representatives began talking about the mission of the NPCA. Seeing this approach wasn't working, I interrupted: "President Obama promised to double the Peace Corps, and the budget you've introduced, a minuscule 10 percent increase, barely keeps the numbers at 7,500. We obtained 132 cosponsors on Congressman Farr's Bill, which authorizes $450 million. A third of the Congress—we built the support *for* you. There are twenty countries that want to open Peace Corps programs and this year alone there were more than fifteen thousand applications," my voice almost cracking.

"We never knew about this," Kosiak said softly, studying the nine-point font list of cosponsors. "You've got a lot of good names on here. Lots of Republicans too," he said.

You never knew about this?

"Yes, and we can get a lot more," I said, "but there's no point in it really, if you introduce these low numbers." While the president's budget wasn't binding, it was an important guide for the State and Foreign Operations Subcommittee members.

At this point another man seated next to Kosiak stirred to life, adding, "Well, you know, there are serious questions about the operations of the Peace Corps," he said. "Why are there more than one hundred volunteers in small, meaningless Pacific islands and none in India, a smattering in China? Why are there volunteers in Eastern Europe at all?" he said, now growing more annoyed, more confident. "A lot of people feel the Peace Corps is a dinosaur." I couldn't believe what I was hearing. He was flipping through some document. I answered that the small Pacific islands like Vanuatu and Kiribati where places most Americans had never heard of. These would be among the first cultures to disappear from climate change and rising ocean tides.

"We need to see Peace Corps in more strategically important countries," Christa Capozzola, herself a Peace Corps alumnus, echoed patronizingly. "All these volunteers in Romania and Bulgaria," she said, pointing to my map of where volunteers were sent. "Are these really third world countries?" she asked.

"The mission of the Peace Corps is cross-cultural exchange," I said, outlining the three goals of the agency. "These countries have rich cultures, languages, societies, as well as real development needs," I reminded her. "Volunteers are working with the Roma in Bulgaria and Romania, one of the most disenfranchised populations," I countered. "It no longer makes sense to discuss the world in terms of first and third world countries."

To my mind one of the best innovations of the Peace Corps was the expansion into former Soviet and Eastern Bloc countries in the late 1980s and early '90s—countries like Albania, Bulgaria, Georgia, Moldova, Poland, Tajikistan, Uzbekistan—the very countries being assailed in this meeting. The Ukraine was now the largest and one of the most successful programs, with more than four hundred volunteers. Even if the experience wasn't the typical thatched-roof, mud-hut experience and the volunteers had ADSL Internet access, these were successful cross-cultural experiences.

"Yes, but we'd just like to see more volunteers in the countries of strategic importance to the United States," Capozzola responded.

Was this really the Obama administration? *What an inane conversation,* I thought.

"Look! You're the number two person in the Office of Management and Budget. You handle billions of dollars of US aid money and you had your start as a know-nothing Peace Corps volunteer in Mauritania," I wanted to say. But the attitude some RPCVs had was a "That was a nice, naive little experience a long time ago before I became an adult."

I folded my arms in anger and stared at my lap. They went on and on, referring to a report that pointed out problems with the Peace Corps administration. I agreed that Peace Corps had become sclerotic in *Washington*. Sargent Shriver was credited with saying, "We don't cut red tape, we shred it," but the Peace Corps in 2009 was a place with entirely too many political appointments, too many lawyers, too much of a top-down structure. This could be changed, though, with a good director.

The point was that Peace Corps was an agency about the volunteers and not the staff. But to act as if it was some bloated bureaucracy, given that it cost less than 1 percent of the State and Foreign Operations bill, twisted the truth. The Obama administration's solution should have been to work internally with the Peace Corps to fix the problems while also growing it, as was promised. As we walked down the spiral stairwell, I looked up and recognized Peter Orszag on the fourth floor staring down at us. Either he looked a little panicked or (more likely) it was just my imagination.

As I walked out of the office, I realized one thing. The first shots of the Peace Corps War had been fired.

CHAPTER 10

ᢍ

A Bold New Peace Corps

Around the time of writing this book, President Obama's support from his own base was eroding. The only issue I followed with any regularity or depth was the Peace Corps, but it illuminated to me part of the reason why the president faltered. The paradox of national politics is that the greatest change is made at the smallest, most granular levels. As former US Speaker of the House Tip O'Neill famously said, "All politics is local." This was just as true in Nepal as it was in the United States. In this respect, politics is not all that different from community organizing. A few hundred million dollars may not save a failing bank or an overextended military, but for programs like the Peace Corps, Fulbright, and Teach for America this "dust" in the budget can be transformational. Second, the president didn't ask ordinary people to actually *do* anything as a component of their citizenship as Kennedy had done.

Like so many people, I believed Obama was my generation's John F. Kennedy. I agreed with the first lady when she said his election was the first moment in her adult life when she felt proud of her country. The Peace Corps seemed so close to the core of the message that elected Obama—a message of idealism and humility, a resurgent primacy of service and volunteerism, peace and people over militaries and wars. "He's got a lot on his plate," aides would respond when asked about the Peace Corps, as if that was a reasonable excuse.

We probably generated more than twenty thousand phone calls to the White House from among the thirty-one thousand RPCVs on our e-mail list. The president never called back. The vice president never called back. All we got was a flimsy postcard from the president's mailman,

Mike Kelleher, thanking us for being good citizens. He was, of course, a former Peace Corps volunteer.

But the good news was that the appropriations subcommittees were not *bound* by the president's budget request, which was only a guideline. It would certainly be harder with the president's low numbers, but if the chairwoman of the State and Foreign Operations Subcommittee, Congresswoman Nita Lowey of the eighteenth district of New York (which covered Westchester and White Plains), wanted the full $450 million, we could still get it. The extraordinary power of the subcommittee leadership was something I didn't understand when I started working on the campaign. Once I realized this, we started focusing all our efforts on this one office.

The crisp summer morning I arrived at the fourth floor of the Rayburn Building to meet with Congresswoman Lowey's appropriations aide, I knew it was perhaps the most important meeting I'd ever have on Capitol Hill.

Sitting on the dark leather sofa with a printed copy of the Peace Corps Expansion Act, I studied everything about the office. There were many pictures of the congresswoman with past presidents. The chair of the State and Foreign Operations Subcommittee was a necessary ally for the White House to implement its foreign policy objectives. The president had his own team of congressional liaisons who worked closely with Lowey's office on issues of importance to them. Erin Patterson came out holding a coffee mug and a binder of papers. She had strawberry curls and was in her twenties. I followed her to a conference room in the back where she set down the large binder, took a deep breath, and curtly asked, "So. How can I help you today?"

"As you may know, the House Foreign Affairs Committee recently authorized the $450 million in Congressman Farr's bill, which was also endorsed by 132 House members," I said, handing her the pages and pages of signatures. She didn't look at it.

"Look, Rajeev, I'm on your list. I'm an RPCV too." I couldn't believe it. The number two for Congresswoman Lowey, also an RPCV! "Listen, Peace Corps isn't going to get this kind of massive increase," she said.

"Look at the funding over the last ten years!" she said pointing at my graph. "It's never gone up more than five or ten million dollars in a year. The Peace Corps cannot absorb such a large increase all at once.

"But there are twenty countries—" I started to say.

"Well, Peace Corps can shut down some of the others and open those."

"But the amount we're asking is so small. We have worked for a year and a half to build this support," I said holding up the signatures, and now on the edge of my chair.

"I was a volunteer in Nicaragua," she said. "It was an experience I treasure greatly, but you know the Peace Corps has real problems in the way it is run."

She was right that the bureaucracy in Washington was bloated, but things could be done about that. The volunteer experience in the field remained strong. Again I wanted to hold up the mirror. I wanted to ask her if she would be having this conversation with me, if she would be managing a $50 billion foreign aid account if she didn't have that experience. But I tried to listen.

"Even if *somehow* you got the $450 million in the House version, do you think you'll get it in the Senate bill? Senator Leahy isn't going to vote for it, you must know that, right?" There was a second step in the appropriations process. Erin was right that even if we got the $450 million in the House bill, it had to be approved by the Senate subcommittee chaired by Senator Leahy. The liberal senator who hailed from the state with the highest density of Peace Corps volunteers (Vermont) had reservations about expanding the Peace Corps, and in past years cut back higher funding levels proposed by the House. There were lots of theories as to why, but one I kept hearing was that every time he called the Peace Corps office in Washington, the secretaries asked him to *spell his name.* I cringed at the thought of the chairman of the Senate State and Foreign Operations Subcommittee, the man who could shut the Peace Corps down, being asked to spell out L-E-A-H-Y. Another time when he called over, they thought he was an applicant.

But more than Senator Leahy, the name I heard everywhere was Tim Rieser, Senator Leahy's powerful appropriations aide, Erin Patterson's counterpart. "How does Tim feel about this?" aides would ask. "Where is Tim on this?" What upset me was that the White House, the House of Representatives, and the Senate were supposed to be distinct strands in the process, but knowing that, politically, the Senate was an obstacle, their position became the ruling one. From the time I had spent on the Hill, I knew it was all a game. If you pushed for one account, another was taken away from you, and these bills were, in many ways, shaped by a last-minute flurry of hundreds if not thousands of one-line e-mails among aides in the hours and minutes before the bill was signed.

"Come on, Erin. You're an RPCV!" I finally blurted frustrated. "You know what this would do for the Peace Corps! It would change everything. President Obama promised this. For just $110 million there would be three thousand more volunteers around the world," I said. "We could open Vietnam and Indonesia. We agree on the point about streamlining administration in Washington, but even that requires resources. It can't be done while the agency struggles to stay afloat."

"I'm sorry, Rajeev, it's not gonna be $450 million no matter how many signatures you get, how many phone calls you make. Each advocacy group wants more just like you," she said. "What are you going to take it out of? Child and maternal health?" It was a familiar tactic: every time we asked for more money for the Peace Corps we were accused of killing babies in Africa. On the Senate side, Rieser compared the cost of Peace Corps volunteers to life-saving malarial vaccinations that he claimed cost "just pennies," overlooking the money spent in pharmaceutical research to make them and the very real costs of delivering them into the right hands.

"The reproductive rights people are ready to burn down the district office in White Plains. You guys just don't understand the appropriations process." This last sentence was something I was told over and over again, but the "appropriations process" was not something mandated in the Constitution, it was not natural law or anything like that. Like the caste system, it was invented to keep order, and the Brahmins at the top didn't like for it to be challenged. US foreign aid was a highly sensitive and vulnerable account. There was a paranoia that starting to move funds around could create unwanted attention and also reveal the deep problems within the bill, which spent billions on questionable objectives in Iraq, Afghanistan, and Pakistan.

I shook her hand firmly and walked down the long halls of Rayburn realizing we had to do something drastic . . . but what?

When I first came to Washington in 2009, I naively read books with titles like *How Bills Are Made into Law*. But after the meeting with OMB and the one with Erin, I threw them into the garbage and picked up Sun Tzu's *The Art of War.*

Peace Corps the agency (our campaign was independent from it) had no real presence to speak of on the Hill. From time to time I'd run into the Peace Corps' congressional liaison, who tended to huddle around offices that already supported the Peace Corps. This was squandered time better spent on winning new allies. Some days I had ten consecutive meetings only in Republican offices with staff who had never met with a Peace Corps representative before and I usually found overwhelming support.

But the military was entrenched on Capitol Hill. It had both a transient and a permanent presence. They were spread out in a large suite in the Rayburn Building. Even the senators saluted the military lobbyists who were bunkered in everywhere—corridors, stairwells, elevators. This entrenchment was part of why the Pentagon's baseline budget was $540 billion, more than a thousand times that of the Peace Corps ($330 million). It cost approximately $1 million to support a solder in Afghanistan for a year. This sum could have fielded twenty volunteers in as many countries. For the cost of four soldiers in Afghanistan, the Peace Corps could have opened up in a new country. There was no discourse about reducing military expenditure, only private lamentations of its largess. Republican senator from Ohio George Voinovich once said to me, "Believe me, if I had my way I'd say we sell a few tanks and give the money to the Peace Corps."

I was surprised to learn that several of the most storied US military officers had spent at least some of their careers serving in the "civilian" world of politics. Senator John McCain, a US Navy captain, for example, spent four years as a US Navy Senate liaison on Capitol Hill. Former national security advisor General James Jones, spent five years in the US Navy-Marine Corps Senate Liaison Office. Both Colin Powell and Wesley Clark were White House fellows in the OMB where they actually helped write the federal budget.

While building the water project, Tanka Sir and I sometimes rode the rickety "express" bus to Dhankuta to meet with the chief district officer (CDO). Seated on dusty sacks of basmati rice in the aisles, bouncing over the slatted bridge atop the Tamur River, he would place his hand on my shoulder and say, "Rajeev Sir, the key is to go directly to the *highest* person if you want to get anything done." But just as often he would say, "Rajeev Sir, it's never the highest person! You have to talk to the number *two*. The number two does all the work!" I'd spent much of my time now trying to reconcile these two contradictory statements. Was it Congresswoman Nita Lowey or her assistant, Erin Patterson? Senator Leahy or Tim Rieser? President Obama or the number two at OMB, Christa Capozzola?

Over the next few days, we sent daily newsletters to all thirty-one thousand volunteers on the list to call Congresswoman Lowey's office. I waited on the wedge of grass near the crosswalk and talked to as many congressmen and congresswomen as I could bird-dog to speak to Chairwoman Nita Lowey. Erin was not budging at all. We had to go directly to Chairwoman Lowey herself. Flipping through the directory I started calling RPCVs living in the eighteenth district of New York.

"Hi, this is Linda," a voice answered.

"Hi, Linda, I'm working on a campaign—"

"Hey, Rajeev, I'm on the list" she said. "We need Congresswoman Lowey right?" The sentence "I'm on the list" was music to my ears.

"Yes. Is there any way you could come to Washington and meet her? We only have ten days till the vote."

The next morning Linda Locke, an executive with MasterCard International who had been a volunteer in Morocco in the 1980s, boarded the train to Grand Central before getting on the Amtrak to Washington. During Locke's meeting with Erin Patterson, which lasted thirty minutes, she handed her letters from her son, her sister, her brother-in-law, and her cousin—all RPCVs. Just as she was leaving, the chairwoman happened to be exiting. Like a persistent lobbyist, Linda jogged with her as they walked to the Capitol.

"Thank you for letting me know how you feel about the Peace Corps!" the chairwoman said. "I'm very interested in seeing the Peace Corps grow and innovate too."

That same afternoon, I went to the triangular wedge of grass near New Jersey Avenue and bird-dogged anyone I could find. My message was the same: "Talk to Congresswoman Lowey!"

Later in the day members of Congress stopped *me* and said, "I talked to Nita."

Something was starting to happen.

"Rajeev, fourteen large boxes are sitting outside our office. What is this all about?" the NPCA representative asked.

"They're books," I said.

"Who is paying for this?" he asked.

"I've put it on my credit card. I'll pay the $4,000 if you won't."

"What are you doing in Washington? We need to know who you are meeting."

"I'm trying to push for $450 million. What else would I be doing?" I asked, growing irritated.

"Where do you want us to send them?"

"Would you mind delivering them to Larry's apartment?"

Laurence Leamer was the best-selling author of thirteen books, including influential biographies on the Kennedy family. He was also a Nepal RPCV who had served in a village barely a day's walk from Namje called Marekhatare from 1964 to 1966. Larry had already been helping by writing blog pieces on the Huffington Post website that were galvanizing the grassroots and drawing attention to the president's broken promise. When I told him how we were struggling to get Chairwoman Lowey's support, he paced for a while in his apartment near the Foggy Bottom metro station and then said he had an idea. In just three days, Larry edited and published his fourteenth book, an eighty-eight-page work full of the passionate letters we were getting from RPCVs all over the United States. On the black cover in white capital letters were the words "WE IMPLORE YOU CHAIRWOMAN LOWEY." As the title of the book, these words were the running headers printed across the top of each page.

Around this time my already soured relationship with the National Peace Corps Association, the national RPCV alumni umbrella association, broke down completely. I was technically a consultant to them, but we had very different working styles. The NPCA constantly wanted to have conference calls and write strategy plans, but I didn't really work well like that. Mention of the NPCA at the grassroots inspired about as much enthusiasm as the waiting room of the Department of Motor

Vehicles. "You're the most exciting guy the NPCA has sent out in years," one RPCV said to me. What made me crazy was that their main focus was to build a memorial on the National Mall, which seemed to me like building a giant gravestone for the Peace Corps.

"Why do we need 535 copies?" I asked Larry when we put in the order.

"536," he corrected me. "One for every member of Congress . . . and one for the president."

"How are we going to reach the president?" I asked.

"What are you doing Thursday night?"

I printed my invitation card and took a cab to Georgetown with Larry. The fancy fund-raiser, which was an event to promote more female Democratic candidates for Congress, to me, was just another committee hearing. I was there to bird-dog one person who I knew would be there. Larry and I made our way through the crowd, passing several US senators and governors. Then, while Larry spoke to Governor Tim Kaine, who was also present, I joined the line, waiting my turn. I inched closer, holding a copy of the Lowey book. And then in a surreal moment, I was face to face with the closest personal advisor to the president of the United States.

"I need you to promise me something," I said.

Valerie Jarrett was a little startled. Then, through her rimless glasses, she looked right in my eyes, and after a pause said, "Okay."

"No, really. I need you to really promise me you'll do something for me."

"I promise you."

I handed her the eighty-eight-page book. "I need you to give this to the president."

Taking it from me, she put it into her black handbag and said, "I'll put it in his hands tomorrow morning." I thanked her and started walking away when she stopped me and said, "I give you my word."

One of the ways the Maoists swelled their ranks from a bunch of shotgun-wielding insurgents to a movement with tens of thousands of supporters was through plays and dramas. In village after village, they put on stage plays about gambling and alcoholism, sexism and caste discrimination, which struck a chord with people. Whether it was life imitating art or art imitating life, these displays greatly expanded their influence.

The interplay between art and politics in Washington ran deep. Many other advocacy campaigns had Hollywood celebrities up on the Hill. This drew the cameras, and where there were cameras there were members of Congress saying what needed to be said. I found this ridiculous—that if you could somehow get a Hollywood actor to walk around with you, that was more important than all the intellectual, economic, and moral arguments underpinning the cause and the hundreds of members of Congress you had painstakingly recruited for it. But still, I thought about this question a lot.

The vote was just one week away on June 18, 2009, and we still had no confirmation either way what the subcommittee was going to vote for. On June 13, five days before the subcommittee vote, we decided to hold a public rally at Freedom Plaza. I went to fill out the paperwork for the permit, and on the form where it asks how many people were expected to attend, I wrote, "10–10,000." We had a stage and a microphone, but we need a celebrity who could draw all the RPCVs to the stone square.

I didn't know any famous people, but Larry did. He scrolled through his iPhone and called Sargent Shriver's eldest son, Bobby, who, of all the Shriver children had the deepest links to Hollywood and the music industry. Bobby put us in touch with the global marketing director of American Express, a powerful man named John Hayes whom I had met before, as he was a great champion of the Peace Corps. Bobby and John had organized the famous Red Campaign and the ONE Campaign and recruited dozens of A-list celebrities to these causes.

The jackhammers were pulverizing the sidewalk in front of the Independence Avenue Starbucks when I got the call from John Hayes two days before the rally.

"Hey, Rajeev, listen I've got ——'s agent on the line," he said. I couldn't hear; the jackhammers kept interrupting as he said the person's name. I kept hearing "Casey" or "Tay-C" or something like that. Though I hadn't heard of these performers, I was relieved he had at least found someone.

"Hang on," I said, jogging to a quiet residential area. "Okay, that's better."

"Can you hear me now?" he said.

"Yes."

"I HAVE JAY-Z'S AGENT ON THE LINE," he said loudly. I had to brace myself on a tree.

"Oh," I said, by which I meant, *Holy Mother of God*.

"I've briefed Steven here, but why don't you give us a rundown of why this is important, why now?"

"Well, we're a few days away from the vote, the most important vote on the Peace Corps in fifty years. We've been pushing for a $110 million increase, which would add several thousand positions and open Vietnam, Indonesia, and other countries. But, to be honest, I don't know how many people are going to come on Saturday," I confessed.

"That's okay. We just want people to be there because they care, not because they're there to see a celebrity."

John called me back immediately after the conference call to explain that Jay-Z *and Beyonce* were both huge fans of the Peace Corps, that they wanted to come and speak at the rally. Around that time I had gone over to meet with a man named Stanley Meisler, an early evaluator at the Peace Corps and the author of a book on the Peace Corps' fifty-year history, *When the World Calls*. When I asked Meisler what the difference was between the Peace Corps today and the Peace Corps of 1961, without missing a beat, he said, "Publicity." The early Peace Corps enlisted the help of some of the best Madison Avenue PR firms to make it into a household name. One appearance by Jay-Z and Beyonce in support of the Peace Corps could bring the flash of national publicity the agency so greatly needed. As a kid growing up on Long Island, my best friend, Amit Saxena, and I would drive around in his teal, beat-up Ford Taurus listening to "Big Pimpin'." Just thinking about Jay-Z standing on that stage gave me goosebumps.

Over the next two days, Larry and I ran all over DC printing flyers and T-shirts. We even had rally towels that said "BOLD NEW PEACE CORPS" on them, which we imagined people would whirl around. We went to ten embassies trying to get ambassadors to speak. Larry called all the journalists he knew to cover the event. The two of us were waiting in the lobby of the Jamaican embassy, when the six-and-a-half-foot-tall ambassador came out and said, "You Peace Corps, mon? Well come on in then!" Taking us into his office he said, "When I was a young man, driving through the streets of Kingston I heard Kennedy's speech about the Peace Corps and that changed my whole life. I'll speak at your rally."

I arrived at Freedom Plaza at 11:00 a.m. A long scroll was being signed by RPCVs—it was a letter to the president. The stage we had arranged looked sharp, with a white banner across the back that read, "MAKE THIS YOUR PEACE CORPS MR. PRESIDENT."

But one of the attendees was missing. Hearing the news that Jay-Z would not be there, I just wanted to go back to my hotel in Woodley Park. When John Hayes had called over to the NPCA and asked them about the rally, they said it was "being run by amateurs." They also underplayed the importance of the June 18 vote, and so instead of Jay-Z a Peruvian flutist was now gallivanting on the stage.

I was standing at the back, behind the crowd of 250 people. Just as I was thinking it was all a bust, the tall Jamaican ambassador climbed the stage wearing a BOLD NEW PEACE CORPS shirt. A few of the Jamaica RPCVs recognized him and cheered. Then he spoke, and I forgot about Jay-Z. I forgot about Beyonce. He put his hand to his mouth and let it rip: "*One love!* I say, *One love!* Let's hear it for Jamaica! And Bob Marley! And the love that Peace Corps represents all over this world!" The place went wild. People were actually whirling the rally towels. I walked closer to the front and stood next to Larry.

First I felt its head rise, then its arms. Now it was upright. Then there it was standing: for the first time we had woken the great sleeping giant, the volunteers were finally raising their voices. Whether it was actually a giant or a great big marshmallow man, it was hard to say, but the passion was there.

The last person to speak was also the one who led the rally to the White House. I had never seen Tim Shriver speak before a crowd. I knew he was the CEO of Special Olympics International. Most RPCVs wanted him to be the new Peace Corps director. His humble, powerful speech stirred up many emotions in the RPCVs who were present. In it, he said:

> Me and my wife, Linda, and my son, Timmy, his friends, Brandon and Clint, got here and, you know, we didn't really care how many people were here. The first person I met was Alexi. And I think I was drawn to Alexi because he's five and a half. He signed his name here on the letter.
>
> I think I was drawn to him because the first time I was at a Peace Corps event I was five and a half. And I think it was my dad and my

mother, my uncles and aunts, my brothers and my sister there. I was the little guy. My dad came home and brought me a Peace Corps suit, one of those Peace Corps sweat suits they used to have. And I can remember I was so proud, I could put on my Peace Corps suit. I think what my parents were saying to me was that it was okay to grow up idealistic. It was okay to believe in something. It's okay to grow up and believe in your country. It's not a bad thing to believe the world is a place you can belong and make a difference.

So Alexi and I were here writing on the banner and I was thinking to myself, you know, my dad is not here. He's ninety-three and very sick. President Kennedy's not here, and Senator Ted Kennedy, who spent fifty years fighting for things like today, he's not here. And all the people of that generation—most of them are not here. They were called the greatest generation. They fought in World War II to fight Nazism and totalitarianism. They built this country. When the call came for the civil rights movement, when our conscience was changed, they joined it. They made the nation something we could all believe in and they're not here. . . . We're here.

And I think . . . if they were here forty years ago, I think they would say, I hope forty years from now, there would be someone named Rajeev and he'll be just as passionate and he'll believe in this country and he'll believe so much in his ideals that he'll sleep on couches and go around the world and go on the Hill and knock on doors and not be afraid, and he'll believe so much that he'll organize the entire nation to say peace is our hope, peace is our destiny, peace is our mission, saying, "I believe in peace."

And here we are, though in our numbers small though they may be, saying we will not be defeated. There was a great generation before us and there is a great generation now. *We* will carry that message. The Peace Corps wasn't founded by a lobbying group. The Peace Corps wasn't created by people that were CEOs. The Peace Corps was created by half the number of people in this plaza with no blueprint, no plan, no agenda, no power base, no constituency, half the people on this plaza. And they built it Harris Wofford because of you. . . . Now, let's march to the White House!"*

---

*"Tim Shriver Speech–More Peace Corps Rally," June 13, 2009, available on YouTube.

"What do we want?" he chanted.

"*A bold new Peace Corps!*" we chanted back.

"When do we want it?"

"*Now!*" we shouted.

Turning the corner, our line of marchers straightened. Harris Wofford was at the front of the Peace Corps contingent, leading the volunteers carrying the banner. The Capitol police, seeing the crowd of now three hundred people marching to the White House, came over, their hands on their holsters, but as they recognized who Shriver was, realizing this was JFK's nephew, I thought for a moment they were going to ask for an autograph. We stood there shouting. I screamed and screamed as loud as I could. "Hear us, Mr. President!" We raised our fists at the White House.

The day before the vote, I rode the Amtrak up to Penn Station in New York City. Before boarding, I sent out a last newsletter to the thirty-one thousand RPCVs asking everyone to make one call to Representative Lowey and, after doing so, to send us a message saying, "I called Chairwoman Lowey." Every half second a new message popped up on my iPhone. I was somewhere between Delaware and Pennsylvania on Amtrak when the phone rang. "Call off the dogs! Call off the dogs!" Marc Hanson said. "Lowey's interns can't go to lunch!" But we didn't call them back. The interns could go to lunch after we got the $450 million.

I woke on June 18, 2009, ready for the worst. I still had a bad feeling about everything. It was so hard to know if we were going too far. My phone rang at 8:15 a.m. It was Maureen Orth.

"Hey, Rajeev, listen: I'm going on *The Chris Matthews Show* with Congresswoman Lowey tonight. What should I say?" she asked. I just stood there, ecstatic, outside the Wall Street Station in the middle of the morning rush hour.

"If it's not $450 million, if you and Chris can plead with her . . ." I said before going over the facts about how many cosponsors we had on the Farr Peace Corps bill. In *The Art of War,* Sun Tzu writes, "Build your opponent a golden bridge to retreat across." As I hung up the phone, I couldn't help thinking about this passage.

Just before six o'clock, I walked over to my brother Rishi's apartment on West Tenth Street, where just a few years before I had stored the Namje hats, to watch *The Chris Matthews Show* with my mother and sister-in-law. Matthews came on and told of how he had himself served in Swaziland from 1968 to 1970. Then he welcomed Maureen, and suddenly there was Congresswoman Lowey standing in front of an American flag. My heart raced and I was too anxious to sit down on the sofa. I had expected a debate, but no sooner had the chairwoman appeared on camera than she announced, smiling brightly, "Well, Chris, now that I know you and Maureen were in the Peace Corps, I am going to do it, and you're the first one to know that I'm going to include $450 million for the Peace Corps this year so we can expand into twenty new countries and put it on an important glide path toward doubling!"

"Thank you, thank you, thank you!" Maureen said. There was a text message on my phone. It was from Maureen: *How 'bout them apples?*

Will Rogers was right, I thought, all politics *is* applesauce. One of the things that made me happy was that we didn't know what did it—whether it was Linda Locke jogging beside the chairwoman pleading, Maureen's brilliant move to have her on *The Chris Matthews Show* just before the vote, the thousands of phone calls, or Larry's book. I was ecstatic, but I knew we had one more challenge to face before getting the $110 million increase: Senator Leahy.

CHAPTER 11

ℒℬ

The Ice Cream Social

By the numbers, we had generated even more support for the $450 million in the Senate than in the House. No fewer than *forty-five* senators, including powerful Republicans like Senators Kit Bond of Missouri and Bob Corker of Tennessee, had signed on to the $110 million increase. But as we were about to discover, the Senate was a far more conservative institution than the House. The longer term limits, lack of racial and gender diversity, and greater collegiality rendered it an old boys' club. In fact, we would find our toughest opponent not to be a Tea Party Republican but rather one of the most liberal senators in American politics—Patrick Leahy of Vermont. Although only in his early seventies, Senator Leahy was already second in seniority in the Senate, the chair of the powerful Judiciary Committee and, most important for us, chair of the key subcommittee that determined the Peace Corps budget.

Getting a direct meeting with Senator Leahy was proving impossible. I had lurked in the elevator wells of the Russell Building and walked in and out of the restroom on the fourth floor of the Russell Building near the senator's office, but I never ran into him. When I asked an aide to Senator Ted Kennedy how to win Senator Leahy's support, her sage counsel was "Dress up in a Batman costume and stand outside his office." Senator Leahy was known for his affinity for Batman, which approached obsession. On one occasion he was seen wheeling around the Senate Russell Building on a toy batmobile he had purchased for his grandson. Realizing the senator's importance and becoming somewhat desperate, I decided to meet him in the only way I could think of. Larry Leamer and I checked the box marked "Scooper-Duper Supporter" and bought fifty-dollar tickets to attend the senator's annual Ben & Jerry's Ice Cream Social, a fund-raiser for his reelection campaign and a low-key love fest for both the senator and Vermont's famous ice cream.

Larry wasted little time and was soon face to face with the senator. "But Senator, I cannot understand your objection to this!" Larry said. "It's just a $110 million increase. There are thousands of young people who want to be Peace Corps volunteers, but there is no money. I am here as a surrogate for them. President Obama promised this during the 2008 election. Please, just take a look at the historic level of support we have built. We spend more than this sum in five hours in Iraq." With two hands Larry was tightly gripping the long legal-sized pages of an op-ed piece he had coauthored with the travel writer Paul Theroux, a Malawi RPCV. He had tracked down Theroux under the canopy of a remote rainforest in South America, where he was leading his latest adventure. The two writers had written a piece about how the $450 million budget would transform the agency.

The senator's face was growing crimson. "Chris Dodd and I can *shut the Peace Corps down!*" he thundered back, startling several of the four hundred guests present. Leahy was a genial and humorous presence in the halls of Congress; very few people had seen him mad. I couldn't help but vaguely recall a disturbing scene from *Batman: The Dark Knight* in which the Joker, played by Heath Ledger, threatens one of the dinner guests (played by Senator Patrick Leahy) before a startled crowd. But Larry was not afraid. "But Senator, more than a third of the Senate and the House of Representatives is behind us. This is a democracy, Senator!"

"I rely on my own judgment," Senator Leahy responded in a gruff voice that reminded me of Bruce Wayne's adopted affect. I nervously looked on from about ten feet away, cradling my Chunky Monkey ice cream cup.

Suddenly, a very tall man, the only person taller than Senator Leahy at the fund-raiser, stepped over with a nervous smile. In his velvety tuxedo, he looked more like a nightclub bouncer than the chief of staff to the chairman of the Senate Judiciary Committee. Putting his hand on Larry's shoulder, the chief of staff slipped him a tiny business card, saying, "My name is Ed Pagano. Why don't you come in and talk to me tomorrow morning?" With that, the band started playing again and the three-minute encounter was over.

"That wasn't good at all!" a seasoned K Street lobbyist said to me as he ladled Rocky Road past his lips using a small wooden paddle. But I wasn't sure *what* to make of what I had just witnessed; probably he was right. But I knew the senator was against any significant increases well before what would become known in Peace Corps circles as the infamous "Ice Cream Social." But we had been left with little choice. At least Larry had succeeded in getting the senator's attention when no one else could. In his eyes, there was simply no line item in the foreign operations bill more important than the Peace Corps. If he erred, it was in being *too* passionate—a misfire that no Peace Corps volunteer could fault him for. Were it not for Leamer's media savvy, the Peace Corps may not have been positioned to gain *any* new funds. Blog pieces that he had written for the *Huffington Post* and a conservative publication called *Newsmax* had galvanized a dormant base and elevated the profile of a tiny campaign to the national stage. Just days before this encounter with Senator Leahy, he had used his press contacts to pretty much single-handedly obtain official support for the $110 million increase from California congressman Howard Berman, the powerful chairman of the House Foreign Affairs Committee. But one of Senator Leahy's major concerns was the lack of a new Peace Corps director. After six months of sitting on their hands, the Obama administration had recently named a solid new Peace Corps director, Aaron Williams, himself a volunteer in the Dominican Republic from 1966 to 1969. He had a distinguished twenty-five-year career with USAID, which included a stint as the head of the South Africa programs where he managed a billion-dollar mission. As for the need for reforms, Senator Chris Dodd had just released the bill, which would require the Peace Corps director to complete a comprehensive global survey of the agency and implement reforms on the basis of the findings.

In a way, Larry and the senator were both right. The Senate was, in theory at least, democratic. Subcommittees took votes. Full committees decided on their recommendations and offered amendments. The revised bill was then voted on by the full Senate. But anyone who has seen the empty aisles of the Senate floor on C-SPAN can guess that this is not at all how things work. The decision on how much money to give to the Peace Corps was Senator Leahy's to make. In a way, having one person make the decision made public advocacy *easier,* since we knew whom we had to convince. The problem for us was that senators who had signed up in support of $450 million would not dare pick a fight with the man who would likely soon be the most senior senator in the entire Senate and the all-powerful chairman of the Appropriations Committee. As long as his colleagues on the subcommittee were appeased with funding for their own favorite projects, they would go along with whatever he decided.

From my vantage point, I felt that Senator Leahy had been irked by years of frustration trying to deal with the Peace Corps bureaucracy during the George W. Bush presidency when the Peace Corps became known as a dumping ground for political appointees. He had concerns about Peace Corps priorities, but no high Peace Corps official ever came to Capitol Hill to talk with him, even though he controlled the purse. In a way, our campaign was pouring salt in his wounds, since he could hardly stroll down a Vermont street without a former volunteer asking him about Peace Corps funding.

We had thrown everything but the kitchen sink at Senator Leahy to show the extensive support for the Peace Corps among his constituents. Vermont is the state that has not only the largest number of serving volunteers per capita but also the largest number of alumni. I called and briefed more than five hundred Vermont Peace Corps veterans and many of them called the senator's office. Many of them were actually shocked that the senator was not one of the leaders in the push for an expanded Peace Corps.

A week before the Ice Cream Social, I reached Ben Cohen, the co-founder of Ben & Jerry's ice cream company who called the senator and pleaded with him. Even the CEO of Ben & Jerry's (who had the delightful name Mr. Freese) had written, offering to name an ice cream flavor *Smore* Peace Corps. With help from his grandson Jason Carter, who was a South Africa RPCV, we tracked down President Jimmy Carter, who was traveling in Lebanon at the time, and Jason urged him to call Leahy. "Pat, please do this for my mother," President Carter implored Senator Leahy, his long-time friend, referring to the beloved Miss Lillian who at age sixty-eight had joined the Peace Corps and had gone to an Indian village to serve as a nurse. "I'll do the best I can" was the senator's vague response.

"Don't you worry; I'll take care of that Leahy!" one RPCV said to me on the phone in a slightly manic voice one evening. "They tried once to stick the fucking capitol police on me again, but that won't contain my activities and—" I quickly pushed the red "END CALL" bar on the screen of my iPhone before he could finish. I was discovering the dangers of too much democracy. One could never know whether the person on the other line wasn't seriously disturbed—but how to balance that with the need to rally grassroots support? This difficult calibration was what made organizing a study in judgment.

After the Ice Cream Social, we clearly needed a different approach. The debate was not about the Peace Corps at all but a larger disagreement about the meaning of democracy. The debate we were having was the same one playing out in the new postmonarchy Nepal, where leaders were trying to build a representative democracy, deciding the proper balance between direct popular referendums and the necessary level of power for state officials to conduct business. Senator Leahy was always one of the senators I truly admired. He fought for basic things like personal privacy, and he was one of the few senators to speak up on issues of impunity by the Royal Nepal Army. But he was not yet coming around on the Peace Corps issue.

Our approach needed to be more oblique, like a wide-arc boomerang flying across the country, sometimes around the world, before it gently tapped Senator Leahy. Former presidents Carter, Bush Sr., Clinton, and Bush Jr. were all supporters of robust Peace Corps growth at one time or another in their administrations. Our hope was that the former presidents would sign a letter to President Obama requesting that he help pass the $450 million budget through the Senate. Through a Nepal RPCV and US ambassador to India, Peter Burleigh, we only got as far as President Carter, who felt it was unwise "to tell a president what he already knows."

The only thing Senator Leahy loved more than Batman was the Grateful Dead. So I tried every angle to reach the guitarist Bob Weir. I called the agency that represented him; I called a nonprofit group called the Rex Foundation, where he was a spokesman, as well as the executive office of the Gibson Guitar Corporation, but I never heard back. The one musician we did reach was Peter Yarrow of Peter, Paul and Mary, who had sung "Puff, the Magic Dragon" at many fund-raisers for Senator Leahy over the years. I was blind copied on an e-mail that began, "This is Puff's 'real' daddy."

One of these long-arc boomerangs got me in hot water. A lobbyist whose wife worked for Senator Lugar advised me to speak to an RPCV aide to Senator Menendez who formerly worked for Senate Majority Leader Harry Reid. I wanted him to ask Senator Reid to step in. It was an incredibly windy October day in 2009 when I got the call from the aide, Mark Johnson, just near Union Station.

"Hi, Rajeev?"

"Hi, Mark, thanks for calling me. I was hoping—"

"Listen. I don't know who the hell you think you are, but I work with advocacy groups that have been around for a hundred years and you RPCVs don't know what you're doing," he said. "You guys are total amateurs. You have no idea how things work here and you look like an idiot."

"Uh . . . okay, thank you," I said, as a gust of wind nearly knocked me into the street. I was standing under the famous Christopher Columbus Memorial Fountain outside Union Station. I braced myself on the leg of a bowing Native American woman crouched before the towering white Columbus, who was standing on the prow of a ship.

I found it strange that RPCVs around Washington seemed to view their Peace Corps experience and all RPCVs as somehow amateurish. Their idealism had hardened so much.

The other part of the strategy was simply shoring up Congresswoman Lowey's support. Theoretically, there would be a "conference" to iron out differences, now that the House and Senate bills were at different levels. One of the ways in which the process frustrated me was that there never was an open conference in which people like Congresswoman Betty McCollum and other supporters would get to participate and negotiate—it was just the chairs and ranking members and their staff, a great deal of backroom decision making, which seemed so contrary to the openness of the Hill.

I found out that the actor Richard Gere, who had deep ties to Nepal and Tibet, had held a fund-raiser for Chairwoman Lowey. Suddenly, I was on conference calls with lamas at the Tibet House in New York trying to reach him. I had conversations with Uma Thurman's father, Robert Thurman, a Tibet scholar at Columbia University, asking him to call Richard Gere who would then call Representative Lowey who would then "stand firm" in the negotiations. These kinds of calls required lots of instructions and explaining, but people cared; the Peace Corps name still kindled an idealism in people that made them really want to help.

When senators, presidents, and CEOs of major companies could not move Senator Leahy, we began lobbying the Dalai Lama, who I was surprised to learn had his own press secretary, chief of staff, and congressional liaisons. It made sense that he had this political structure, but the idea of the Dalai Lama receiving BlackBerry messages from his personal secretary, Mr. Chhime Rigzing Chhoekyapa, always kind of shocked me.

The reply from the spokesman for His Holiness the Dalai Lama to my request for him to call Senator Leahy was at least a gentle no:

> Of course the Peace Corps has done wonderful service in many countries around the world. During His Holiness' travels, especially in Japan, he also suggested to the Japanese youth to visit and work short periods in other countries like the Peace Corps. That way they will not only be able to help poor and needy people, but will also benefit themselves immensely through the rich experience of helping others, especially poor or developing countries.

Finally in the early fall of 2009, I was thrown out of the campaign by the NPCA. The last straw was that they wanted to do all newsletter design in house, which basically would have left me out of the process. "Thank you Rajeev!" read a small blurb in the NPCA newsletter below a progress report on the Peace Corps Memorial on the Mall. It included a picture of me with Nepalese children, my arms raised.

Annoyed, I sent out a message titled "A Message from Rajeev" in which I said I was not quitting but rather we were forming a new campaign completely independent of the National Peace Corps Association.

After five months of trying to win Senator Leahy's support, the moment had come. The evening of Tuesday, December 8, 2009, hundreds of Peace Corps luminaries gathered at a black-tie event at the prestigious Meridian International Center in Washington, DC, where the new director of the Peace Corps was to be introduced to members of Congress. There were rumors that the 2010 Peace Corps budget had been decided and this was going to be announced.

When I saw Congressman Farr walking toward me in the reception room, something about the look he wore told me it was bad news. He put his arm around me and leaned in close and said:

"It's four hundred. You did everything you could. I saw Senator Leahy. He said Ben Cohen had him on the phone from Australia for an hour! He said to him, 'Pat, I've supported you for years and I'm not letting you off the phone till you say to me it's four hundred fifty,' but even this couldn't do it. But listen, because of what we did, a thousand volunteers are going to get on a plane that wouldn't have otherwise." But I was no longer hearing the words, everything went silent. I felt like disappearing from the place, and I think Congressman Farr knew it. He looked sad too. I walked over to the bar, depressed, and tried to get drunk.

In a daze, I rode the Amtrak home. The next morning I woke up at my parents' house on Long Island and felt like I'd been hit by a truck. I wondered if it had all been a dream. I started writing e-mails about amendments.

Just before Christmas I halfheartedly sent out a newsletter with two clinking champagne glasses and the headline, "A toast to $60 million!" It was the largest one-year dollar increase since 1961, but all I could see was the half-filled champagne glass, the one thousand volunteers that would never find their river town, their Kalambayi, their Namje.

I moved to Toronto that year with my wife, Priyanka, but I stayed with the new campaign, which we called "Push for Peace Corps." "That sounds like an exercise!" one RPCV joked. Push for Peace Corps struggled financially, but the independence from NPCA was a real breath of fresh air. Donald Ross, who had created and overseen the More Peace Corps campaign, was able to get another grant to keep the new campaign, Push for Peace Corps, operating.

Though I don't think I lost my passion, I did become more robotic and mechanical. I decided I would just work harder, be more stoic, cover more offices in DC. Senators saw me laboring around. I would be carrying my papers and get caught in the rain. I think they all felt sorry for us. This pity was a very good thing, and I started to learn how sometimes the most important thing you can do in a campaign is simply continue on.

I liked the idea that the command center of the Peace Corps campaign had now seceded to Canada. It was like my own private protest. After a week or two in DC I would usually need a few weeks or even months away from it. Being able to get on a plane and leave not only the Hill but the United States was rejuvenating. Campaigns can become really unhealthy. You get obsessed with numbers and blame yourself when you don't reach targets. It took me a long time to realize that the $60 million increase was truly historic, the largest one-year gain since 1961, the year the agency was founded. It was when I read that Indonesia had opened and then Sierra Leone, Colombia, and Haiti that I started to understand we had achieved something. Articles began appearing in *USA Today* and the *LA Times* hailing a resurgence of the Peace Corps. The volunteer numbers started rising from 7,200 to 7,500 to 7,800 all the way to 8,700, which was apparently the highest number since 1968. It wasn't sixteen thousand, but it was a start.

In March of 2010, I returned to Washington to advocate another increase in Peace Corps funding for 2011. This time we were trying to raise the budget by $46 million, from $400 million to $446 million. I was amazed at how some senators who were on the State and Foreign Operations Subcommittee didn't know much about the details of the budget their subcommittee was charged with approving.

"$446 billion?" one three-term senator asked.

"No, *million*," I said.

"Okay, I'll take a look at that."

Every Thursday morning a breakfast was held for Illinois constituents on the top floor of the Hart Building at which both Senators Dick Durbin and Roland Burris fielded questions from their constituents. When I learned about the breakfast meeting, I decided to attend.

"And where in Illinois are you from?" Senator Durbin, a member of SFOPS, asked.

"Long Island," I said.

"Long Island, Illinois!" he said laughing sardonically and looking at the crowd.

"Senator, President Obama promised to double the Peace Corps. Will you support $446 million in the 2011 bill?"

"Look, in this time of tough decisions, we can't go above the president."

"This *is* the president's request," I said.

"Why don't we talk about this after."

Afterwards I went up to him, and he was upset with me. "You know, this is no forum to talk about this."

As we continued pushing for the $46 million increase in funding that year, we again garnered more than 130 signatures on the Peace Corps funding letter. But problems were emerging.

"Rajeev, *stop* this advocacy," Erin Patterson said to me over the phone. "You're just pissing off Leahy, pissing everyone off. You've done *enough*."

"But without the advocacy, we wouldn't have even gotten $400 million, Erin," I responded. My feet hurt from the hard marble floors.

"Let us handle this and just stop doing everything."

Tactically, what the House funding commitee had started to do was make our hard-nosed advocacy the scapegoat for the lack of funding. In the end, Senator Leahy and Tim won. As of March 2012, the budget of the Peace Corps is not even $400 million. It is $374 million—the exact amount Senator Leahy wanted back in 2009.

Whether the Ice Cream Social, issues with where the volunteers were being sent, or the Tea Party and the need to rein in spending, always an excuse emerged. They had made their painful point; they had relied on their *own* judgment.

I often think about what would have happened if Jay-Z had come to Freedom Plaza. And like a tide, periodically my thoughts flow back to the president. It was painful to finally realize that he and his administration really couldn't care less about the Peace Corps. The president didn't lift a finger.

In the village, Tanka Sir used to always say, "Politics is the *dur-tee* game." To me it was always a tactical, wily game to be played, not to be taken too seriously. But in Washington I felt the severity of Tanka Sir's statement.

The Peace Corps, on both the left and the right, remains misunderstood. While Senator Leahy and OMB wanted to see far *more* volunteers in China, a Republican congressman from Colorado, Mike Coffman, had initiated a campaign to suspend the China Peace Corps program. In September of 2011, he circulated a letter to President Obama in the Congress that stated, "Having the Peace Corps in China, where we have to borrow money from the Chinese to fund it, is an insult to every American taxpayer and to so many of our manufacturing workers who have lost their jobs to China." Coffman's letter characterized the Peace Corps as a giveaway aid program, overlooking that it is the American volunteers who usually benefit the most by learning the language and gaining international field experience. No one was losing their job in a Ford manufacturing plant because of a few hundred Peace Corps volunteers in China.

Discussions have surfaced about whether it is time to privatize the Peace Corps in light of this annual appropriations saga, which, in the current climate of scaling down government, is bound to get worse. When I was in Nepal, I felt that being a part of the government made me far more professional and serious about my role. It also made the host country nationals take me more seriously. Peace Corps brought to you by Walmart or American Express would compromise the independence and cheapen the stature of the program, even if it meant we wouldn't be beholden to subcommittee chairs. The talk of corporatizing the Peace Corps really made me nervous.

In the absence of necessary support from the state and foreign operations subcommittee, Peace Corps has already started to partner with the President's Emergency Plan for AIDS Relief and other global health and clean water initiatives to finance the fielding of more volunteers, but the Senate subcommittee is using this cofinancing to justify a lower Congressional appropriation level. There have been discussions of turning the Peace Corps into a public corporation governed by a board of directors a la the American Red Cross, for example, but this would mean that federal funding from Congress could diminish substantially, as Bill Josephson, who was the coauthor of the paper that defined the Peace Corps in 1961, has pointed out. Experts were proposing a new public corporation for global service that would fund the Peace Corps, AmeriCorps, Teach for America, Volunteers for Prosperity, and other service programs. But in 2011 there was a near-successful attempt by Congress to completely defund *all* service programs, and my own feeling was that Peace Corps should stay out of this service category altogether. As hard as it was to acquire the funding, the State and Foreign Operations bill was still a much safer home.

In August of 2011, I woke up one morning and put on my suit. That day was the culmination of another year's work. The Senate was about to announce its budget, and I'd been bird-dogging senators. In the last two and a half days, I had spoken to twenty-six of them about the Peace Corps. As the coffee was percolating and I was putting on my tie, nervously, frantically thinking of whom to call, the phone rang with a blocked number. Usually this meant someone important in Washington was calling.

"*Rajeev Sir ho? Ma Chandra boleko! Sir, ma Malaysia puge! Ma yaha factory ma job paye sir!*" ("Rajeev Sir? It's me Chandra! I made it to Malaysia! I'm in the chicken factory!")

It was hardly seven in the morning, but I had always told myself that the day Chandra ji, my landlord in Namje, finally made it to the wing-clipping sweatshop in Malaysia, I'd have a drink. I opened the minibar and poured a Styrofoam cup of wine. Suddenly, I didn't care about the vote or any of it. I close my eyes and pictured Chandra ji.

After three years in Washington, it was time to go home.

PART III

CHAPTER 12

∽

A Road to Namje

Bouncing over the slatted bridge north of the Char Koshe Jhadi jungle, I peered at the rising massif for the first time in a year. I had certainly changed a lot but the mountain, except for a few more blinking pink lights in the fog, was as I remembered it. The villagers would remind me it was my twenty-first journey to Namje in ten years.

The Maruti minivan pierced the clouds. Cold white wisps were coming through the broken air vents. I had taken the twenty-minute ride from Bhedetar to Namje more than a hundred times but it never ceased to thrill me. A *kolej* (wild turkey) fluttered as we passed, kicking up dirt and dry leaves. The oblong boulders draped in ropey vines symbolized the journey into nature. Curving along the arc, the Maruti lurched leftward as the road continued over a dramatic drop.

Namje was just four kilometers from Bhedetar, but it felt more like four hundred. A curve or subtle twist in the Himalayan landscape could tuck a village into isolation. The broad base of Thumki Hill was a curtain of rock, leaving the hotels and watering holes of Bhedetar completely out of sight. Of the many gifts nature had bestowed to Namje and Thumki, it was this wide turn in the landscape for which I felt most grateful. Too steep to build anything, the western edge of Thumki was a pristine jungle. The exposed rocks on the promontory were plated with the bright purple leaves of a rare medicinal plant called *pakhambed,* a salve protecting the villages from the ghastly "development" just minutes away.

But something felt different. The Maruti wasn't rocking left and right as it usually did. I suddenly realized what it was: the road to Namje had been *paved.*

Without actually seeing the changes, it is difficult to comprehend just how much a few inches of asphalt blacktop can transfigure the environment, economy, and social structure of a village. Between 2000 and 2010 rural roads in Nepal had expanded by more than 50 percent, adding thousands of kilometers of new transportation infrastructure. Some of the most remote places on Earth where villagers had never even seen an automobile were now linked to major transportation systems. It wasn't just the topography that was flattening. Each farmer now had a cell phone in his or her hand. This transportation and communications infrastructure, combined with more than a billion US dollars per anum pouring into the rural corners of Nepal (from migrant workers abroad), was transforming the built fabric and land ownership patterns.

The driver pulled the handbrake exactly at the interface where the new asphalt road ended and the uneven rocks began. I put my croc onto the blacktop for the first time and watched as the slow-turning wheel of the biggest tractor I'd ever seen in the hills leveled a frightened green sapling. Tiny men in tangerine vests marked "*Sadak Vibhaag*" (Road Department) were hurriedly laying smoking globs of asphalt, which were being flattened into a hard surface. "*Pani aayo!*" another cried as he dumped a *gagri* of water into a volcano of sand and aggregate. The mixture consumed the water until it was a distant memory. Up ahead, men with iron *jhampals* were prodding at the rocky cliff to widen the road, which caused the terraces above to crack and soil and roots to bleed downwards over the rocks.

This road was begetting even more roads, as villagers were picking away at new streets leading up and down the hill. It wasn't only the road that was being paved but much of the soil adjacent to it as well. Even the villagers were caked in a thin layer of cement powder from their own construction projects. I suspect if they could have, the villagers would have covered the entire mountain in *Satna* cement. The new four-story buildings, replicas of the ones in Bhedetar and Dharan (or any other industrialized South Asian city), were essentially identical to each other. The entrance of each house was composed of two iron shutters. The windows had bars. If it weren't for the bright pastel exteriors (they were painted purple, pink, orange, and other colors), they would look like jails.

Standing in his new castle, framed by a ridiculous-looking Shakespearean balcony, I spotted Hangsa Magar, who had worked as a plumber on the water project. He was wearing a bushy sheepskin sweater that looked like he had gutted the animal and stepped inside its woolen exterior. I gasped, observing his wife, Kumari, who was balancing her toes along the back lip of the house as she held an iron *aari* (plate) full of cement globs and a sharp spade. It was a fifty-foot drop. Hangsa dai's case was fairly typical. To finance construction of this building, he had sold more than twenty *ropanis* (about one hundred thousand square feet) of his family's agriculture land. He was now landless and over budget, plunging deeper and deeper into debt. He was actually in negotiations to buy back a small piece because he had nothing left to farm, nowhere to house the pigs. The ill-suited design of these buildings was bad enough, but what they represented was more problematic: the transformation of an active, diverse, and ecological village economy into a passive state of renting out rooms and iron shutters.

Just as I was wondering what in the world had happened to this once beautiful radish-farming village of saffron-striped mud abodes, I spotted the new headmaster of Namje school, my old friend Tanka Bhujel, raised fifteen feet in the air and framed by his own balcony. He waved and disappeared into an internal staircase, reappearing with a fistful of limp marigolds:

"Welcome to Namje Bazaar!" he beamed.

"Do you like it, sir?" Vishnu Acharya, a local dairy farmer, asked. As villagers handed me fistfuls of cut flowers, I wished I could go back and plant them in the forest.

"It's nice," I said halfheartedly.

A cheerful voice called from inside the shuttered storefront: "Namaste, sir! You probably didn't even recognize the village, right?" I almost didn't see Goma didi's round, smiling face camouflaged between the rows of stuffed animals and pink balloons. Their shop had been transformed. There were streams of tiny shampoo packets and fashionable sequin tikas, crates of a new brew called "White Mischief." I could tell that a whole lot of white mischief was going on in the village.

It wasn't the use of modern construction materials that troubled me—far from it. On some level I felt happy for people like Hangsa dai and Kumari didi who probably never imagined they would one day live in a big cement house. These structures were symbols of progress and permanence. What irked me, though, was the complete lack of imagination and creativity in the design of these homes. They were large and clumsy, paid no heed to the existing trees, water, and sunlight. They were out of proportion, and where there should have been tall windows facing the Himalayas, there were cramped, windowless toilets. The older homes had melded lyrically with the surroundings. They curved around tree trunks, were positioned in relation to the sun. The issue with cement was that once it was set, it would have to be air blasted to be removed.

Mostly, I couldn't believe the pace of this new development. The growth had begun back in 2003, but in the last year Namje had undergone a black, billowing industrial revolution. I don't know what was more surprising: that this was all happening or that the people were so readily embracing it. I had always thought the water project would green the village. I had dreams of lush jungles and myriad organic farms and fishponds in the misty fog. But here it was, hard and grey.

One attribute of village life I truly loved was living in Chandra ji's house: the grainy texture of the walls, the fragrance of eucalyptus and smoked meats, the way the floors sloped to meet the ground outside. Having lived in an American suburb most of my life, I had never experienced a home made of the same materials and elements found immediately outside it. It was literally living within earth. I studied the bumps and recesses in the mud walls, which bore impressions of the stacked stones beneath. There were no borders between people's homes; nothing was a right angle, not even the frame of the house.

I had also imagined the water project would bolster education, particularly for girls who bore the brunt of the water crisis, but in some ways it created more gender gaps. Before, women and girls were out in the fields, but now they were locked in these cement homes. Tanka Sir and Goma didi's thirteen-year-old daughter was hunched over a tower of dirty dishes. A small, square washing area had been etched into the ground with a perimeter of plastered bricks. I watched as the spigot shot out pulses of water like bullets, which careened off the hard surface. Chicken bones and greenish vegetable shreds lay next to the washing area.

"Now, the village is developed," Tanka Sir said. "Water, electricity, roads, cement school buildings. If anyone is poor in Namje, it is truly their own fault. Next time you visit, the road will be crammed with buildings. See all that land over there? It has been bought up for construction," he said, pointing to a five-hundred-meter forested bend in the road, beyond the last house along the road.

"But isn't that a community forest?" I asked.

"No, it's all private land. Before the road came, no one cared about it. Now it is divided up into thirty *gharedis* owned by people from Bhedetar." A *gharedi* was a colloquial land unit referring to a parcel just big enough to build a small *ghar* (house).

"How much for one *ropani*?" I asked. A *ropani* was about five thousand square feet, a fifty-by-one-hundred-foot parcel of land.

"*Ropani*?" he laughed. "Forget *ropanis*. Now, people speak only in *aanas* and *paisas*." These were measurements I had never heard before. An *aana* was one-sixteenth of a *ropani*, about the size of two parking spaces. Each *aana* was further divided into four *paisas*. A *paisa* was about the size of a coffin. "One *ropani* costs two million rupees [$30,000]."

To give a sense of how much the simple act of paving over a gravel road was causing land prices to explode, when I was a Peace Corps volunteer back in 2003, a *ropani* was just fifty dollars. *Ropanis* were given away for free. In just eight years, it was six hundred times as much—$30,000—for the same piece of land. The father of one of my students once offered to give me four *ropanis* to settle down and build a house. Had I accepted the gift, I would have been rich not only by Nepalese standards but also by US and European standards, with $120,000 (and growing) in land capital.

The insidious result of this explosion in pricing was, of course, that the village was being displaced. This sum of, twenty *lakhs* or $30,000 per *ropani* was unimaginable wealth for the average villager.

Karna ji, the builder of the water project, was less enthusiastic about the new changes. "The plotters have bought more than one hundred *ropanis* in Thumki," he said. "What to do? I told my brothers and sisters not to sell it or else to sell it to someone within the village, but the plotters pay more. No one even knows who owns the land now because the plotters converted it into two hundred *gharedis* and sold them all to people in Dharan and Kathmandu. They cut it down even more and sell it to others."

"*Sabai khaisakyo*" ("It has all been eaten up"), an older man from Thumki, Dhan Bahadur Magar, said, flicking his hand cynically in the direction of Thumki Hill. The verb being used to describe the acquisition of land by the plotters, *khaisakyo,* means "has been devoured" or "eaten."

In Namje, the steel tips of six towers transmitted cell phone, TV, and radio signals all over the eastern region of Nepal. But Thumki, which was on a slightly lower hill abutting Namje's western edge, had no towers and only a smattering of homes that, because of their thatched roofs and sandy mud exteriors, were hardly visible. Rather than steel towers, a copse of majestic fifty-foot alder trees stood sentry over Thumki, with fountain-like bamboos cascading all the way down to the road, the arching tips of the last bamboos just a hair's breadth from the asphalt. Its walls along the road were steep. Unlike Namje, there was no construction along the inner face of the hill, which buttressed long stretches of mustard and millet. Deer and even wild monkeys could be seen traveling through its raspberry-filled edges at dawn. Gunjaman dai, the mayor of Namje, whose family leased a small tract of land on Thumki Hill, told a story of how he once encountered on the hill a small bear, with long bangs that covered its eyes. A bird always found in pairs, called the dukur because of the sound it made, lived in the tufted centers of the bamboos, as did grasshoppers, crickets, and all kinds of other insects. As more than two hundred of the village ancestors were buried within the alder forest, it was also a sacred hill.

Men known as "land plotters" embodied Oscar Wilde's famous expression of "knowing the price of everything, the value of nothing." Though there were only eight main plotters, they oversaw a complex network of underlings and runners. The head plotter was a fifty-year-old named Vishnu Katuwal, a Nepali Congress party leader. At one point he was a lowly school teacher, born in a remote VDC situated on the Nepalese border with Tibet. From a few land sales, he earned a huge amount of money that he then invested into more land sales and also into his political career.

Like a gang, the plotters usually arrived in Namje and Thumki in a formation of motorbikes and parked outside one of the mud homes. They showered money and opportunity to those villagers who tipped them off about who was selling land, who was under financial stress, where the good plots were. Information, timing, and liquid capital were everything in this process.

In the evenings the motorcycles would shuttle back to Bhedetar, where the plotters would drink with the bureaucrats who worked in the VDC office, where all the land maps were kept and each transaction had to be registered. If the plotters learned someone was about to make a sale, they called them and offered a better price. They sweetened the deal with a chicken and a bottle of rum or else a cut from an unrelated deal in another village. The banks would then loan the money and take a cut of the profits. Mostly, these were illegal speculative investments. As far as I could tell, there was absolutely nothing redeeming about this practice.

In a VDC three hours east of Namje, called Rajarani, the plotters purchased all the land surrounding two huge, pristine lakes, "Raja" and "Rani," which were the namesake of the village. They had even purchased land on hilltops surrounding the lakes because of their views of the water. Soon a ring of forest around the water would be a ring of noisy cement hotels. Anywhere there were scenic views of water or the Himalayas, the land was vulnerable to plotting. Anywhere there was a road about to be paved, the plotters were there before the tractors.

A friend from Dharan who owned a rice mill, Ram Barakoti, emerged with a bowed head from inside Tanka Sir's house. "Namaste, sir," he said. He was trailed by three others from Dharan whom I didn't recognize. One of them had a red ring around his mouth from the beetle nut he was chewing.

"I'm a Namje man now too!" Ram dai exclaimed excitedly.

"Me too," one of the others said, waving a one-hundred-rupee note and motioning to Srijana to give him a packet of beetle nut.

"What do you mean?" I asked.

"That's our new land over there!" he said, pointing to a field just under the road line of Thumki Hill. "Actually, only one-third belongs to me. I purchased it together with two friends from Dharan."

I instantly recognized the plot. It used to belong to Tanka Sir. My landlords Chandra ji and his wife, Nanda Maya didi, whose home I had lived in for two years, farmed this land. Nanda Maya didi was standing at the edge of the road, a *doko* against her hip and her head down, listening to the conversation.

"I had to sell it," Tanka Sir said, now looking a bit regretful. "We acquired a huge amount of debt building this new house. My father raised us with that land."

"What will you do with the plot?" I asked Ram dai.

"I won't do anything to my portion. I may grow tea, but the others will probably build a resort for the tourists," These words—*resort* and *tourist*—were English borrow-words used with quite a bit of poetic license. They weren't talking about Aman resorts, ecolodges, or anything fancy but more of the same cement buildings chock full of cheap whisky. The "tourists" came in two categories. They were either bands of men from Dharan, Biratnagar, and India seeking drugs and prostitutes or rich families who would trash the place for a few hours every Saturday and leave complaining about how dirty the locals were. This was the only brand of tourism I had seen in Bhedetar for years, and the paved road was pushing it closer and closer to Thumki. I looked on as Nanda didi's cow put its front hooves against a trunk and tore dark *Gagun* leaves with its mouth from a tree that now belonged to a businessman in Dharan.

Part of what troubled me, though, about the land plotters was that I shared the same subcaste as several of them. Like them, I belonged to the Indian subcaste Marwari, a mercantile caste originating in Rajasthan that was part of the third caste category, Vaishya. Several of the land grabbers in eastern Nepal were wealthy Marwaris. Years ago, an old man from Mejuwa village known as Kepchaki Budho had sold the entire mountain above Saacho Khola to a Marwari named Brijulal Agrawal. As Brijulal had made his vast fortune as a garbage collector, he went by the nickname "Kabadi," which means "garbage" or "useless." Thus in this way, his most enduring legacy is that an entire mountain in Namje was now called "Useless Mountain."

A paradox of the developing world is that the most resource-rich landscapes, from diamond mines in Zambia to the rainforests of the Amazon, contain some of the highest levels of human poverty. Until I witnessed the land displacement occurring in Namje, I did not understand why this was so. Namje was a case study of how infrastructure development could *create* poverty. The new paved road brought one lane coming in and many more leading out, carting away its beautiful land, water, plants, rocks, timber, and even people. It wasn't the road or greater mobility in the abstract that was a problem. Globalization, trade, and migrations have always existed in Nepal. Even Magars of Namje and Thumki were believed to have migrated from western Nepal in the late eighteenth century.

Rather, the problem was the land *splicing*, which bore no relation to the natural contours of the land or to any conception of public good. Cutting up the landscape and selling the small plots to people who had no intention of sustainable farming or doing anything else beneficial on the land was an insidious trend motivated by the greed of a few powerful men, under the guise of "development." All this predatory land plotting involved not just a breaking of the public trust but also a repudiation of laws and regulations. Today, this practice is happening not only in one VDC but in most of the 3,913 VDCs of Nepal as road access grows.

On the face, it would seem that the exploding land prices in Namje and Thumki was a great thing, like discovering a gushing oil well. But the practical effect of the overnight six-hundred-fold increase in land value was that many villagers sold their land and became landless. It wasn't a *forced* relocation, but it was basically a coerced sale. Some of these men were national-level leaders of industry and politics; others were professional middlemen who were relentless in trying to convince a villager to sell his or her land. For an ordinary farmer, saying no was dangerous, because most of the land plotters were, not surprising, also loan sharks who held their debt.

At the same time, certain villagers were giving these plotters a foothold. They were trapped in a narrow view of rural development that was essentially just urbanization. If you asked anyone in Namje the question, "What is development?" the answer was always the three Bs: *Batti. Baato. Bhawan.* (Electricity. Roads. Buildings.)

While the conversion of a village into an ugly cement town was seen as evolutionary or inevitable, a specific catalyst flushed the corners, added stories, and consumed more agricultural land: the exploding land price. As prices shot up and land was consequently sold off, there was less of it to go around. The only direction left to build was skyward. Taller buildings required *wider* foundations, and so the cornerstones were set back farther, displacing more forest, fields, and people. The space between buildings tightened, they grew flush against each other, because even the smallest sliver was suddenly too expensive to leave green. What was more valuable, a tree or a *lakh?* And suddenly one day, a beautiful farming village like Namje was the younger twin of Bhedetar. Land was no longer valuable for the food, water, and biofuel it provided but for cold, hard cash. Land was now elastic, its uniqueness obfuscated by fungible measurements: *ropani, aana,* and *paisa.*

While the ten-year Maoist conflict is credited with weakening the economy and infrastructure of Nepal, in a strange way it functioned as a savings program for millions of farmers. Almost every household in Namje and Thumki had at least one adult member overseas, sending money home throughout the war. But the insurgency was, in addition to being a physical power struggle, an ideological and political war against privatized land. Maoists kept intricate networks of information. They knew when land was being bought or sold and levied a People's Tax accordingly, or worse, persecuted someone for being against the spirit of the revolution. Thus, out of fear, families saved up the remittances sent home by a son or daughter over the ten-year period. When the conflict finally subsided, it was like a bursting dam. Naturally, everyone wanted to use their savings to build a more permanent cement house. Land prices were no longer measured in cornstalks and radish loads, not even Nepali rupees, but ringgits, riyals, dirhams, dinars, wons, and shekels. In this way, a major legacy of a leftist insurgency was a crazed, Wild West capitalism.

As the government levied taxes on these remittances, it was the pennies skimmed from Nepali laborers in the Middle East that were paying for each drip of tar on the Namje road. It was easy to rail against the new growth and long for the old, idyllic way of life, but the villagers greatly desired modernity. They wanted to be a part of the modern globalized economy. What we needed to help them find was what they referred to as *bikalpa,* which means "alternative." What was the alternative to Bhedetar? Many villagers expressed that they wanted develop a unique village different from Bhedetar, but they needed a model.

It was becoming clear that the villagers didn't need more infrastructure. Rather, they needed ideas, policies, knowledge, education, skills, design support: an *invisible* infrastructure to better guide the development that was already going to happen, regardless of any foreign aid money.

Land plotting paid no regard to natural habitats, communal gathering places, and sacred spaces within the community. However, these elements—nature, community, and sacred space—were *themselves* the raw elements for combating land plotting. For example, knowing that a particular forest or river system was a unique habitat could trigger certain legal or regulatory protections emanating from national or international environmental covenants that protected such ecosystems. Various kinds of collectivization and land-sharing practices, in other words, a deepening of communal structures, diminished the elasticity of land and made it much harder to subdivide. For example, if twenty farmers in Thumki got together and created a cooperative and established certain rules and restrictions limiting how the land could be used, it was more complicated to sell. Perhaps the only parts of the village that went untouched by the plotters were ancestral grave sites and other sacred spaces. Another strategy for fighting the unsustainable land-use patterns was to somehow enhance this sacred character of land and water.

In 2011, when they realized the long-term consequences of land plotting, the villagers in Thumki and Rajarani villages uncovered three other creative strategies for dealing with it. The first strategy was conceived by a young lawyer and environmentalist in Thumki named Dil Krishna Rai. "Without water, the soil is sand," he reasoned. To attenuate plotting, he led the villagers to try to deny water connections to the subdivided plots. The attempt created just enough press that the investors backed out and the plotters lost large sums of money. Dil Krishna also pointed out that Nepal was party to a vast array of international environmental protocols that had extremely localized impacts, so long as the villagers knew about them. One of these provisions was in the International Labour Organization's (ILO) Convention No. 169. Article 7 of the convention stated that indigenous and tribal people have the right to "decide their own priorities for the process of development as it affects their lives, beliefs, institutions and spiritual well-being and the lands they occupy or otherwise use, and to exercise control over their economic, social and cultural development." ILO 169 was generally interpreted to mean that indigenous people possessed the *first* right over land, water, and natural resources. When we mentioned ILO 169 to the plotters, however, they laughed at us and said, "This is Nepal, not America."

To halt destruction of the land surrounding the lakes in Rajarani, community members, led by another talented local lawyer named Dharma Rai, were reaching out to government ministers about something called *Adhikaran,* which was essentially a form of public domain.

By exerting *Adhikaran* over the land surrounding lakes Raja and Rani, it would become government property, subject to stringent environmental covenants and restrictions. Part of the reason the land plotters were so deeply involved in national-level politics was so that they could exert influence to block such decisions.

Insofar as roads were crucial for land plotting, obstructing them was the third strategy which the villagers developed. Seventeen families in Thumki owned land adjacent to the road. These families ultimately denied what was called a *mukh,* or "mouth," to allow a new road to be paved from the existing gravel road up the hill to where Katuwal's plot was located. Had this new road been built, it would have trampled many more *ropanis* and caused the prices to rise so much that the seventeen families would probably have sold their land. In the end, the plotters opened a *mukh* from their own plot along the gravel road and built a dangerous, almost vertical road. On the day they began construction, a shaman performed an elaborate *puja*. Three *khasis* (he-goats) were decapitated. Viewing the ugly incision in the mountainside, the collapsed rocks and trees, and the dangerous vertical new road, I felt really upset about all the greed. But Dil Krishna could see only the glass half full:

"We lost half the mountain," he remarked. "But we saved half the mountain too."

There was of course another, more straightforward way to fight the plotters: buy the land ourselves.

"Hello? Punya bhai?" I asked.

"Yes."

"How much to keep you from selling the tomato field to someone else?" I asked.

"My father says five lakh twenty-five thousand. But he says it's a bargain. He says he could sell it for twice as much, but because it's for the school, he'll do it for five lakh fifty thousand." One lakh is equal to one hundred thousand rupees, or roughly $1,300.

"We can do five lakh," I said.

"Come on Rajeev Sir, you're from *America* and you're going to nickel and dime us for 50,000 rupees?" he responded.

"Five lakh," I repeated.

"Five lakh twenty-five and you've got a deal. We're only doing this because it's for the school."

"Okay," I said flatly.

"Okay."

My second Samsung flip-phone phone rang. "Hello?"

"I found the owner—he lives in Lazimpat in Kathmandu, next to the milk dairy." It was Uttar Man dai's familiar baritone voice. He was calling from Jimi Gaun down the mountain. "He says the land is not exactly as described on the deed. The district map only shows a small tract, but it's much larger and connected to a community forest."

"How many *ropanis*?" I inquired.

"On paper it's only twelve, but in actuality more than twenty."

"Why is it less on paper?"

"He did that so he wouldn't have to pay as much tax," Uttar Man dai explained.

"Okay. Well, how much?"

"One lakh twenty thousand."

"Deal."

If you didn't know any better, observing the four of us in the cement SWSC office, you would believe we were land plotters. All that was missing was cigar smoke and the stench of cheap whisky. We didn't have a blank check from the banks in Dharan, but we did have donors back in the United States who were firmly behind our effort. One of these individuals was an attorney from Chicago named Marvin Brustin, who is also the honorary consul general to Nepal. Brustin made the largest donation, helping to save many acres of land from plotting.

Lama Sir developed an ingenious new strategy that somewhat deterred the plotters. Under Nepalese law, government schools could *acquire* land, but they were prohibited from *selling* it, and in this small fact we discovered a kind of land trust mechanism to conserve hundreds of *ropanis*.

The results of this effort were most astonishing in the village of Mukten, where six years earlier we had built a school building. More than ninety *ropanis* or about five hectares of forested land was saved. A road was expected to come to Mukten in 2013, but the land plotters weren't as focused there yet.

"Is this it too?" I asked, standing in one of the most beautiful fields I'd ever seen. It seemed to go on forever. The variety of plants and trees was absolutely breathtaking to me. Rajak Sir and Nirola Sir, the two teachers from Mukten school who were working day and night to acquire the land, were sitting on a boulder next to a tuft of lemongrass.

"Yes," they said in unison, unable to control the smirks on their faces.

It was a delicate process that involved navigating all kinds of family relationships. Though the land deed was in a single person's name, often he or she was in Kathmandu or in Kuala Lumpur or Dubai. The sale of land could lead to family battles and disagreements. Making the negotiation too public could catalyze an avalanche of land sales, defeating the whole purpose of what we were trying to do. We also had to be sure that we weren't inadvertently displacing the village ourselves. The VDC was feeding information to the plotters, so once we began a negotiation, we had to have the liquidity to finish it. Standing on this peaceful mountainside, I couldn't imagine how anyone could put a price on this. A man was about to sell an entire lake in Mukten to a plotter, but we stalled him. Even though we offered less than what the plotters were offering, he gave it to us because it was for the school.

But this process naturally had limits. How much more land could we buy? Maybe we could buy one hundred *ropanis* or even one thousand, and of course that was a very positive thing, but was there a way to make more villagers understand the value of their land? What was so interesting was that we and the land plotters were using the same term to describe our opposite activities: *development*. Was there a definition of development that could include ecological stewardship and better design? Also, the teachers kept asking us what they should *do* on the newly acquired land. The villagers needed to travel and see examples of development that went beyond the simple density of cement buildings. Each time we suggested they build their home differently, the answer was the same, "*Bikalpa dinus na ta!*" ("So give us an alternative!") And so eight village leaders boarded a rickety bus to meet me in Kathmandu to try to find the *bikalpa*.

☙

CHAPTER 13

Sacred Hill

Careful not to touch the railing, Laxmi Magar, the president of the Namje women's cooperative, inspected the source of the stench, shielding her nose and mouth with a silk shawl. Gunjaman dai was also observing it with one hand covering his nostrils. Walking away, Laxmi didi shook her head and grunted: "*Chya!*" *Chya* was a slang expression denoting not only physical but also moral abhorrence. In this case both meanings were fitting.

I had never experienced Kathmandu in this way: through the eyes (and noses) of the villagers of Namje. Just walking down the street had been awful. There were so many swerving cars and motorbikes in every direction, regardless of traffic rules, that I kept expecting someone to get hit. A common practice was for drivers to replace the horns with blaring ones that made you squint your eyes in pain and stop in your tracks. It was hard to fathom that just a few decades ago the first cars had been carried on bamboos over the mountains.

It was a small, unnamed spring under a ten-meter bridge that I probably would have walked right by—a slick of water over a heinous pile of festering garbage, which included condoms, instant noodle packets, a hairy and bloody carcass of an unrecognizable animal, a rack of ribs perhaps belonging to a dog, and colorful plastic substances. Just a few hundred meters away, the stream (or whatever it was) joined with the Bagmati River, which itself looked like an open sewer. Gunjaman dai and I made eye contact as he walked away from the railing. He could not speak. With his cuff, he wiped the tears from his eyes.

HUTA RAM BAIDYA—the name was etched into a shard of metal next to a tin sign that read, "Nepalese Society of Agriculture Engineers." A boy unlatched the large door and led us past a clothesline and what appeared to be a junkyard. Entering a cool, quiet sitting room was a relief. Huta Ram Baidya was Nepal's first agricultural engineer, but he looked more like a wizard or genius inventor. The fifteen-power magnification of his glasses made it seem like his eyes were holograms separated from his head. When he entered and sat down on a raised cushion, the curious manner in which he folded his legs reminded me of Gandhi, to whom he bore an uncanny resemblance. The old man rubbed his hands together, and just when I expected Huta Ram to bestow upon us the answers we were searching for he said, "Why are you here? Who are you all? Do I know you?"

Laxmi didi whispered something in Magar to Gunjaman dai from under her shawl, trying not to laugh.

"We're coming from Bhedetar VDC," Lama Sir explained, speaking very loudly. Lama Sir was sitting cross-legged, his hands in his lap, like a schoolchild. "We're visiting organizations, NGOs, and organic farms to find examples of 'alternative development.' I am sorry to admit, I don't know who you are but you could say that is why I am here."

"Tell me something," Huta Ram said, adjusting his hearing aid. "Are there any *sheep* in Bhedetar?"

The villagers laughed. The Nepali word *bheda* means sheep and *tar* refers to a flat parcel of land. Historically, Bhedetar was a bazaar where sheep traders from the high Himalayas came to sell livestock in exchange for salt carried up from the lowlands.

"No," Laxmi didi said, giggling. "No *bhedas* in Bhedetar. We have *baakhras* [goats]."

"Well that's a shame . . .," Huta Ram said. "So why isn't it called *Bakhrataar?*"

Gunjaman dai's shoulders shook up and down as he laughed.

"The next time you visit me, I want to hear that there is a *bheda* in Bhedetar. . . . So, I suppose you want to hear about the Bagmati River," Huta Ram said, turning toward the window. "That's why everybody comes to talk to me, you know."

Huta Ram Baidya had devoted his life to trying to save what was considered the most sacred river of Nepal. The place where it met the steps of Pashupatinath Temple was a site of religious ritual. Pure water bubbled from the Shivapuri hills north of the valley, but by the time it reached the city center, thousands of sewer pipes were connected to it. The Bagmati was dying from this filth and pollution. Its present state was perhaps the most poignant symbol of the ecological costs of growth in what was being called *Naya Nepal* (the New Nepal). Across Nepal, this octogenarian represented the slim hope that it was not yet too late to save the Bagmati.

"You will be surprised to know that I've never once touched the river," said Huta Ram. "It has been twenty-five years since I began my struggle to save the Bagmati, but I have not felt its water. When I was a young man, many years ago, I studied agricultural engineering in India. They taught us about the miracle of chemical fertilizers, the marvels of the modern agricultural revolution. I thought I would bring these ideas to Nepal, but as I watched the river die, as the whole city became cement, I realized the problem lay in the word *technology* itself. What is technology?" he asked. We watched him enraptured, not shifting at all.

He motioned for his fifty-year-old assistant, a professor of engineering at the local college, to retrieve a chalkboard. Huta Ram drew a triangle and wrote something next to the three corners. Laxmi didi leaned in closer, trying to make out the words. When we had invited her on the trip, she demurred claiming she had never gone to school and was illiterate. But on a few occasions we saw her writing things down, sounding words out. She was in her early forties, had never married. She was strong and confident about everything, except when it came to reading and writing.

Pointing to the base of the triangle, Huta Ram said, "Land was once valuable not for its *mulya* [price] but for its five elements: *jal* [water], *prithvi* [soil or earth], *vayu* [air], *agni* [fire], and *akash* [space or void]. But at some moment," Huta Ram said, pulling down on the corner of the chalkboard with his shaking index and middle fingers, trying to flip over the triangle, "We lost our minds! Land became a currency, a piece of stock. The triangle cannot balance on its tip."

Hari bhai looked very serious. He raised his hand and asked, "What can we do to save the Bagmati River?" Heads turned to Huta Ram for the answer.

"Oh, no one can save it!" he said. "It's too late."

We were silent, hoping he would go on. His hologram eyes looked again toward the window.

"It's over, unless . . ." he said, looking at Hari, "we stop thinking *big*. Unless we stop thinking that throwing bills of money into a river can save it. See all that *kachara* [waste] in the river? It is not garbage—it is floating *rupees*."

Then the old man motioned for his assistant to fetch something. He returned with a large rectangular piece of metal with magnetic numbers and letters stuck to it. Holding this metal board Huta Ram Baidya, the first agricultural engineer of his country, grinned and seemed more energetic suddenly. "Now you won't believe me, but this is the technology that will save the world."

We all leaned in, wondering what in the world he was talking about. I thought it was some kind of super electromagnetic sensor.

"This is a computer and PowerPoint projector," Huta Ram said, plucking the letter A and slapping it back on the metal board loudly. "See?" He plucked another letter and playfully slapped it back on the board.

For a moment I thought it was a joke, but I was the only one laughing.

A green, white, and red arrow marked the entrance to the farm. A few feet beyond the courtyard a Samsonite suitcase sat literally full of soil with cornstalks growing out of it. Next to it, a worn leather boot with scallions growing from it. I expected an elf or hobbit to be living in this place, but Govinda Sharma looked more like a barrister in a court of law than a permaculture farmer. His black coat and glasses belied a cheerful and enthusiastic personality.

Lama Sir was already drawing pictures of the plants. Placards pinned to the stalks and stumps of things identified their Latin and Nepali names. He started teaching Gunjaman dai, pointing out everything he saw to the board chairman of Namje school. "Look at this! We are fools. We throw our shoes away but here they use them as a vase. We use a suitcase to carry things, but it could also be a giant pot!" Hari was with the other two students we had invited on the trip, which was being supported by the Phulmaya Foundation. He was carefully observing what appeared to be a vertical garden made of bamboo sections. Laxmi didi could not sit still. Like a curious school-child, she was down on her knees smelling a plant, which she soon identified as lemongrass. She was now out in the field, pointing out everything from pomegranates to rice to tea. "This needs more water," she would say, and, "It's time for pruning!" Observing her, I realized the complete emptiness of the term *illiterate*.

"If you look around, you'll see that there are no flat spaces," Govinda ji explained. "This is because the curves help channel water through swales. Nature, gravity, sunlight, rain—it can do all the work for you," he said, pulling on the lip of the tin roof, which caused beads of water to fall into the bamboo vertical garden, which overfilled until they tipped and poured neatly onto the base of a potted plant directly below. "This is probably the only fish pond you'll ever see," he said, standing over a rather natural-looking pond with uneven edges, "where you never have to feed the fish." He turned on a lightbulb hanging above the water, which caused bugs to crash into the surface and become fish flakes. He explained how the uneven edges of the pond helped create what are known as microclimates, which enhance diversity of flora and fauna.

The permaculture farms I had visited in Northern California in preparation for the Nepal field trip were truly mind blowing. A small American *gharedi* in a suburban neighborhood near Laytonville, California, had more than two hundred crop species. Everything was intricately organized into what were known as guilds, with one plant species serving as a natural insecticide to another. A core principle of permaculture was "stacking functions," or having one plant or one structure play many different functions, and in this way it was good for creating diversity and self-sufficiency on small plots of land.

Permaculture—a term most people, including many experienced farmers, have never heard of—is the verbal marriage of the words *permanent* and *agriculture*. The term was coined by two Australian environmentalists, Bill Mollison and David Holmgren in the 1970s and refers to an approach to designing human settlements and agricultural systems modeled on relationships found in nature. In their book *Permaculture One*, Mollison described permaculture as a food production system "of working with, rather than against nature; of protracted and thoughtful observation rather than protracted and thoughtless labor; and of looking at plants and animals in all their functions, rather than treating any area as a single project system." I was not very familiar with permaculture, but given the dwindling size of land plots in Namje and the increasing use of chemical fertilizers, it seemed like something to explore.

As we traversed the farm, Govinda ji pointed out that fewer than sixteen *ropanis* of land had more than one hundred crop species. There were no fields of corn—just a few stalks. It was all intended for Robinson Crusoe–like, individualized consumption and ideally meant to be a closed loop, reliant only on sun, rain, air, and human activity. The three permaculture farmers we visited in different regions of Nepal told a similar story of being heckled by their neighbors for initiating farms in the middle of a forest, but this idea of ecological farming that mirrors and sometimes originates in the wild is central to this style of agriculture. One farm we visited in Chitwan belonged to a man named Chandra Adhikari, who had integrated his farm so fully into nature that wild birds and reptiles from the nearby Chitwan National Park were nesting there.

The charm of permaculture lies in its comprehensibility—its scale—which made intuitive, visceral sense to us. It seemed to "flip the triangle," as Huta Ram had put it. I believed that if there was a way to make everyone in Namje and Thumki practice permaculture, it could create a deeper relationship between people and land. The focus on microclimates and the concern for every inch of land and water, each edge, and every microhabitat seemed like the elusive antidote to the bulldozer approach of the plotters.

When we returned to Namje and Thumki, we were all set to launch a village-wide permaculture movement. But the effort never got out of the gates. "How do we *earn* from this? Where do we get the capital to start a plot like this? What do we do to feed our families during the seven years it takes for the permaculture system to mature?" These were just some of the basic questions the villagers wanted to know the answers to. They saw this style of subsistence agriculture as a step backwards: "That's how our grandparents used to farm!"

Discussions about sustainability drew blank stares from villagers for whom economic concerns were paramount. Rather than wholesale adoption of permaculture, Gunjaman dai and Lama Sir suggested a more reasonable approach, which was to cherry-pick and use discrete aspects and approaches from permaculture that were beneficial and useful, not adopting it wholesale. This was another lesson of the trip—there was no magic-bullet solution, and it was acceptable to grab bits and pieces that worked.

Where permaculture had more traction was in the context of schools. Between 2005 and 2011, we had constructed five new primary school buildings with the objective of eventually creating a network of "farms schools" that would practice and teach sustainable agriculture and alternative energy. This idea never actually came to fruition. The organic plots we visited throughout Nepal represented the outdoor classrooms we were envisioning for the farm schools. Everywhere, there was life and activity to be observed and there was a natural link to community education. The beehives, fishponds, compost systems, biogas, grey water—these were all teaching tools. When we looked, we found places in the Nepali curricula where these ideas could be taught through practical demonstration.

With hopes of creating our own permaculture plot, we supported Namje high school to purchase a beautiful 19-*ropani* (1-hectare) plot of land on the crest of Thumki Hill. From this peaceful plot, there is a panoramic view of the snow-crested Himalayas to the north and the steamy Char Koshe Jhadi jungle to the south. It was one of the only points in the village where you could see all the way to the border with China *and* India. Our plan was to use this plot to demonstrate organic farming and alternative energy for the community. "You got the best land! We were going to build a resort up there," one of the plotters said to me. Govinda Sharma and another expert named Prasad Chetry guided Hari Magar. Within a year, more than fifty crop species had been planted by Hari. Rainwater collection and composting systems were also set up. By 2012, organic lemongrass tea, cornmeal, and mushrooms were being sold from the plot. But permaculture had not yet caught on among many farmers in the community because of the lack of immediate financial return and the five to seven years it took to establish.

One sustainable agriculture project that did catch on among local farmers was the cultivation of medicinal and aromatic plants (the MAPs Project). In January 2011, we came in contact with Karma Bhutia, a former World Wildlife Fund Young Conservationist Award recipient and an expert with the Mountain Institute, a Kathmandu-based INGO. When we described to Karma ji the land plotting issues in Bhedetar VDC and the need to develop an alternative livelihood, he decided to support our effort, and together we launched a new VDC-wide effort to cultivate *jadibuti* (medicinal plants). Karma ji's story was truly inspiring. In 2000, he started a small project to create a new, ecologically based livelihood that would financially support a group of Buddhist monks in Mabu VDC in Ilam district (also in eastern Nepal). What began as an experiment in growing a lucrative medicinal plant known as *chiraito* (an anti-inflammatory medicine) expanded, over the next seven years, to similar efforts in more than forty VDCs. The project spread to so many communities that it now goes by the name "Ten Thousand Farmers Project." Our concept was to seed a similar movement in Dhankuta district.

We discovered that *chiraito* grows in the wild all along the ridge system that comprised Namje, Thumki, Ochre, Dada Bazaar, Rajarani, and the entire succession of hills down the road. Other MAPs, such as lemongrass and aloe vera, were found at lower altitudes within Bhedetar and in surrounding VDCs. At slightly higher altitudes north of Dhankuta district center, rare cancer medications were growing in the wild.

The MAPs Project was one we never had to push with the villagers because it was so tightly integrated into a market. The collection center was in Dharan. Access to the global market was ninety minutes from the village. Another reason the MAPs cultivation project was popular among villagers was that the plants could be grown *between* other crops. They often grew on the walls of the terraces, where nothing was usually planted. They didn't require irrigation or much change in the existing landscape. When only a few farmers showed up to the first trainings, I was nervous, but Karma ji saw it as a good sign. "This is what we want!" he said. "Once the villagers see the plants grow, there will be a lineup outside. We won't need to push anyone," he said.

There were of course complex challenges in MAPs cultivation. The seeds tended to be expensive. For example, in January of 2012 it cost about $70 per kilogram of *chiraito* seeds. Farmers needed training in how to plant and protect the young saplings, especially in the earliest stages. For example with *chiraito,* it took three years for the first shoots to grow, but after that growth was continuous. As the project grew, more trained staff would be needed to manage this growth. This also entailed new costs. When we had met Huta Ram Baidya, he said to us that the longer he worked in agriculture, the more he moved in the direction of *management,* and looking at how the MAPs Project worked, I was beginning to understand why.

Like everything else, medicinal plants cultivation wasn't self-executing. It was not as if you could distribute seeds and walk away. Karma ji and his team were almost always in the field working with individual farmers and cooperatives. Trainings related to monitoring had to be continually administered. The changing demands and desires of the farmers also had to be researched. Disputes over pricing would erupt, and these conflicts had to be carefully resolved. The markets and price points for the plants were constantly shifting and the farmers needed to be educated about how to monitor the financial landscape. There was always politics to iron out as the forest department often obstructed cultivation.

The appeal of the MAPs cultivation was that, potentially at least, the medicinal plants could make it more lucrative to keep land than sell it to the plotters, especially if seeds, trainings, and market support could be provided. The scientific *depth* of this field also related to its capacity for combating land plotting. In a bookstore in Kathmandu, I purchased an encyclopedia of medicinal plants native to the Himalayas. The book was a thousand pages of fine print and plant diagrams, about forty pounds in weight. This was a field about which one could spend a lifetime learning only a small sliver. I believed that if the villagers could get interested in the intellectual and scientific challenge of growing MAPs, they would see the limitless possibilities for what they could do with their land and be less likely to sell it.

Karma ji educated us about the many small-scale cottage industries associated with processing the raw plants into liquids, soaps, candles, fabrics, and organic dyes. The women's cooperative we had established in 2004 for hat sales had been a debacle but these cottage industries were the ideal activity for the women's cooperative, WADE. The skill and creativity associated with MAPs (and also permaculture) enhanced the dignity of farming as an avocation—perhaps the most long-lasting weapon against land plotting.

I found it hard not to be nostalgic about the old architecture. The mud homes were inseparable from the soul and spirit of the people, and it was painful to see them disappearing. But if you tried to tell a villager to stay in that house and not build a new cement one (as I naively tried), you would accomplish little. Villagers wanted modernity. They wanted to be on the world map. The issue wasn't really the building *materials:* the steel, glass, cement, and tin. With better design and sense of proportionality, those materials could be manipulated beautifully with the environments. The trend in construction was to level the ground flat, cut down all the trees, and put up a cement block. The Nepali verb used for this process, *sammaunu,* means razing what was already there into a flat plane. One of the simple things that could be done was training the builders in keeping the curvature of the land and working with the existing trees and plants.

One particular experience taught me how complex sustainable design really is. In the school we built in Falametar village, about an hour below Namje by bus, I insisted on a tile roof and bamboo verandas, thinking this would somehow be more "green." As the tiles weren't native to Dhankuta, they had to be transported from two hours away in the Terai. No one in Falametar had ever worked with tile, and so three masons had to be transported over as well. When we finally installed the tiles, they cracked and fell into the classrooms. The school, which was otherwise quite beautiful, with huge windows looking out onto the Seuti River, was now leaking. In the end, we had to attach a galvanized iron roof and *cover* it with tiles. Though it was known all over the district as *tile bhaeko school* (the school with the tile roof), the blue tin that showed where the tiles didn't quite meet was a constant reminder of just how complicated sustainability really is. In fact, the most sustainable thing was probably to build nothing at all or use discarded tins and pieces of rubber for construction material, as the locals had done. These homes were nothing more than thin walls made of flattened tins nailed together and sitting on a foundation of reclaimed wood and truck tires.

While there are no large temples in Namje, the houses themselves are sacred spaces. The second story of most homes in Namje and Thumki contain an object called the *pithri,* which is a small urn that is hung from the roof and symbolizes the ancestors and gods worshiped by the family members of the house. The *pithri* was the energy and spirit being lost in the conversion from mud homes to cement buildings. The challenge was to help the villagers develop a modern but spiritually rooted design language. This question led us to a design–build program based in Washington, DC, called Spirit of Place–Spirit of Design. Many colleges and universities in the United States offer design–build educational programs that allow architecture students to implement what they learn in the classroom by physically constructing a building.

Spirit of Place was created by Travis Price, an architect based in Washington, DC. Through this program, each year architecture students at Catholic University of America (CUA) travel to a different sacred site around the world to understand the local cultures, narratives, and myths. After spending a semester modeling and designing, they build, over a nine-day period, what is called a "legacy marker," an architectural metaphor representing these myths and stories in a modern structure. Through this program, seventeen such structures had been constructed from Machu Picchu to Helsinki Finland to the hills of Ireland. In 2011 Spirit of Place accepted our application to build their eighteenth structure in Thumki, but we needed to find the right site on which to build it.

Our permaculture plot, it turned out, was one of the most sacred sites in the village. The Magar tradition was to bury their dead on the highest mountaintop in the village and commemorate the locations with coffin-like, three-foot by six-foot structures called *chihans* and made of stacked dry rocks. Several of the 229 Magar graves on Thumki Hill were at the edges of our plot. Some were painted white while others were left unpainted. Watching thick fog curling between the sepulchers in the plot was surreal.

From the village *dhamis* (shamans) we learned that Magars were neither Hindu nor Buddhist, and that their faith was closer to animism. The head shaman was the eighty-two-year-old father of Karna Magar, the builder of the water project. One night every year Karna's father (who was also named Karna) spent the night up on the hill fighting off evil spirits to protect the village. He was apparently the only one brave enough to do so. When the plotters planned to construct a road right through Karna's own field in Thumki, he dared them to try. I couldn't help but think the image of the village elders fighting the evil spirits atop Thumki Hill was a metaphor for what was happening with the land plotters. We had found our sacred site.

On June 9, 2011, thirty architecture students from the United States arrived on Thumki Hill to build the structure they had designed, which was a Magar ancestral memorial. They built the beautiful structure over nine days, working alongside Karna and other local masons with technical assistance form a civil engineer from Kathmandu named Uday Sunder Shrestha. The structure sat on a twenty-by-twenty meter square plinth made of dry stones, many of which were the grave stones scattered throughout the plot over the years. Along the outer edge of the plinth, were eight seven-foot walls made of stone, with nooks on the insides of these walls to place butter lamps. Once inside, there was another set of walls with quarter-meter-wide gaps. From the outside, you could not tell what was inside, but it drew you in and you wanted to see what was there. In the center, surrounded by jagged rocks placed perpendicularly so that no one could step on them, was a piece of toughened glass about an inch thick, three feet by six feet, covering a hole in the ground, which was about a meter deep and painted all black. Looking at this glass, you saw your own face against the reflection of the sky. All around the memorial was permaculture—fields of mustard, ginger, garlic, marigolds, asparagus, avocados, pear, rhododendrons, orchids. To the north were the white Himalayas and behind, to the southwest, was the faint sound of blaring Bollywood music from picnics in Bhedetar.

On the last day of construction, the land plotters made the fifteen-minute trek to the top of Thumki Hill to see the memorial. "What is the purpose of this? Shouldn't you build a roof over it?" one of them asked.

"It's not a house," I tried to explain.

"It's just a statue," another plotter explained. "They should have built a model house. That would actually have a use."

But the villagers, who labored for more than half a year to carry all of the stones for it, understood what the structure signified. When someone asked what the glass in the center represented, I overheard Hari bhai say, "That's the soul of our village."

Why the Peace
Corps Still Matters

What did I learn in my years in Nepal, my travels across America, and my days roaming the halls of Congress? I am not an academic expert in third world development, but here are some of the things I learned.

Development should enhance, not destroy, the often hidden human and cultural capital that exists in every village. Underlying each community is a substratum of invisible infrastructure. Namje had rings of political structure that comprised *tol* (neighborhood), ward, VDC, district- and national-level political power. Its economic infrastructure included microcredit savings groups and village banks, the workings of which I only discovered years into my Peace Corps experience. A complex community-managed forest system was behind the survival of the large forests that spanned the VDC. The longer I spent in the village, the more I understood how the position of each terrace, each house, and each tree was for a reason.

The water project illustrated the depths of this human and cultural capital. I did not build the project nor was it constructed by an outside engineer. Rather a village plumber with a ninth-grade education designed it. The labor of more than five hundred people built it, and eight years later, the pump continues to operate, probably because of this bottom-up approach. In the end, when no one, including the district engineer, could turn the motor on, it was a peon who recognized the voltage needed to be increased. These experiences taught me a central lesson that I have tried not to forget: each villager, regardless of education or social standing, is an integral pillar for the success of a project.

For development projects to be sustainable, the local people who are the most affected need to be involved in the planning, construction, and future maintenance of the project. The Namje water project has survived because it is financially integrated into the existing public and private institutions: the school, agricultural cooperative, VDC office, and local FM and television transmission towers. In 2010, Dada Bazaar village, two hours from Namje, embarked on a similar water project, but so far has not succeeded in pumping water up the hill, despite having a budget of more than $250,000 (five times the cost of the Namje project). The engineers that designed the Dada Bazaar water project spent little time in the village itself. Local builders were not given significant responsibility. To save on costs and time, pipes were hung above ground, which resulted in leaks due to water pressure. The contrast between the Namje and Dada Bazaar water projects illustrates the importance of the grassroots, bottom-up approach over the top-down approach.

It was only after many years working on the project that I discovered human and educational capital existed not just within Namje but also in nearby cities and towns, which are just a bus ride away. Four hours north of Namje in a village called Uttarpani, we discovered an agricultural college with expert professors who are supporting our organic agriculture initiative. In Dharan, just ninety minutes from Namje, we discovered the regional office for the International Union for the Conservation of Nature, a global environmental organization.

But the most important lesson I learned from the water project I acquired during the long walks down to Saacho Khola. These walks were lessons in botany. The villagers would point out the name of every tree, every flower, every species of bamboo and their particular uses. The more I learned about how much the villagers knew, how much skilled labor they could perform, the richness of the natural resources surrounding them, the more I realized the complete emptiness of the word *poverty*.

Namje was a globalized village. Each time I transited through airports in the Middle East on my way to Kathmandu, I met Nepali migrant workers from places not far from Namje. By 2012 millions of Nepalis were working in more than a hundred countries around the world, returning to their homeland with new skills and knowledge of social conditions in other countries as well as an understanding of the global economy.

They weren't just spending a year or two overseas but typically between five and ten years. New experiences, abilities, and languages—all this was coming back into the village. While overseas, their colleagues were other migrants, not just from Nepal but India, Bangladesh, Sir Lanka, the Philippines, and other Asian countries. In addition to these physical migrations, communications infrastructure was also globalizing the village. By 2012 almost every villager in Bhedetar VDC had a cell phone. Many villagers were using the Internet. It was easy to dismiss these new trends, because they do not fit with the stereotypical vision of an isolated, rural village, but it is important not to ignore these realities. A village is not a physical place but a changing, constantly evolving identity.

Perhaps because it was simply easier to do so, or perhaps because donors and funding agencies were more likely to make a donation to a village that seems helpless and miserable, I sometimes portrayed the villages in a simple light. I exaggerated the problems and set aside the complexity and nuance. In time, through my Peace Corps experience, I learned how these representations greatly hurt the agency of villagers. They also set a very low bar so that project quality and process go unquestioned. With diminished standards, it is enough to simply report that a well or a school wing was constructed in a poor village somewhere, without evaluating whether or not these projects are sustainable or well designed.

Initially I thought we would keep building more and more schools and water systems in more VDCs. But when I realized how little this accomplished and also how much harm this approach can do, my interests drifted from rote infrastructural void filling toward deeper, more integrated approaches. If we could design just *one* great project, it could reverberate and have a catalytic effect. I started to see how it was fine for a project to be confined to an extremely small scale, and that in fact sometimes this smallness in itself can be powerful. The smaller the project, the more planning and detail it required. These small-scale projects became more holistic and global, drawing in local and international policy makers, architects and designers, agriculturalists, education specialists, and natural resource experts.

None of us could have predicted the massive scale on which land plotting would occur in Namje and, in fact, all across Nepal. My first impulse was to try to protect the villagers from it. We tried competing with the plotters by supporting government schools in buying land, but it was impossible to keep up with the plotters, who were supported by wealthy financial institutions. We needed a more creative conservation strategy. Also, it wasn't really my place to tell the villagers what they should or shouldn't do with their own land. Some villagers had huge debts to repay or other financial needs. It was in trying to tackle this difficult problem that our attention shifted to public and community space. Rather than telling villagers what to do on their own private land, if we could demonstrate sustainable alternatives in the public spaces, these alternatives could speak for themselves.

As environmental challenges in the villages deepened, I urged the villagers to forego modern construction, stay in their mud homes, and engage in permaculture. I learned an important lesson from the failure of this approach. Environmental sustainability must rest on *economic* sustainability. We needed to create and demonstrate an alternative livelihood. This was the strength of the Medicinal and Aromatic Plants (MAPs) Project. There was a strong market for the organic medicinal plants in Dharan, and so we never had to urge anyone to grow the plants because the economic advantages of doing so were obvious. In 2012 the villagers initiated a rural home-stay program. Through this program suddenly there *was* an economic incentive to preserve the village homes and deepen organic farming. Finding the economic incentive to protect the environment was crucial.

In addition to economics, religion and spirituality proved absolutely critical in shaping an effective conservation strategy. The Spirit of Place project illustrates how a single structure, which is culturally and spiritually rooted and also modern in its design, in a public space can help define a new direction for a village. Moved by the Magar ancestral memorial the villagers had built, a Buddhist organization based in Malaysia, in 2012, decided to construct a stupa on the crest of Thumki Hill. Even the land plotters are now trying to create a different kind of tourism, rooted in Magar culture, organic farming, and spirituality. When in 2011 the village was named by CNN as "One of the 12 best unheard of destinations in the world," the villagers started to realize it was their Magar culture, natural surroundings, and rural identity that made the village unique.

The question of how to fortify public space in Namje and the surrounding villages led us to the idea of creating small-scale, integrated catalysts within school plots and other community spaces. These catalysts didn't need to be four walls and a roof. Something as simple as a community bench, a plinth in the landscape, a pathway, a rainwater collection system, a gutter, or any small structure that suggested and demonstrated sustainability was helpful. There was a need for more forms of public art (sculptures, murals, installations) within these community spaces that could influence the more functional infrastructure. As we saw in Namje, development was already happening in the most remote corners of Nepal, and huge amounts of capital were flowing into these communities. If the catalysts were done well, they could influence the growth that was already taking place.

Over and over again, I learned how easy it was to talk about "sustainability" but how hard it was to actually achieve it. In 2011 I learned about a Finish organization in Nepal that was planning to implement a "Green Village" initiative in five VDCs in Dhankuta, including Bhedetar. When I asked them more about the project, I learned it was a campaign to build one thousand cement toilets. This, to me, was an example of development work as it is currently practiced—without much depth, research, or integration. If the toilets were going to be creatively designed or employ compost systems, that could be a very positive project. But the rote replication of infrastructure seemed to me a wasted opportunity.

Through these various projects, I started to understand the importance of public space. Visiting Kathmandu today, everywhere public and community spaces are vanishing as land values explode and roads and buildings clog the valley. I started to think more about why public and sacred spaces were important and what role they play in a society. Whether in Kathmandu or in Namje, community spaces hold social, environmental, and educational importance. Parks, *chowks*, community forests, bus shelters, and other public gathering places establish the very identity of a place. The main village gathering space in Namje was the high school. This was the center of public life.

In trying to protect public space, we learned another important lesson: the villagers wanted to have fun and explore new, creative directions. The nostalgic approach of trying to preserve the village as it had always been had no traction. People were interested in modernity and a sense of moving forward not backward. When we asked the community what should be built in the Thumki plot, the answers transcended rote functionality and utilitarianism. They wanted tree houses, amphitheaters, and fifty-foot viewing towers. They had an appetite for design projects (like Spirit of Place) with abstract and metaphorical implications. Even the Namje water project was exciting because it was more than a rote infrastructure project. The villagers were designing and strategizing it together from the bottom up, and the sense that we could have failed was very real. What excited them more than anything else was the possibility of their village being unique from the others. In Dharapani, a village two hours west of Namje, rather than constructing another building or water pipeline, one of the teachers, Mohan Rai, suggested we create a swimming pool or another creative water structure.

Still, it took a great deal of discussion to get the villagers to articulate these creative desires. The Nepali phrase for rural development, *gramin bikas,* denotes electricity, water supply, bridges, and other basic infrastructure. We needed to encourage them to forget this definition, to go beyond the checklist approach to rural development, and think deeper. For the first five years I worked in Namje, I would simply ask the villagers what they wanted. Invariably, the answer was more cement buildings. I could rest my conscience on knowing I was supporting the community's own self-articulated goals. In my estimation I was being humble and deferential to the community, just as the Peace Corps had taught me. What I initially failed to recognize then was that it was also within my role to present alternatives and case studies from other contexts. I didn't realize that when villagers were expressing what they "wanted," they were assuming a closed set of possibilities.

When we first began building projects, I was highly skeptical of any outside partnerships. I worried that international groups would not speak the language or understand the culture. I worried about exploitation and loss of the villagers' voices in the process. But gradually I realized villages were already integrated into the global economy, whether I chose to see it or not. Moreover, the land plotters weren't from the United States or Europe but neighboring villages. I increasingly became more open and enthusiastic about the global-local partnerships in helping to generate the imaginative ideas that the villagers wanted. While not every international partnership is appropriate, the excitement that comes from volunteers and experts from other countries coming to a village can itself serve as a catalyst for positive change. It also broadens the network.

The villagers kept asking for the *namuna* (model) house or the *namuna* permaculture farm. While I kept thinking we needed to build the one perfectly sustainable model, I later realized that we were modeling a process for designing and implementing good projects.

No matter how geographically remote a village is, it is still affected by national and international public interest laws. Knowing these laws was sometimes important for our project. From a young lawyer in Thumki, Dil Krishna Rai, we learned about ILO 169 and how certain provisions within it could be used to protect against land plotting. From another lawyer, Dharma Rai, in Rajarani village, we learned how important national public domain laws could be for protecting bodies of water. At the very least, public education about these legal provisions stimulated dialogue and debate. Even when working in the most localized settings, knowledge of national and international laws and policies could be helpful.

When I was a Peace Corps volunteer, I believed that many of the challenges in the village could be solved with technology and capital. However, the greatest challenge we faced in the water project was not technical but related to the greater dynamics of the Maoist war and smaller internal political and social conflicts that emerge when doing a project. As Huta Ram Baidya pointed out, the real struggle is political, psychological, and sociological in nature and has more to do with attitudes and behaviors than innovating a technology.

I think the reason I kept going back to Namje was a curiosity about how things had changed since the last time I was there. Each trip revealed a new, previously unknown layer of the village. The constantly evolving context in the village meant that our projects needed to adapt.

The problems confronting Namje and Thumki embody the larger crises of the new world we live in: the loss of agricultural land to roads and highways, the displacement of indigenous people and cultures, the replacement of sustainable building typologies with unsustainable housing, the substitution of diverse farming methodologies with industrialized monocultures, and the dangerous conflation of government and private interest. These problems are interconnected and constantly changing, presenting an even more complicated picture. The problems cannot be solved by an atomized, top-down approach.

Driving throughout America meeting volunteers, I realized the Peace Corps matters because, beyond the work of individual volunteers, the Peace Corps is critical in producing thousands of young Americans who see and understand the developing world as the complex place that it is and who can share that understanding with others. Many of these volunteers enter government service abroad where their language abilities and understanding of communities strengthen their ability to better assist people in other countries.

For me the Peace Corps was an invaluable first step into a rural community. This immersion is needed before beginning any development project. Prior to building the water project, my landlord's entire livelihood was derived from carrying water up the hill for the towers. Had I not known this, I never would have realized that the water project would displace his job and the role of other professional water carriers in village. Traveling to the river to wash my clothes, I saw how carrying water was an important ritual and part of what bound the community together. Had I been designing the water project from a distant location or had I hired outside engineers to build it, I never would have understood these implications or realized the importance of returning to Namje once the water pump turned on.

The Peace Corps in Washington needs to revamp its present ineffective approach to Congress. The agency should be bold about what it is and clear about what it is not in making its case for a greater share of federal tax dollars. On the Hill, I found that most lawmakers and congressional staff I met viewed the developing world as poor and helpless. I found it difficult to explain to them the importance of listening and observing rather than immediately intervening in the community. But when I told them the stories from Namje, people listened and were inspired. The Peace Corps has more than two hundred thousand such stories to tell on the Hill.

Senator Leahy is right that the Washington bureaucracy has calcified. Today there are half as many volunteers as there were in 1966 but four times as many lawyers. The Peace Corps director could reduce bureaucracy and move precious funds out into the field by firing half the headquarters staff in Washington, DC. Having fewer administrative staff in Washington would not only save resources but would also make the agency more nimble. The Peace Corps staff should always be secondary to the volunteers and not the other way around.

While the Peace Corps needs to make a stronger case to Congress about its valuable contribution to America and the world, it must avoid entanglement with US political and economic objectives while doing so. Most important, the Peace Corps must be careful not to play into the discussion about smart power. The Peace Corps is in many ways the very opposite of the smart power approach. At every level, it stands for humility, friendship, and seeing the sameness in people who come from different walks of life. It is a program centered on cultural exchange, not imposing the ideas or influence of the United States onto another country.

The Peace Corps needs to independently, without coercion from Congress, decide where the volunteers are placed. A criticism I heard from congressional staff and senior advisors within the Obama administration was that Peace Corps volunteers were not in the "important" countries. While most RPCVs would agree that the Peace Corps presence in China, Brazil, India, and Indonesia should be large, this should not come at the expense of the smaller countries. It is just as vital for people to learn about Kiribati or Moldova as it is to learn about the larger countries.

As great a program as the Peace Corps is, it can be made better and more relevant to the new world we live in today. While the Peace Corps is not really a development organization in the way that USAID is, volunteers do often take on development projects. Many of these projects are of the traditional sort—building schools, libraries, water projects, and sanitation facilities. Partnerships with design and engineering organizations that share the Peace Corps' core values of environmental sustainability and community participation would help volunteers develop projects that serve the needs of the communities even better.

Partnerships with global design-build NGOs and educational programs like Architecture for Humanity would enrich the Peace Corps with a new source of ideas and creative energy.

In Peace Corps circles, the topic of how to make the Peace Corps better is hotly debated. A running inside joke in the agency is that among the two hundred thousand RPCVs, there are two hundred thousand *and one* opinions about how to run the Peace Corps. But there is one thing that almost all volunteers would agree with. The two-year model should not be shortened, and if anything, third-year extensions should be more easily granted. The strength of the Peace Corps is *time*. It is the uninterrupted two years that leads to the deep attachments and friendships that make the program so special. There is no substitute for this immersion experience.

Most Peace Corps volunteers are teachers. I came to feel that the two years I spent teaching in a village school were the most important of my development career. In most village settings in Nepal, the school is the center of political, economic, and social life. The development impact being made by Peace Corps volunteers in schools around the world is significant. For example, since 1961 Peace Corps volunteers have taught more than four million children in Africa alone.

Based on my more recent experiences working in Namje and Thumki, I feel the Peace Corps can enhance its relevance and meet a vital need by expanding and deepening its arts education program. In Namje, I saw repeatedly how imagination and creativity were essential as the villages modernized. The Peace Corps should launch a campaign to send a large number of art and design educators into classrooms and college campuses throughout the developing world.

The More Peace Corps and Push for Peace Corps campaigns serve as proof that for Congress to respond grassroots activity is crucial. Today, though there are more than two hundred thousand Peace Corps alumni, less than 5 percent of them are involved in Peace Corps advocacy. If the Peace Corps is to continue to grow in numbers and funding, an informed and educated grassroots voice is indispensible. We saw firsthand how even a single constituent can make a difference of millions of dollars in the Peace Corps budget.

As I think about the last ten years and what they have taught me, I realize it is that small numbers of people can be effective. Margaret Mead was right when she said, "A small group of thoughtful people can change the world. Indeed, it's the only thing that ever has."

"Hello?" I answered.

"I'm with the *Kathmandu Post*. I had a few questions about Sargent Shriver. He made several trips to Nepal in the early 1960s, but I can't find the dates. Do you know when those were?"

"I don't know. . . . I can try to find out," I said. "But what's your story about?" As I asked the question, I realized what had happened.

"You must have heard the news. Sargent Shriver passed away yesterday."

I set down the phone, my heart feeling heavy, and walked out into the bright streets near the Bagmati River. I took the dirt pathway that goes along the quieter side of the river, farther from the main street. I walked and walked for a long time with my hands in my pockets. I passed a narrow, black iron walking bridge. A man on a motorcycle was trying to force his way across it as men and women, as well as farm animals, crossed in the other direction. But soon it was very peaceful and I was almost totally alone. This part of the river was somewhat cleaner and deeper. As I watched the fast-flowing waters of the Bagmati, my heart felt heavy. For the first time in my life that I could remember, I felt a personal debt to a historical public figure. I rushed back to my computer in the hotel. Asking myself "What would Shriver do?" I shook off the sadness. I hailed a Maruti to Thamel. I spent the night racing through the alleys of Kathmandu trying to get online.

It was my turn to speak. I looked out at the Namje school ground. It was raining viciously. The tent the villagers had erected for the opening of the Thumki plot was flapping wildly. Lama Sir was drenched and hugging the pole that held up the tent. As I spoke about what the plot meant, I talked about the graves. I said that when I looked into the fog, I saw my old student Bhageswar, who had recently died in Saudi Arabia in a factory accident. I talked about how I saw Purna, who died of cirrhosis of the liver from too much drinking. Purna had written the beautiful song "*Tanna Rassile*" ("Pull It Up with a Lasso") about the water project.

I looked up at Thumki Hill. The fog covering the permaculture plot was pure white. This seemed appropriate, as the fate of the hill hung in the balance. Finally, I said that when I looked in the mirror, I saw my dear friend Dalle, who had died recently from an alcohol overdose, only in his late twenties. We had worked together on so many building projects. Dalle had always said to me, "Even if it's on your back, can you carry me to America?" The villagers laughed hearing this story. Dalle was now up in the clouds, the village ancestor protecting the sacred hill.

Acknowledgments

Were it not for the people of Namje and Thumki, this book would not exist. I only hope I have done justice to their spirit, voice, and agency. For the kindness they have shown me, I especially wish to think Harka Lama, Tanka Bhujel, Gunjaman Magar, Laxmi Magar, Hari Ale Magar, N. B. Chemjong, Karna Magar, Durga Katuwal, and Goma didi. In Silanga village, I wish to thank Krishna Air, Fagendra Pant, Premraj Pant, and Shivy.

I have been extremely lucky to work with fantastic people at Beacon Press who took a big chance on a first-time author. I especially wish to thank my editor, Gayatri Patnaik, for her excellent instincts and for giving me the opportunity to share my story. I am also very grateful to Helene Atwan, Rachael Marks, and Tom Hallock for their support of this project.

I am fortunate to have not one but two wonderful mentors. Donald K. Ross trusted me with the reins of a national campaign when I had no experience to speak of in organizing and taught me so much. Scott Skinner, who has supported and mentored my work with the Phulmaya Foundation, read the early drafts of the manuscript, judiciously mailed comments and revisions, and kept me going psychologically. During the copyediting phase, he again provided invaluable help. Many thanks to my friend Andrew Burtless for providing spot-on feedback on early drafts and allowing me to defeat him in our epic one-on-one basketball sessions in Queens when I needed a confidence booster. I am grateful to Michael Melamedoff. It was exciting to watch *The Exhibitionists* grow up alongside this project. Your comments on the draft were exceedingly helpful. Our meetings at the Mustang Kitchen in Jackson Heights must continue. I'm very grateful to Amit Saxena for all his friendship over the years. I promise to return your Darryl Strawberry T-shirt one day soon. Jules and Lisa, I need to make sure we go on a trip to Nepal this year so that you can see what your generous support has accomplished.

I have been humbled to work with Peace Corps legends and luminaries over the last three years. I would be remiss not to thank Senator Harris Wofford, Bill Josephson, June Little, Bill Moyers, Tim, Mark, and Bobby Shriver, Senator Chris Dodd, Stephanie Odegard, Michael McCaskey, Jason Carter, Chris Matthews, Ken Hill, John Chromy, Stephen Heintz, Representative Gene Ward, Kim Biggs, Collier Perry, Juliet Sorenson, Mark Gearan, Dick Ottinger, Carol Bellamy, Pat Waak, Betty Curry, Jack and Leftie Vaughn, Laurence Leamer, Fred O'Regan, Broughton Coburn, Bob Arias, Mal Warwick, and George Packer for guiding this movement and for using your pen and your voice to move Congress. No one has done more to support and highlight RPCV writers than John Coyne and Marian Beil, and I am grateful to them as well. I fear mentioning any single person among the thousands of grassroots activists who have powered "Push for Peace Corps" because of the likelihood of leaving out so many, but thank you collectively for your advocacy that has enabled thousands more to be volunteers.

Two Colombia RPCVs are doing more to lift the Peace Corps budget than anyone else. For Maureen Orth, my deepest thanks for always pushing me to get it right and for believing in me. And for "Mr. Peace Corps," Congressman Sam Farr, thank you for your inspiring leadership and for reminding us never to be shy or bashful in our advocacy.

I don't think most people appreciate how crucial communications can be in a fast-moving campaign. Were it not for the tireless, around-the-clock efforts of the dedicated staff at Barrel, who cared about this project as much as we did, we would not have been able to engage and inform the growing support base. I wish to thank Peter Kang, Sei-Wook Kim, Zack Lerner, Jane Song, and Andy Ni for designing the beautiful newsletters, often at 3:00 a.m., and developing all the communications systems that powered the effort.

For my N/193 *saathiharu:* Mitho, Rene, Elise, Adam Palpali Baaje, Kurt "Old Beijing" Brosef, Andrew, Matt Steele, Katie, Tony, Chris, and Eloy. I couldn't ask for better friends with whom to have shared this journey. From the days at Phora to the long afternoons in the VDRC in Gaindakot—these are among my most wonderful memories. David O'Connor and Prem ji, thank you and all the outstanding Peace Corps training staff for taking such great care of us while we were in Nepal.

To my former colleagues at OHCHR in Kathmandu: Thank you, Lok dai, for teaching me the *art* of translation, and Mark Flummerfelt, the painful *science* of it. Were it not for fellow NYU law school alum Fred Rawski, who handed me his business card at Indira Gandhi Airport, I may never have had the chance to be a small part of an organization doing important work to protect the human rights of so many people every day.

We have been fortunate to have the support and encouragament of donors who understand the complexity of the issues as well as the personal agency of the stakeholders. Thank you Marvin and Allison Brustin, Sheila and Matthew Chellgren, Sajjan Agrawal, Shanti Kumar, Rashmi and Sanjay Shrestha, and Gil Asher for your support. In Kathmandu, several pioneers are doing more to shape *Naya Nepal* than anyone I've come across. I'm grateful for the opportunity to work with Karma Bhutia of the Mountain Institute, Uday Shrestha of *Spaces* magazine, and Nayantara Kakshyapati and Bhushan Shilpakar of *Photo.Circle*.

Were it not for a piece in the December 20 and 28, 2010, double issue of the *New Yorker* magazine by Peter Hessler, this book project likely would never have materialized. To Peter, thanks so much for everything, including your friendship. I constantly flipped through *Rivertown* and *Country Driving* throughout this process and found much inspiration. I count myself among the thousands of your and Leslie's fans who can't wait to read your books about the new journeys across Egypt. I'm grateful also to Lynsey Addario for the beautiful image that graces the cover of this book and for encouraging me to think about writing something about my experiences.

For the historical sections on Peace Corps, I relied on another Beacon publication, which is the best institutional history ever written on the Peace Corps, Stanley Meisler's *When the World Calls*.

My wonderful parents have supported me in more ways than I can express. For your love and support, thank you Mom, Dad, Rishi, Reena Bhabi, Sourabh, Uncle, Auntie, Priyash, Pi Anku, Nita Auntie, Ayasha, and Shabu. I'm grateful to my astute brother, Raghav, who helped articulate questions I needed to answer in part III. Just as I was finishing the manuscript, my grandfather, Chotaji, passed away. Though I wish he could have read this book, I take solace in knowing that so many of the ideas in its pages were shaped by the childhood conversations we had about politics and government.

For Priyanka, my partner and fellow gypsy: Thank you for the blunt though necessary criticisms and the encouragement when I didn't think I had anything worth saying. Some of the best ideas in this book were shaped by the hundreds of hours of drinking Americanos, brainstorming together, and me looking over your shoulder at course packets from Brookes University. I hope that some of the early chapters carry the quaint warmth of our attic apartment in Marston, Oxford, where it was so wonderful to be able to write (and procrastinate) alongside you.